An Independent Folk

A history of early Wheeler County, Oregon

Mary Fitzgerald

Printed in the United States of America
By Lightning Source Publications
1246 Heil Quaker Boulevard
LaVergne, Tennessee

To order additional copies of this book, contact Mary Fitzgerald at:
39499 N. Twickenham Rd.
Mitchell, Oregon 97750
or
marytwickenham@yahoo.com

Dedication...

For my Aunt Judy — an inspiration to me since
I was knee-high to a bummer lamb.

Acknowledgments

There are many folk — all independent souls —whose support and help made this book possible.

Thanks to those wonderful old-timers who enthralled me with their stories — Mary Beldon; Marbel Blann; Bob and Dan Cannon; Effie Jackson Carroll; Lyle and Dale Cole; Bob, Jack, and Ruth Collins; Roy Critchlow; Fred Dunn; Bobby Ferenstein; Evelyn, Joe, and Tom Fitzgerald; Audrey Jackson; Lee and Patsy Hoover; Candy and Virginia "Ginny" Humphreys; Bob Huntington; John McCulloch; Ethel McFadden; Sandy McKay; John and Mary Misener; Richard Mortimore; Carl Naas; Carlyle "Cork" Norton; Betty Potter; Kent Powell; Loretta and Ron Quant; George Schnee; and Elsie Simmons. I wish we could have visited longer; there are more stories to be told.

I appreciate the sharing of materials and advice and the support of my aunt, Judy Keyes Kenny, who has such a keen interest in history. Special recognition goes to Mac Stinchfield, Marilyn Garcia and Randa Liston at the Fossil museum, and Nancy Allen and Jennifer Hudson at the Spray museum for their help. I'd like to thank Kari Anderson for her web sites advice and to Steve Lent for his publishing guidance.

Yoma Ulman and Sue Brooks, I am thankful for your encouraging words that helped me keep focused.

Bobby Ferenstein, your friendship and your expertise and the endless hours of editing and advising me has been invaluable. Though you were "…taught that the editor doesn't just take a back seat to the author, but actually hides in the trunk, under the spare tire and jumper cables," I deeply appreciate your coming out of that trunk and helping me when I most needed it. I admire your independent old-timer ethics greatly. Thank you.

Foreword

The United States was a fairly new nation in the 1840s and was suffering growing pains. In 1804 President Jefferson had sent Meriwether Lewis and William Clark to lead an expedition to the West to gather information about the land included in the Louisiana Purchase, the greatest real estate bargain the U.S. ever made: $10 million for the vast territory ranging west from the Mississippi River to the Rocky Mountains and north to Canada. This opened the land for the settlement that followed, and the movement to the West began in earnest during the 1840s.

The wagon train of '43 was the first major move to the West, but more followed until 1886. In '44 a second key wagon train of emigrants left Missouri, heading for the Oregon country. Many descendants of those emigrants, including the Hoover, Parrish, Gilliam, and Cave families, to name a few, remain in the Wheeler County area. Through the years, families have intermarried to the extent that to list all those descendants of the wagon train of '44 would take several pages, the genealogy becoming as mixed up as a hound's breakfast.

Jacob Hoover had a double connection to the Cave family; he married Jeriah Cave in '34 and the couple had three children and after Jeriah's death, Jacob married her sister, Malinda Cave, in '44. She gave birth to a son, Jackson, on the trail. One of Jacob and Jeriah's great-great-grandsons, Lee, lives near Fossil with his wife, Patsy; their five children also live in the area.

Also on this train was a minister, Edward Evans Parrish, whose granddaughter May Parrish Barry would live in Wheeler County for several years until her death. Another descendent of the Parrish family is Georgia Loomis, who has also made her home in Wheeler County for many years. Reverend Parrish performed weddings and funeral services while on the Oregon Trail, and two of the funerals would be for Henry and Naomi Sager, parents of seven orphaned children who would complete the trip to Oregon alone.

The wagon train of '45 is perhaps best known for the disaster following the decision of some of the emigrants to follow Stephen Meek on his "short cut," which led to tragedy for his followers. Lost in the southern Oregon desert, the emigrants struggled to survive and suffered deaths beyond the norm for wagon trains. Another well-known story concerning this wagon train is the one of some of the children wandering off from the main body of emigrants and finding gold nuggets which they put in a blue bucket and then misplaced, leading to the legend of the Blue Bucket Mine. The emigrants on this train included little four-year-old John Frier whose granddaughter, Vada Lowrey Fitzgerald, would be born on one end of High Street in Mitchell and would be living on the other end at the time of her death, a month short of her ninety-fourth birthday. Two of Vada's sons, Joe and Tom, still live in Wheeler County.

In the years the Oregon Trail was used as the route to the West, the estimated 350,000 emigrants making their way from the East would leave an average of ten graves per mile, about 5 percent of all those who started the journey. Most of those burial sites were unmarked save for names scratched in a rock or a barrel stave or spare piece of wood, most of which soon weathered away to become part of the landscape. The wagon train of 1843 had suffered a relatively low number of deaths compared to those emigrants who followed, but for the families who lost loved ones, statistics didn't mean much.

Also of note is the fact that the Indians along the Oregon Trail didn't bother the emigrants on that first wagon train. However, the white men continued to roll across the natives' homeland, killing the buffalo that provided so many of the essentials to the Indians' way of life. Soon the emigrants indiscriminately began abusing the natives, who understandably became aggressive, and wagon trains in the future would have the hostility of the natives to contend with along with the physical hardships of the Oregon Trail. The actual number and severity of the attacks, however, have been greatly exaggerated by authors and movie directors for their financial gain and for their audience's entertainment.

The destination of the early emigrants was the western coast of the Oregon Territory. There they recovered from their arduous trip, mending bodies and spirits, before filtering out from the Willamette Valley to various destinations to the south and to the east. The Homestead Act would be established in 1862 but not all land in the territory would be surveyed for several years. This meant that in parts of eastern Oregon, the settlers would have to rely on their own resources to find a parcel on which to squat and to later file a deed for the homestead when the boundaries had been surveyed.

As early as the late 1850s, occasional parties of men made their way up the John Day River and across country to the area of Wheeler County. There are no records of the earliest of these forays into the interior of Oregon. It wasn't until in '59 that Captain D. H. Wallen was dispatched by General William S. Harney, who was in charge of the Department of Oregon, to find a feasible route up the John Day valley, to the Malheur valley, and on to the Snake River.

Wallen's party explored as far as the Malheur country, doubtlessly passing through the area of Wheeler County. They met up with the Indians and the whites on the Warm Springs reservation, and their passage was taxed by the natives with their creative and unauthorized procurement of some of Wallen's stock. The Indians were pursued by Wallen's group and some of the horses were recovered, a few native women and children were captured, and several of the men were killed.

The following year, in '60, Major E. Stein and Captain A. J. Smith were sent out by General Harney. Their intrusion on the Indians' land was met with resistance, and there were several conflicts during the exploration efforts. Stein traveled as far as the mountains that now carry his name; Harney County would be named after the general who was instrumental in a route being opened up in the uncharted lands.[1]

In '62, gold was discovered in what is now known as the Canyon Creek area on the route to the Malheur Valley. The dream of becoming rich overnight caught the fancy of many young — and some not-so-young — adventurers. Men began discarding jobs, families, and common sense as they hurried to the gold field in eastern Oregon, their route taking them through the area that is now Wheeler County. To repeat that often-used phrase, the rest is history, and a colorful part of that account was made by the uniquely independent souls who located in Wheeler County.

James Biffle was the first known homesteader in the area, followed by the farmers Christian Meyer and Frank Hewot, Samuel Carroll, and Sam and Nancy Wilson. Ezekial Waterman established productive grain fields, Henry Wheeler a stage line, and Jerome Parsons a reputation for telling tall tales. T. B. Hoover, Broadie Johnson, and John Spray were the first of the city fathers. The Keyes and Steiwer families would be known as some of the first sheepmen and Henry Wheeler one of the premier cattlemen. James Keeton would establish one of the first sawmills necessary for development of the settlements in the area. These characters are only a smattering of the first of the folks who made Wheeler County their home, and not necessarily the most important; they just have colorful stories to be told.

No one person or single family can be claimed to be the best known

---

1. F. A. Shaver, Arthur P. Rose, R. F. Steele, and A. E. Adams. An illustrated History of Central Oregon. Spokane, Washington: Western Historical Publishing Co. 1905, p. 635

or the most important of the settlers. The person telling the story can show bias while telling the tales, but the listener or the reader will have to choose the importance of each character in the saga of the building of the county. Told with a mix of both creative history and straight facts, all somewhat in chronological order, the following pages will shares stories of some of the independent personalities who formed the backbone of Wheeler County. Homesteads will be filed, ranches and cities built, and a county formed — all in a few short pages bound in a single book that, I hope, will give readers cause to pause and reflect and interpret as they see fit.

They are unique individuals, they are. Folks in Wheeler County, those who have been born and reared in the most impoverished county in the state of Oregon, seem to be a breed of their own. Independent to a fault at times, determinedly clinging to their conservative principles, kind-hearted and neighborly and content with their surroundings, the old-timers stand apart from the rest of the world.

Who are the old-timers? An old-timer might be someone whose ancestors traveled to Oregon during the first of the emigrations of the 1840s. An old-timer might be someone who eked out a living from the soil, working always from daylight to dark, wearing clothes with patches patched, hoping to have a crop good enough to sell to pay taxes and buy flour and beans to feed the family through the winter.

The old-timers can be farmers or ranchers, sheepmen or cattlemen, loggers or businessmen, city fathers or politicians. These old-timers stick together, helping their neighbors in times of emergencies — a prolonged and difficult birth for a first-calf heifer; a crop threatened with failure because a man with a broken leg couldn't stack his hay; forest fires that in a few hours destroy years and years of forest growth; flashfloods roaring and ripping through a recently planted grain field or through the middle of a small town; unusually cold winter weather freezing newly born lambs and calves fast to the ground; coyotes eating calves as they were being born, still half inside their mothers, or killing a dozen lambs in the night, eating on the small bloody carcasses for the sheepmen to find in the morning. These are emergencies and neighbors have to depend on each other to survive.

Sometimes the old-timers just can't find a solution locally to their problems and begrudgingly ask for help from outside the area, hoping the government they pay taxes to might lend a hand. The bottom line is, with Wheeler County's 1,500 square miles inhabited by an average of one person per square mile, there is a price to pay for the privilege of living there: the politicians and large populations west of the Cascade Mountains that divide Oregon in half have the numbers to rule the state; from where the majority of voters sit, the points of view of the distant county's residents are often misunderstood and neglected in favor of the larger populations who want to recreate on the land. Often those recreationists are zealous conservationists whose superior attitudes rankle the old-timers; but Wheeler County folks adjust as best they can and dig deep for a sense of humor to help cope with the change that has come, for come it has and the county will never be the same as it is in the memories of the old-timers.

This is where the stories of times gone by come in handy; when old-timers gather together, there will always be stories of "the good old days" and the "good old folks" and, for a time, fenced-off watering holes and swimming holes and rutted four-wheeler trails are forgotten as neighbors gather to share tales of the characters they have heard of or have known. Old-timers may have no say in the fate of the lands they have worked and on which they and their families have eked out a living for many years, but they take pride in having been a part of something great — the building of Wheeler County, an ongoing symbol of life in "the good old days."

Researching for information about the history of an area is a never-completed task. The more I dug into records the more information I found, much of it contradictory. I finally decided to always, if possible, locate three sources for each bit of information I would use and to settle on the two accounts out of the three that were most similar. Sometimes it had to be three out of five, because the first three bits of information were inconsistent. If what I've relied on is not what someone else would find to be accurate, I'll just have to apologize in advance. As a retired teacher, I cringe when I think of a textbook I used in my classroom which, when I began to do more extensive research, contained misinformation. Though I'm certain beyond a doubt that none of my students were as enthusiastic about their history lessons as I was, I still regret misleading them. I don't want to repeat that mistake with the readers of this book, so have researched the content carefully, knowing there will still be misinformation of which I am not aware.

Naturally, the folks I interviewed for this story each came into our meeting from a different and individual point of view. Therefore, I trust that will be taken into consideration and with a grain of salt; it is the first-hand accounts that make a story so enjoyable for me to tell and, I hope, enjoyable for my readers. I realize there are those bibliophiles who want facts only, and for those who do, please make use of my bibliography to find a wealth of information. For those so inclined, it's great reading.

I thoroughly enjoyed doing the research and quite often bored my family and friends unmercifully with what I'd found; however, I like sharing a story and I find writing the account on paper is my strength and my preferred venue for sharing. While gathering information, I interviewed folks I knew well and I did research on the area of the county I knew best. My efforts include just a very small bit of the rich history of Wheeler County and I hope that others will be inspired by what they read here and will put together a book with stories from their acquaintances and from their points of view.

I did embellish with relish the dry, hard facts, to make them more interesting for the average reader. There are written records of each place, event, and named character in my story and those are as accurate as I could make them based on my research. I did include a few unnamed individuals to make the story more coherent, and those characters will be obvious.

The most thoroughly enjoyable part of my efforts was the collecting of information for the book, much of it gathered while listening to old-timers share their memories. I grew up hearing stories of the "good old days" and the tellers of the tales were my idols; they haven't diminished in stature, but have grown in importance as I recount their anecdotes here. They are a vanishing breed and are irreplaceable. No amount of recordings, written or oral, can take the place of a story well told. I've been blessed to hear stories from the best, and am privileged to be able to share.

WHEELER COUNTY, OREGON

Locations in <u>An Independent Folk</u>

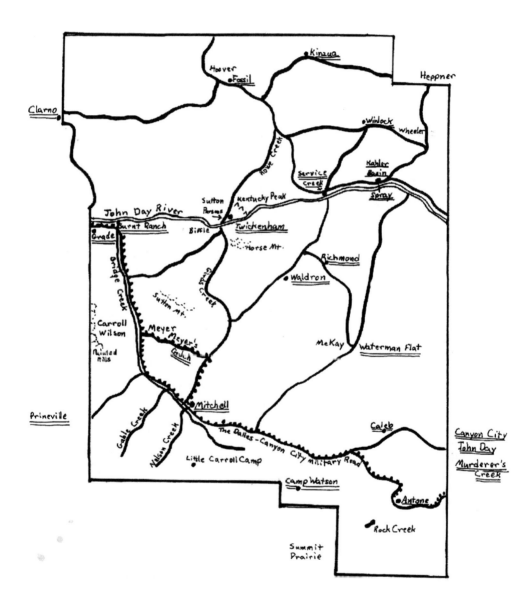

Chapter 1
1862 — James Biffle

He was heading east from The Dalles towards the gold field in Canyon City, bound for the homesteading land in between. The lone traveler was riding a sore-footed bay overloaded with a heavily packed canvas roll tied securely behind his worn saddle. Occasionally he tugged impatiently on the long lead rope tied to his sway-backed mule's halter, urging the tired gray animal along.

"We're almost there," the man his friends called James Biffle promised his animals, though where "there" was he had only a vague idea. The earliest immigrants to the Oregon territory had settled in the western part of what had become the thirty-third state in 1859, arriving at the hub of activity established by earlier settlers sailing around the tip of South America and up the Pacific Coast or traveling across the wide and desolate plains to the same destination. Discovery of gold in the eastern part of the new state was encouraging movement towards that area and from the westernmost regions.

Biffle was following the route established by the men sent out by merchants from The Dalles earlier in this spring of 1862. These enterprising souls had wanted a passable road to use for shipping their goods to the gold field that had begun the year before near Canyon Creek, hoping to capitalize on the miners' needs. Adding to the trails left by the members of the U.S. Cavalry and the prospectors heading east, the freighters and the packers with mules had established a fairly distinctive roadway.

Somewhere near this road, Biffle hoped he'd find a place to squat where he would develop the plot of land and later, after the land had

1

been surveyed, file a homestead. He didn't know where his home would be, for sure. What he was looking for was a likely location for a cabin and for a garden where he could grow enough produce to feed himself. Too, the holdings would have to be flat enough and large enough to develop some fields for the crops he'd need to feed the sheep he planned to run on his farm. He felt he'd know his homestead spot when he found it, even if in the light of day the directions he carried with him didn't look so promising.

He was carrying a map of sorts with him, crudely drawn on the brown paper which the storekeeper in The Dalles had used to wrap his new jeans. He'd sat at an over-crowded, poorly lit bar late one night, his dark eyes focused on the weathered face of the soldier just in from the Canyon Creek mining camp to the east, buying him a drink to keep him talking while Biffle recorded the directions to Canyon Creek.

The inebriated cavalryman had stabbed a wavering finger at different locations on the map, remembering an area here or there or another place that would be a good location for a large garden and fields, being flat and near water. He'd traveled along John Day's river a few times with a small group of soldiers scouting for a quicker way to the gold field from The Dalles, so he figured he had a bit of knowledge of the country.

"John Day was a trapper. Did lot of exploring in that area," the soldier explained. "Got lost, Indians found him, took all his clothes and rifle, turned him lose. Boy, was he glad to see the cavalry ride up! So the story goes." Biffle had joined the storyteller in laughter, thinking he was relieved that he'd not been in Day's footsteps. "Anyway, they named the river after him," and the cavalryman stabbed at the wavy line indicating the waterway on the map.

"Betcha could grow just about anything, too," the soldier had encouraged Biffle. He looked his companion over from head to toe, noting his lean and muscled body, his work-hardened hands, and his weathered face. Here was a man not afraid of hard work, and hard work was what it'd take to succeed in this new land.

The unkempt private licked his lips, wiped them dry with his shaky hand, and eyed his glass, nearly empty. Biffle signaled the bartender for a refill. He'd been hungry for talk of the area he planned to call home and here was a ready-made source of first-hand information, though he knew he'd have to get all the news he could from the cavalryman before he consumed much more of the watered down beverage the bar was selling. After ten more minutes or so of meandering conversation, Biffle left the befuddled fellow talking to himself, knowing the soldier's sergeant could straighten him out the next morning.

"'N' watch out for those road agents," were the last words the soldier mumbled. "Watch out for the road agents. Rob ya blind, they will."

Biffle was mulling over his conversation with the man as he guided his horse along the dusty road traveled by the military and the prospectors, packers, and freighters going back and forth between the gold field and The Dalles. He'd left that city early a few mornings before and now his fourth day on the road to Canyon City was winding down, and he'd reached what he knew to be the John Day River.

Leaving the river, Biffle guided his saddle horse up mounded hills covered with tan and red and green adobe soil interspersed with what looked like somewhat fertile soil. He could see why he'd heard these hills referred to as "potato hills" with the huge lumps of soil from a distance resembling that vegetable somewhat. Here small, mean-looking clumps of grass struggled to make a living. From the scarcity of vegetation, and that pretty sorry looking, the lone traveler surmised there was little rainfall in this country. Too, it looked like the backbone of the earth was pretty close to the surface with the occasional basalt rocks jutting up to make obstacles to maneuver around.

At the top of a rise, Biffle pulled his horse to a stop and the pack mule gratefully pulled up beside him, blowing from the effort of the climb. Across the river from their vantage point an imposing rock bluff rose from the waterway. Possibly 500 feet high, the sheer face of the brown basalt landmark appeared to be fairly smooth and was punctuated with small patches of lighter colorations.

Looking at the majestic bluff tinged orange, then red, and then purple with the last rays of the setting sun, the horseman drew in a deep breath. The massive rock bluff overshadowed the smaller rock formations on either side; to the east, as far as he could see, were lesser rock-covered rounded hills, some red or white with clay banks, some covered with light-colored dried grasses and low shrubs. Though not frequenting church and seldom opening the Bible at the bottom of his pack, Biffle nonetheless felt that some being larger than man had been at work here.

He sat long, marveling at the massive rock face, drinking in the majestic scene, until his horse began to shift impatiently, bringing him back to the task at hand. He lifted the reins in one of his broad hands and then without warning was suddenly overcome by one of the coughing spells he frequently had, causing him to slump over in the saddle. The coughs seemed to emanate from deep within his chest, body-wracking coughs that teared his eyes and left his body weak for a time. The coughing subsided and he straightened in his saddle; pulling his handkerchief from his hip pocket, he wiped his eyes, blew his nose, and lifted his horse's reins again.

The evening breezes were sharpening, carrying the scent of sagebrush with them and, perhaps, the smell of a campfire. Night birds were beginning to make their hunting cries and a coyote howled from a distance and was answered by another one a bit closer. In the fading light, Biffle could just make out the rabbit tracks paralleling the road he'd been following and the zigzag marks of a rattlesnake that had crossed the hoof prints in the dusty pathway. It was time to make camp for the night, and he headed down the hill towards a flat area near the river.

The smoke he'd caught a whiff of was from a campfire and Biffle shouted out a "Hello!" to warn the campsite of an approaching stranger. Two men worked near the fire, feeding the flames and adjusting their coffee pot on the coals to find the hottest spot. A large cast-iron frying pan butted up against the coffee pot and Biffle could smell meat cooking. His stomach growling as he dismounted, he accepted the men's invitation to light and have a bite.

He and his hosts visited long into the night, smoking hand-rolled cigarettes and drinking cup after cup of strong black coffee, catching up on news of the gold rush and President Lincoln elected in '60 and Oregon becoming a state in '59 and of the Cayuse Indian war ended in '50, they supposed, though they all three carried a loaded rifle each time they mounted a horse, "For insurance," the younger of the two fellows stated, nodding his head.

The men talked of how, a little more than ten short years before, and doesn't time go by fast? the Yakima and Nez Perce, the Umatilla and Cayuse and Walla Walla Indians, had given up their land — 30,000,000 acres for about $650,000, or two cents per acre. The Indians were probably still pretty pissed about that, the men figured, and would welcome a chance to retaliate. The men kept their rifles close, the two campers favoring their Springfield .58s and Biffle explaining he just wasn't comfortable without his Enfield .577, beings as how he'd heard there were still renegade Indians on the loose, not to mention the road agents that waited for easy pickings from travelers to the gold field near Canyon City. He sneaked a glance at his hosts and wondered what their story was, noticing the shifty eyes and the constantly nervous hand of the older fellow regularly pushing his long straggly silver-gray hair from his eyes or pushing it behind an ear.

"And, then, there was the Whitman Massacre," the younger of the campfire hosts volunteered, the glow from the campfire's flickering flames highlighting the gray streaks in his dark brown hair. As he began his tale, shifting his body yet once again on his rock seat, it was obvious to Biffle the story was well rehearsed and had been repeated time and again with other travelers. The Sager family had started for Oregon and the parents had died on the way. The oldest child at thirteen, John had led his six siblings the last leg of the journey and struggled on foot through the early, heavy snow into the Whitman Mission in '44 and doesn't that seem like yesterday?

The local Indians had contacted measles and many of their tribe died. The survivors blamed the disease on the Whitmans and the other white folks and, in their grief, wanted revenge. And after all he'd done for them, the Indians had burst into Whitman's mission in '47 and killed him and his wife and two of the Sager children, those poor little waifs. To have survived the horrors of being seven children alone in the Blue Mountains in the early winter and then to be killed by savages was just too hard to take.

They'd keep their rifles close. Not that there weren't good Indians; they all knew some that were dandy folks. It was just that a fella had to look out for the ones that would like to slit a man's throat and take his scalp. Never knew when you'd run across one, and the three men sneaked furtive glances into the darkness outside the glow of the campfire.

Too, there was always the damn gold to dream about. Biffle shoved a small juniper branch into the diminishing fire, stirring the hot coals around. He didn't want to leave this conversation unfinished. The first gold in Canyon Creek had been discovered in '61, and ever since there had been a steady flow of men headed for the gold field, all sure they'd be the one to find the mother lode.

The three men around the campfire had been planning to make the journey ever since they'd heard of the nuggets being found, but it'd taken them all time to prepare. And, now, they were on their way, though Biffle felt he preferred to make his fortune supplying the miners. Or not. He might be content to take advantage of the Homestead Act of '62 and take up a claim and support himself on what the land would produce. He'd see. Gold was tempting, but he didn't think it was the life for him. There was more than one way to benefit from the gold rush.

The established route for The Dalles-Canyon City Military Road passed near where the three men sat visiting. From there it turned to the south to follow the small but fast-flowing creek that was known as Bridge Creek, so named because two prospectors headed for Canyon City had felled junipers to create a bridge across the waterway. "So we heard," volunteered one of the men sharing the fire with the traveler.

Several miles further on, to the northeast, according to Biffle's brown wrapping-paper map, the road wound its way along the north branch of Badger Creek where it was said hundreds of badgers lived. One of the men drew a crude map in the dirt, the glow from the camp-fire dimly lighting his efforts. The road then followed the fast-flowing Mountain Creek through a rocky gorge and on east to an open, lush valley about three miles west of the John Day River and, finally, to the gold field. This was the route his hosts would be taking, they said, and they exchanged a quick, secretive glance that Biffle caught. "What was going on?" he wondered, and his feeling of unease grew.

Biffle planned to more-or-less follow the river east a ways, looking for a homestead spot not too far from the main trail, he explained. That there would be water, he knew; if not from the river, then from one of the many creeks that fed the main waterway. And, he was confident there would be a valley suited for his purpose. He'd heard how ever so often a basin opened up alongside the river and the sketchily drawn map in the dirt showed one of those valleys to be not too far up the river. Maybe that was where he'd wind up.

Hesitant to end the last conversation he might have for weeks, Biffel mentally searched for other topics to discuss. He carried copies of Dickens's two new books, <u>A Tale of Two Cities</u> and <u>Great Expectations</u>, in his pack but he had a sense his companions weren't much interested in reading or even that they could. Better to save those two books for savoring in his camp later. Finally, sighing, he rose to his feet and ground out the last little stub of his cigarette under his boot heel.

He reached out a hand, thanked his hosts for his supper and good conversation and wished them luck in the gold field. Then Biffle turned to his own bedroll for the night, settling in a short distance from the camp, his hand resting lightly on his loaded Enfield. He didn't know the men he had shared supper with; they appeared to be okay but there was a funny feeling in the air. A man couldn't be too careful. Between rattlesnakes and coyotes and renegade Indians and road agents, he'd better be prepared. As an afterthought, he sat upright, lifted his Enfield rifle, and, as he jacked a shell into the chamber, saw the two men jerk their heads in his direction, their hands reaching towards their Springfield guns.

"Just gettin' ready in case of varmints," Biffle called out. "Never know." He grinned from the darkness as he saw the men look at each other in the dimness of the fading light of the campfire, then drop their hands from their rifles. He settled into his bedroll for a restless night, shifting his uncomfortable body often, his mind alert for any sign of movement from the direction of his hosts.

As he quietly prepared to leave the camp in the false light preceding dawn the next morning, he saw the shapes of his hosts deep in their bedrolls and he listened to their steady snoring. Biffle saw by the early dayglow parts of the camp he'd not noticed when riding in the previous night.

There was a large pile of sagebrush nearby, a larger pile than would be needed for a cooking fire and for warmth for one night. The hanging carcass of the deer he'd fed from the night before had the back-strap and most of the two hind quarters cut away; obviously, it had served several meals to the men he'd had coffee and conversation with.

He surmised the two men might just well be some of the road agents he'd been warned about. The location would be a good one to set up a base camp for their operations, all right. There would be a stream of folks traveling the nearby road, carrying the cash for their mining venture. Easy pickings out here in this desolate country with no law nearby, except the occasional soldier riding past.

"Bad luck to you!" he called out softly in the direction of the sleeping men when he'd furtively led his horse and mule some ways from the camp. "Bad luck, and may the good Lord not help you!" he added with a grin, and he headed towards the brightening sky in the east.

There was a broad silted plain paralleling the river, formed by years of flooding waters depositing their rich sediment, and it was over this sandy course that Biffle rode. The occasional odor of a rotting fish carcass, washed up on the sand and half eaten by a raccoon or some other carnivore, drifted along the shore, mingling with the mud smell and the fragrance of the grasses his horse's hooves walked upon. He listened to the morning call of the blackbirds darting through the willows ahead of his passage and a red-tailed hawk giving out an occasional call as it circled above the river.

Massive brown rocky bluffs lined the north side of the river, giving way to rock-strewn bare hills eroded by centuries of wind and rain on the south side. Startled mule deer burst from their early morning drinks as soon as they heard the horseman and his pack mule, and Biffle laughed at their panic, watching the gray-brown animals with their large ears bound away in long, bouncing leaps.

They were safe from him for now. He'd chew on a piece of jerky for breakfast and later that day, closer to time to camp, he'd replenish his meat supply with a rabbit or a sage grouse. He didn't want to shoot an animal and leave most of the carcass behind as he continued his quest to find his new homestead site. Not that there didn't seem to be plenty of the big-eared mule deer in this country, but he hated to waste the meat.

A chocolate-colored rocky outcrop blocked his passage along the clear flowing, gurgling river and Biffle turned to the south, angling up a wide gully with a small muddy stream trickling slowly but steadily among the rounded rocks in the bottom of the small canyon. His sure-footed horse picked his way among the scrubby gray-green sagebrush and dark green bunch grass, spooked occasionally by a startled grouse exploding from nearby.

Not far from the river, a hunk of loosely packed brown columnar rock rose to the east of the creek he was following, and Biffle angled his horse around the stony obstacle. As he passed by, red symbols on the rock caught his eye and he pulled his horse to a stop, dismounting for a closer look. He knew nothing about Indian writing, but apparently some native had recorded an event to share with others who followed. Or, perhaps, Biffle smiled, some young sprout had left a bit of a naughty message behind to amuse his peers and, with luck, escape the watchful eyes of his parents. That's what Biffle guessed he would've done, when he was a young 'un, but he supposed he'd never know what the symbols meant.

Most of the day was spent guiding his horse in a roughly eastward direction, tugging at his mule's lead rope as they made their way up steep bunch-grass-covered hillsides, avoiding an occasional pile of cactus with spines that seemed to jump out and grab a man, and moving around clumps of rocks.

"Just follow your nose, old fella," he advised his mount as he gently pulled the bridle reins one way or the other. Once his horse spooked, jumping sideways, and the dry rattle of a snake told Biffle why. He patted the horse's neck, quieting him, and urging him on again.

The soft soil, at times adobe and at times sandy loam, made the horse's hooves dig in deeply as he struggled up the steep hillsides, his ascent made harder by the balking mule pulling back on his lead rope. At the top of each rounded hill, Biffle would rest his animals, letting them crop at the clumps of bunch-grass as he nibbled on pieces of dried apple or jerky, looking at the lay of the land. Always there was another smoothed hill blocking the larger view to the east, and the unknown lured the traveler eastward, the feeling of a pending discovery growing as the day progressed.

To the south rose a low mountain, soft tan and brown shrub-covered folds leading up to the rocky basalt top, forming a barrier to travelers. Some of the rolling hills were dotted with layered white banks, then red, indicating worthless clay soil, but there were areas covered with sparse grass in between the useless dirt. The rounded tops of the hills showed the results of wind and rain erosion, and small draws leading to the bases of mounds marked the path of the runoff.

"It'd take a lot of acres to fatten a steer in this area," Biffle guessed, though the bunch grass was high and looked as if it had potential for grazing. So far, he'd not located the flat surface he'd need for a garden, though he'd made his way through several little draws and gullies with evidence of water. He kept alert, sometimes standing in his stirrups to give short relief to his bony buttocks tired from a day in the saddle, constantly watching for rattlesnakes and for the badger hole that could break a horse's leg if he stumbled into it. Some red adobe banks he traveled around sloped downward to pathetic looking creek beds that hadn't carried much water for quite a while, though the tufts of grass indicated there had been adequate spring rains to start those small bits of vegetation.

Alongside a narrow waterway, on a semi-level spot on a bank, Biffle spied the remnants of a scattered campfire made some time previously and, on closer observation, he noticed chips of flint and a half-finished broken arrowhead. The natives had obviously spent a day or two here, resting and making use of their leisure by chipping away at the chunks of the obsidian rocks they carried with them for just such an opportunity to replenish their supply of arrowheads.

"Were the arrowheads made by Paiute?" Biffle wondered. "Or Bannock or Snake or Umatilla?" He supposed 'most all arrowheads were similar, regardless of the tribe making them.

He picked up a shiny shard of the black glass-like rock, marveling at its sharpness. He was amazed at the even chips he knew had been made with a deer antler, the knapper chipping, chipping, chipping patiently away, forming the sharp point that would kill a bird or a deer — or a human, if need be. He wondered how many miles the rock had been carried; the broken glassy-black arrowhead was made of rock foreign to this terrain, for sure, and had probably been traded for.

Far below, to the north and west, Biffle could catch glimpses of the river he'd left that morning. He knew he'd come to the river again and hoped to do so before he made his night camp. It had been a warm day and he could smell his own sweat mingled with that of his horse and of the pack mule and he wanted to bathe before he crawled into his bedroll with himself.

He hated to make a dry camp, and knew he could noodle his way down through the smaller draws and the larger canyons to the waterway, if he had to, though he wanted to take a more direct route, one that could be developed into a thoroughfare he could travel to reach the main military road. He goaded his horse slightly, urging him on, tugging impatiently on his mule's rope, wanting to reach the stream for his night camp. He'd round one more hill, he decided, and then he'd have to head for the river for the night and continue his search for his intended roadway the next day.

Suddenly, there was the valley.

Biffle caught his breath as he took in the panorama before him. From his place on the top of a tall hill covered with small tufts of bunch grass and an occasional rounded group of basalt rocks, he could see the broad, flat-bottomed valley he had previously only dared to dream of.

Biffle's view, looking north from his homestead site.

The willow-lined river he'd followed formed the backbone of the basin. To the north lay strips of fertile flood plain backed by gently rising hills of white and red clay banks with rolling grassy tops. Behind them rose a steep escarpment, thrust up eons ago by some underground force and twitch of nature, the disruption forming an inspiring flat base for the clay hills that led to the foothills of the rimrocks beyond.

The rims. Fading sunlight played on the rocky face formed by volcanic action and then millions of years of receding ocean waters wearing away at their rocky shores. The long basalt ledge stood proud and straight atop the base of shale and soil holding the roots of grasses and small brush. Behind the rimrock ledge arose yet another layered hill capped by a high peak with a small and flat rocky top looking somewhat like an inverted coffee can.

Ancient volcanoes had formed this land with their immense turbulences, the fiery molten lava flowing for hundreds of miles to form the base of the rock structures before him. As the magma flowed, it covered all vegetation and animals in its way, the heat and pressure of the lava helping to form the fossils buried below the surface. Sometimes the gigantic earth tremors had lifted the ocean floor, sometimes pushed it below the surface of the waters. The process had taken millions of years, the formation of the streams he'd crossed and the river below the result of waters from the prehistoric oceans seeking the lower levels of the terrain. In time, the natural streams had conformed to the landscape, wearing away the rock, depositing the particles as soil in the land near the waterway. Wind and rains and freezing temperatures had all done their share of the erosion, sculpting the river valley.

From his vantage point, Biffle could see the rims vanish from his view, the river out of sight between the hills on both the north and south sides. On the southern side of the waterway rose another high mountain layered with rocky outcrops and with steep canyons running to the river. More flood plains spread out from the southern side of the river, wide enough to make good grazing land. He could see the steeply rising foothills leading to the top of the rock-topped mountain. Perhaps 2,500 feet high, Biffle guessed. Not as tall as some he'd seen, but tall, nonetheless, and forming a barrier on the south side of the valley.

His horse stomped impatiently, pulling at his bit, and the mule edged nearer Biffle's stirrup, sensing the end of a day spent watching the rear end of the horse. Sighing, Biffle reluctantly allowed the animals to move on. It'd be 'most dark by the time he reached the river and set up camp. He'd come back to this hilltop in the morning, again to sit and to look and to wonder. This valley would be home. That he knew. He'd choose his exact home site in the morning.

Biffle's homestead cabin would be about fifteen feet per side, the size recommended by the fellow in the county clerk's office in The Dalles.[2] This was the unofficially required size for a homesteader's cabin — well, maybe twelve feet on a side would do — and one window was needed, the pompous little clerk had informed Biffle, as if daring him to leave the

---

2 An old-timer, Fred Dunn, remembers seeing a dugout in an adobe hillside on Biffle's homestead site. Dunn says this is where Biffle lived for a time.

window out. Completion of his new home, "Properly constructed," the clerk emphasized, peering at Biffle from under his silly green celluloid visor, would mark the plot of land as his own.

"You'd better make a pile of rocks on each corner of your claim to prevent anyone else from infringin' on your territory," the records clerk had advised, and he'd made a crudely drawn map for Biffle to use as a guide for marking his property. "Surveyor will come out one day and make it official." When that official would arrive at his homestead, the clerk didn't say and Biffle didn't ask. He figured it would be several years yet before the government could spare men and the money to get as far to the east as he planned to settle, so for now he'd just establish himself with squatters' rights.

He'd had to buy a small wagon, large enough to transport the rough-sawn lumber — and the window — from The Dalles, where he'd gone to purchase what he'd need to develop his plot of land. He found a satis-factory horse to pull the wagon, a sturdy little grey mare that could also pull a plow when it was time to establish a field. His saddle horse would be tied behind the wagon for the trip back to the valley as he'd never been harnessed and Biffle had no time to fool around teaching him how to pull a load.

The round trip, which he had estimated to be a total of just over 200 miles, had taken him a bit over a week as he'd had to file his claim, pay the required fee for the land, and buy the wagon and the lumber for his cabin. He'd stopped to buy a few months' supply of flour, coffee, and tobacco and other staples he'd need. He added a small cast-iron cook stove to his purchases and then headed back up the military road to his chosen parcel of 160 acres. By the time he left The Dalles, Biffle had spent much of the cash he carried in a money belt worn next to his body. He'd not wanted to put any money in a bank that would be a good three days' ride away from him when he finally settled.

While in the city, he had also learned more from the garrulous clerk in the court house than he'd ever thought he'd need to know about the Homestead Act of '62 that had just been talk when he had started his venture to eastern Oregon. Signed by President Abraham Lincoln on May 20, 1862, the Act required Biffle or any other interested home-steader to file an application, improve the land, and file for a deed of title. He'd get a clear deed to the land when he had lived there for five years in his small cabin — with one window. Biffle met the requirement that he be twenty-one years old or older, and that he had never taken up arms against the U.S. government; staying the five years might be the challenge. For now, he'd just squat on the land.

As he looked at the sketchily drawn map showing his holdings, Bif-fle figured there'd be a whole lot of problems coming with folks trying to ascertain where their exact property lines lay. If all the maps coming out of the court house in The Dalles were as loosely drawn as his, and there was no doubt they would be, that little weasel of a clerk was setting the stage for a multitude of land disputes. Being the first homesteader in his valley, Biffle hoped, could help him avoid any clashes with ensuing settlers, but he'd not be surprised if he had to fight to keep his holdings as he'd marked them.

Biffle was no carpenter. He'd known that before he started on the structure. He'd been reminded of that as he'd scratched his head and run his fingers through his thick brown hair, absent-mindedly finger-combing the tangled mass. The taciturn worker in the lumber yard had helped him choose enough lumber for a cabin, though Biffle realized he'd been sold more than a good carpenter would need. He figured much of the wood he had purchased was green, from the weight of it, and would shrink in the summer sun, but he needed his building sup-plies and couldn't be choosey. The fellow taking his money knew the boards might shrink too, but he was taking advantage of the boom in house-building in the new settlements and homesteads east of The Dalles and he was selling any wood he could get into his lumber yard and he was grinning all the way to the bank.

While gathering information, wondering if his savings would cover the cost of his venture, Biffle had read an old newspaper plastered on his very small hotel room wall that in '52, lumber was selling for $25 per thousand board feet.[3] The homesteader knew the price had increased sharply with the boom in building in eastern Oregon, but he needed to make his money stretch as far as it could. Knowing he'd make mistakes as he built, ruining some of the lumber, he didn't begrudge the money he'd spent; he could always use a few extra boards, he figured, and he knew the price had gone up considerably in the past ten years, so perhaps — just perhaps — he'd not been overcharged too much.

The first of the extra boards he'd purchased had come in handy when he'd laid a few pieces across the narrowest part of the creek they called Bridge Creek, trying to pad out the crudely made log bridge he'd heard about on his first trip. As he focused on getting his loaded wagon across the watery obstacle, the weak pine boards cracked with the weight of the loaded wagon on them, but he got his cart full of supplies safely across. He'd picked up the shattered boards, cursing the damage as he placed them on top of his load. Some of the pieces would be large enough to make a small shelf or to frame the window so they wouldn't be a total loss, he figured.

He had to carve a very rough road just wide enough for the wagon across the rounded hills and following the gullies leading to his valley, angling his pathways to keep the wagon upright. He used his shovel on occasion, moving the smaller rocks that blocked the way through the narrow passageways or, if the rocks were too big to be moved, build-

---

3 End of the Oregon Trail Interpretive Center. "Provisions and Places. Prices in Oregon 1852." http://www.historicoregoncity.org/HOC/index

ing dirt beds up and around the obstruction. It was a rough corridor from Bridge Creek to his homestead site and the first heavy rain would wash much of it away, but he planned to take the trip with his wagon only once. Well, maybe another time or two, he admitted to himself. He might need more lumber and he'd need to get a plow to turn the soil for a crop. But, he'd use his pack mule to haul almost anything else he might need in the future.

Three days after he'd pulled his loaded wagon up on top of the white bank rising fifteen feet or so from the flood plain in the southwest side of the valley, Biffle framed the one window that was required for his home-stead cabin. The roof would leak, no doubt about that, as he could see daylight through knotholes and where the crudely sawn boards failed to butt up snugly against each other. He'd work on that later, using scraps of lumber to patch the holes or, if he had enough left, strips of wood placed over each joint, both on the roof and the walls. At least the shack would break the wind for now and Biffle was glad to have the shelter.

Before he worried about patching gaps and knotholes, though, he'd finish making a wooden platform for a bed of a sort that he'd use both to sleep on and to sit on as he ate from the table he'd made. He heard sounds in the night that could've been mice or rats, and he didn't want to share his bedroll with them, though he knew well they could climb right up a wall.

The table he'd built had one leg longer than the other three, and Biffle had trimmed the longer leg, but the table still rocked. Rather than cutting again, and perhaps again, to level the table, Biffle had solved that problem by digging down an inch or so in the dirt floor and settling the longest leg there and wedging a flat piece of shale under another leg. It was a tempo-rary fix, but it'd be fine as long as he didn't have to move the table.

Each time Biffle shut the door, hanging loosely on its leather hinges, the little shack shook a bit and seemed to dislodge a rock or two from the foundation. He'd tried to collect enough flat rocks to rest the crudely built walls on, but it seemed as if they'd never settle in. Maybe later on, perhaps his next trip to The Dalles, he could get more boards and put in a complete floor. Or, maybe he could head down to the Military Road and wait for a lumber wagon to come by, buying some of the load headed for the gold field at Canyon City.

For the time being, he'd laid the few remaining boards he had on the packed dirt, forming a makeshift floor that helped to keep some of the foundation from rolling away from the walls, and he left a gap in the boards around the longest table leg. Pounding large nails in the walls to hold cotton sacks full of his staples and his spare pair of pants and shirt, he called it a day.

Early in the evening as the sun's last rays played their light show on the face of the northern rims, Biffle sat on the large flat-topped rock he'd rolled against his cabin to use as a seat. He pulled a sack of tobacco and a small packet of cigarette papers from his shirt pocket and licked the tip of his index finger. Selecting one thin piece of paper, he gently squeezed it and made a trough with the thumb and middle finger of his left hand. He separated the gathered top of the tobacco pouch with his right forefinger and shook a small amount of tobacco on the paper. Then, holding one string between his teeth, the other between his fingers, he pulled the ties tightly and put the small cotton sack back into his shirt pocket. He lightly spread the tobacco almost the full length of the paper, tapping it slightly, and licked one long edge of the paper. Rolling the tobacco-filled paper carefully into a long cigarette, Biffle smoothed the wetted edge of the paper over the tube, forming a bond that would hold the tobacco while he enjoyed his last cigarette of the day. He absently raked a match against the wall of his shack, cupping his hand around the cigarette as he lit it, protecting the small flame from the evening breeze that came from the west.

This had become his favorite time of day, sitting on his dry hillside above his bottom land, drinking in the sights and smells and sounds of his valley. Biffle watched as the usual group of large black ravens settled into the tops of the taller trees lining the river bank, their raucous voices penetrating the evening as they "caw-cussed" everything in their limited bird world. Night birds were beginning their plaintive calls, darting in and out of the willows in search of insects that were thick above the waterway. Occasional nighthawks uttered their deep-throated cries, sounding almost like distant bulls bellowing for lost cows. Frogs croaked in the wet reeds and crickets began their nightly symphony, their sounds all part of the evening concert in the valley. The pungent smell of the sage grew heavier in the evening when the night breezes blew from the river to the south and the musky smell of the waterlogged reeds and willows tagged along.

Deer grazed slowly towards the river, picking at the tall bunch grass and nibbling at the willows as they approached the stream. Once he'd cleared the flat land of the sagebrush, Biffle figured the deer would skirt their way around the clearing, their survival instincts telling them they were too exposed in the open to an unknown enemy. The native animals wandered wide around his tethered horse and mule, avoiding the animals that were unfamiliar to them, not liking the smell of creatures to which they were unaccustomed, yet not seeming too afraid of them.

The show of light on the rimrock to the north fascinated the lone man sitting against the wall of his home. The sun lowered itself in the western sky, the colors on the basalt face of the rim changing from brown to yellow to orange to red to violet, and finally to dark brown as the light faded from the valley. Each evening Biffle noted a new feature on the rock face that he'd not taken in before and each evening it seemed as if the colors highlighted a different piece of the rim.

If he lived to be a hundred and spent each evening on his rock by the cabin, Biffle allowed, he'd see something new each day in the fading light. He felt the essence of the valley wrap itself around him and fill his heart with contentment as he sat propped against his shaky shack on his alkaline bank.

Almost without thinking, the homesteader rose from his seat and entered his home, reaching for the Bible he'd placed on a shelf made especially for the gift his mother had given him. Returning to his outside chair, Biffle opened the book to the place marked by a worn piece of wall-paper cut into a book marker and he saw Psalm 121 underlined in pencil. "I will lift up mine eyes unto the hills, from whence cometh my help," he read. How did Mother know when I'd read this? he mused, and, closing the book gently, he sat quietly for some time, his thoughts rambling, returning to the psalm, drifting off to past conversations and books read, taking in the vista before him, and, always, his thoughts reconnecting with the psalm.

As he absorbed the sights and the sounds of his valley every evening, the homesteader began to realize it wouldn't be money in the bank that would make this land his. He knew farming couldn't be extremely profitable here in the isolated valley, but he was conscious of another fortune that was his. He was becoming a part of the sagebrush and the rolling hills and the strength of the rims. Life here was beginning to feel like a good fit, his independent soul satisfied with making the sacrifices he knew were ahead in order to live the style of life he'd dreamed of for years.

He knew he'd have to struggle to keep body and soul together financially, but he was aware that his riches would not be in gold stored in the bank in The Dalles, that his wealth would lie in his life on his homestead. His way of life would be the fortune he knew the bankers and the lawyers and the rich merchants in the cities would envy, yet they would cling to their pursuit of material things for their artificial happiness. Biffle would be the first of the independent folks who would call the area their home.

"Old Ben Franklin was a pretty wise fella," Biffle thought. "He said that the Constitution gave men the right to life, liberty, and the pursuit of happiness — but, it didn't guarantee it. I've got my life and, thanks to the folks who fought for it, I've got my liberty. And now, after pursuin' it for the past several years, I do believe I've found the happiness."

Establishing a farm was back-breaking work and one day rolled into another, and then the next and the next. Each morning as the sky lightened and the valley awakened from the night's darkness, Biffle rolled over on his sleeping platform, the hard boards encouraging his sore body to leave its resting place. He shoved his well-worn and stained patchwork quilt and the one woven wool blanket he owned to the wall side of the raised area, along with the coat he'd folded into a pillow, and his bed was made.

Often, as he arose from his hard bed in the mornings, Biffle was struck with a bout of uncontrollable coughing. Cough after deep cough, he hacked and spit, ridding his body of the heavy mucous that had seemed to gather during the night. Oftentimes, he bent double with the effort, sitting back down onto the side of his bunk until the session had subsided and he could stand upright, wiping his eyes and blowing his nose. Occasionally, the coughing would not stop so Biffle would scoop up half a spoonful of sugar, put a small dollop of kerosene in the spoon, and down the cough suppressant, often feeling that the cure might be worse than the cough.

He kneeled by his small cook stove and unlatched the handle, noting it was still warm. That meant there would be enough coals to start a fire, and he pushed the red embers together, using a piece of kindling as a poker. Adding a few twigs and pieces of dried grass, he quickly had a small blaze flickering and then he added larger pieces of sage branches he'd gathered not far from his cabin.

Satisfied with the cook fire, he scooped a six-quart rounded enameled pot into his tin water bucket, put it on the stove and took a small handful of coffee from the flour sack he'd filled in The Dalles, and tossed it into the water. He set the pot on the hottest part of the stove, where the stovepipe left the small cast-iron range to run through the wall, and left the water to come to a boil while he went outside to relieve himself several feet from the cabin.

As he ambled to the place of his morning toilet, he perused the landscape, looking for the sight of an Indian who might be watching him, not being modest but being cautious. He wasn't too concerned about the natives, but it didn't hurt to be on the lookout. After he'd scanned the sloping hills to the south and the west, the open bottom land to the north and east, he turned to the business at hand, unbuttoning his canvas pants.

He'd developed this morning ritual, standing with his legs slightly apart while relieving himself, looking at his homestead and the valley, deciding his schedule for the day. He'd continue pulling sage on the bottom land just under the hill where his shack sat. He figured he had been able to clear an average of around an acre a day, about 200 feet by 200 feet — well, closer to 209 feet a side, or about 69 paces.

It depended on the mule and on Biffle's patience. The little sage, he could dig under that with his pick and his shovel and toss it aside to move later. Bigger sage, though, he had to dig down a foot or so around the roots and then hook a piece of rope around the base of the plant, tie the lose end to the mule's harness, and get the beast to pull. That was the trick; that mule had a mind of his own. Where the sage entered the ground, sometimes the base would be six inches across, maybe more. Big base meant big roots, long roots. The bigger the plant, the bigger the problem.

After he'd cleared a sizeable area and the mule was balking more than he was working, Biffle would remove the harness from the tired animal, lead him to the river for water, and then stake him out in a patch of bunch grass near the river bank. He'd hook the wagon she'd pulled from The Dalles to the grey mare and toss the loose sage onto the bed. Then, the load would be hauled to his wood pile where he'd toss it off and later cut or break it up for firewood.

With the sage pulled off the area he'd set for the day's clearing job, Biffle would tackle the bunch grass. Some of the clumps were large and it took a fair amount of digging to free the roots from the brown topsoil. Again, he'd leave the results of his work where they lay until he tired of bending and digging. Then he'd hook the mare to the wagon again, lift the bunches of grass up on the bed, and haul the load to the sides of the area he'd marked out for his field. He'd paced off an area about 600 feet by 600 feet, figuring that would be enough work for his first year. Almost ten acres, he reckoned.

He figured he'd plant oats for both his animals and for himself. A bit of wheat, too, and a sizeable garden. There ought to be enough spring rains to start his grain crops, and if he planted his garden near the river, he could carry water to the plants during the summer when he knew there'd be little moisture. The scrub brush and lack of trees away from the river were sure signs that there was little rainfall in this area. The soil, though, that was fertile.

He'd picked up handful after handful of the rich soil in the flood plain, smelling the freshness of the dark earth. With enough water, a man could grow just about anything he'd ever want or need in this valley. The water would be vital, though. He'd have to figure out a way to irrigate if he wanted a really good crop, but this year he'd just get the grains planted and see how they would do with dry-land farming.

The breeze shifted and brought the smell of coffee to the morning air. Biffle snapped his mind back to the business at hand, buttoning up the stiff flap of his canvas pants as he hurried to his cabin to pull the boiling pot full of coffee off the heat.

He took the glazed top off the small sourdough crock he kept on his table and used a spoon to scoop some of the thin batter into a tin pan. Adding a bit of flour, a pinch of salt, and a few pinches of saleratus, commonly called 'baking powder,' he made a stiff dough, then lay his spoon aside and kneaded the mix with a calloused hand. He wiped the top of the small cast-iron cook stove with a piece of flour sacking, and then he patted the soft dough into four flat rounds, laying each on the stove top as he finished shaping the bread. That would be much faster than baking the rounds in the small oven, and he could have two pieces of the bread for breakfast, two for dinner.

He poured a cup of the strong black coffee into his tin enameled cup and kept a wary eye on the biscuits cooking on the stove top. As he stood near the cook stove, he absent-mindedly rubbed the backs of his hands, noticing the skin was getting rougher. He picked up the container of kerosene from the floor and tipped a small amount on the palm of his hand. This he rubbed into the backs of both hands, knowing that kerosene was good for healing rough skin.

When the top of the cooking dough appeared to lose all shininess, he ran his pocketknife under the rounds, turning them to cook the other side, scraping small bits of browned sourdough off the cast iron and onto the floor. While the biscuits finished cooking, he scooped a handful of dried apples out of the sack hanging from a nail on the wall and chewed the fruit, wrinkling his nose at the lingering smell and taste of the kerosene he'd rubbed on his hands.

Maybe tonight, if he finished early, he could boil up some of the apples with a bit of sugar and make some apple butter to add to his biscuits for supper. With that in mind, he put several large handfuls of dried apples in his largest pan, but before he added water to soak the fruit, he thought better of the idea and dumped the apples back into their sack. He was out of cooked beans and needed to make up a batch. With only one large pan, he'd better take care of the beans today, do the jam tomorrow night. He replaced the dried apples with a few large handfuls of brown beans, poured in enough water to cover them, and set them on the fire to take advantage of the last of the heat in the stove. They would soak all day and take only an hour or so to cook for supper.

Biffle ate one of the sourdough biscuits in four bites, washing down the dense bread with swallows of his cooling coffee. Then, taking the second biscuit and a fresh cup of coffee, he went outside to sit on his rock by the side of his shack where he could survey the land spread below him. As he folded his legs to sit down, he noticed the small fossilized marine shells in the large rock he used as a chair.

Just about every time he'd gone out looking for firewood, he'd found petrified bones of ancient animals far larger than any deer or coyotes he'd seen in his valley. Too, he'd found chunks of sandstone with leaves of prehistoric plants in the white clay banks above his home

site. These he had picked up, examined, and tossed aside. That the area on which he was establishing his farm had once been underwater, there was no doubt. Biffle knew the winds and the rains through the ages had pounded and worn these ancient life forms into the rich soil he would work.

"It's good bottom land," he mused aloud, nodding his head. "It's big bottom land," and he looked at the land spread below his perch, then across the river where the flat land stretched to the foothills of the rim-rocks and to the east out of sight between the rims on the north and the hills on the south.

"Big Bottom. Good Bottom." He tried the names out loud. "Big Bottom," he decided. "Good name for a homestead," he chuckled to himself. "Not so good for a woman, but it describes the land. Big Bottom."

Chapter 2
1863 — Meyer and Hewot

They were heading east from The Dalles, the big German bouncing along on the unforgiving wooden plank seat, each jolt of the loaded wagon jostling the thick mat of light blonde hair on his rounded head and flapping the cropped beard that covered his square jaw, the tall, sharp-featured Englishman pacing alongside on his bay mare.

Occasionally the German tugged impatiently on the leather reins leading to the two mismatched horses, one black and one a dappled gray, pulling the wagon piled high with supplies for a new homestead. A reluctant mule, her black coat powdered with dust thrown up from the wheels of the conveyance, gave a sporadic jerk on the rope tying her to the tailgate, reminding her owners that she was not happy with her lot in life.

"We should be almost there," the hulk of a man on the wagon said as he worked the reins, encouraging the team, though he had only a vague idea of where "there" was. He and Frank Hewot were following the route taken by Biffle the year before and, like him, they hoped to find land that would be suitable for their needs.

The trail left by the members of the U. S. Cavalry and the prospectors heading east since the discovery of gold near Canyon City two years before in '61 was distinctive. Though well-marked and easily followed, it was still definitely rough and uneven, each rain causing the soft mud to rut up from the traffic passing over the roadbed.

Somewhere near this road Meyer and Hewot hoped they'd find a place to squat where they would develop 160 acres and file a homestead. They didn't know where their home would be, for sure. What they were looking for was a likely location for a cabin and for a garden where they could grow enough produce to feed themselves and to sell to the travelers on The Dalles to Canyon City Military Road. They'd know the right homestead spot when they saw it.

Meyer absent-mindedly ran his fingers through his shortly cropped blonde beard, his thick eyebrows jutting out above his intensely blue eyes as he carefully watched the road ahead for signs of deep ruts that he would guide his team around. The motion caught Hewot's eye and he took in the hulk of a man, his massive arms stretching the cloth of his shirt, his belly straining the buttons almost to the point of popping off. His bulky body, however, showed no signs of softness though it contrasted sharply with Hewot's lean and muscled body. Both men had work-hardened hands and weathered faces that told of days spent laboring under the sun.

The partners guided their horses up the winding road snaking between mounded hills often showing patches of tan and red and green adobe soil. Occasional areas of rank bunch grass indicated spots of fertile soil that were watered by springs higher in the draws. From the smallness and the scarcity of vegetation on most of the dry hills, the travelers assumed there was little rainfall in this country.

At the top of a rise in the road, Hewot reined his horse to a stop and reached into his shirt pocket for the makings of a cigarette. His dark hair blew back from his forehead when he bent against the breeze threatening to extinguish the flame of the match he used to light his smoke, his bushy eyebrows pulled together as he squinted against the smoke curling up from the fag.

Meyer's team gratefully pulled up beside him, blowing slightly from the effort of the climb and the mule gave a snort as if reminding the travelers that she had long thought it was about time she was allowed to rest. Ahead of them and across the river from their resting place, an impressive rock bluff rose into the sky. The face of the brown basalt landmark appeared to be made of rock thrust up from below the surface eons ago, the columnar face melded together from some ancient inferno deep under the ground. The rock rested on a base of sloping grassy hills leading down to the river called the John Day and the setting sun was casting rays of orange, then red, then purple on the rocks.

Following the base of the massive rock formation to the east were lesser rounded hills covered with light-colored dried grasses and low shrubs. The sharpening of the night breezes reminded the travelers they needed to make camp before darkness set in, and Meyer clucked to his team as Hewot pulled away from the wagon on his horse.

They set up camp facing the massive rock across the river where they had watered their horses. Wood was scarce near the obviously well-used campsite, but the small fire they managed to build felt good in the coolness of nightfall. As they drank their coffee, Hewot puffed on his cigarette and Meyer chewed on an unlit pipe. They both felt they would reach their homestead site in the next day or so and they felt excitement at the probable fruition of long-held dreams.

The German had been born in 1819 and as a young man had traveled to California in '49 when news of the gold rush there had spread to Germany. He and Hewot had struck up a friendship that developed into a partnership, and here they were, planning to develop a farm and pursue a livelihood in a manner to which Meyer was familiar, that of farming. He'd had enough of digging for gold, as had Hewot.

The next day the partners followed the route for The Dalles-Canyon City Military Road along the river for just a short while until it turned south along the small but fast-flowing creek that was marked "Bridge Creek" on their rumpled map. Another few miles and the road would turn sharply to the east, and then wind through a valley beside a creek — if the map they carried was even somewhat accurate. Perhaps they could find their garden spot somewhere soon, fairly near the middle of the roughly 200-mile trip from The Dalles to Canyon City. They figured they were close to their destination, estimating that they'd pushed their team hard, traveling about thirty miles each day, and this was the end of their third day on the road.

The men hated to end their conversation, anticipation of the next few days exciting them almost to the point of sleeplessness. Meyer finally begrudgingly admitted he'd better get some rest before the next day of travel. Sighing, they rose to their feet, Hewot grinding out the stub of his cigarette under his boot heel. Meyer smoothed his dusty beard over his chin as he knocked the last of the tobacco out of his pipe, stuck the pipe in his shirt pocket, and rolled his broad shoulders to loosen them under the tightly stretched cotton of his shirt.

The men turned to their bedrolls for the night, placing their loaded Enfield rifles close. The partners slept lightly, waking several times in the darkness to listen to the sounds of distant coyotes and nocturnal birds, the soughing of wind in the willows, and the gurgling of the flowing John Day.

Both men woke early in the morning to the false dawn of the day, moving as one as they rolled out of their hard beds and reached for their hats. They stood and stretched, yawning loudly and shaking their bodies, sore from the hard ground. There was no need for talk; the men had long ago established their daily routine and they each began their chores. Hewot moved to lead the horses and their mule to water while Meyer rebuilt the cooking fire and prepared a pot of coffee and began to fry bacon for breakfast.

Once he'd had a plate of food and a cup of coffee, Hewot broke the morning silence by volunteering to replenish their meat supply with a rabbit or a grouse sometime during the day. He looked over at his friend; the big German needed a lot of meat, all right, to keep that body healthy. Hewot glanced at the well-used .58 caliber Tennessee mountain rifle packed into the scabbard mounted onto his saddle. That he'd get one of the plentiful deer they had been seeing as soon as they picked a place to settle was a certainty. Taking aim on a piece of meat and bringing it down with one shot was an act as natural as breathing to the marksman.

Meyer guided the wagon along the road as it turned south onto the small flood plain paralleling the creek that ran into the river. The morning air sharpened the call of the blackbirds darting through the willows ahead of their passage and a deer, startled from its morning drink, bounded away from the creek. Overhead a red-tailed hawk gave out a piercing call as he circled above the stream and a bald eagle flapped his powerful wings effortlessly over the travelers. The men found and then carefully crossed the crudely built bridge shown on their map and continued following the waterway.

The passage along the creek was bordered by scrubby sagebrush and bunch grass, and an occasional grouse exploded from near the trail. The men had been traveling for an hour or more when the rolling hills began to drop their coverings of bunch grass. Red clay, streaked with white, then greenish-brown, shone brightly on the hillsides. More and more of the rounded colored domes appeared among the bunch-grass-covered hills, the hues more vivid than either of the travelers had ever imagined soil could be.

Some of the rolling hills were dotted with layered white banks, then red, indicating worthless clay soil. These were interspersed with grass-covered areas near Bridge Creek, showing fertile patches of dirt. The smooth tops of the hills showed the results of wind and rain erosion, and small draws leading to the bases of the mounds marked the path of the runoff.

Meyer looked toward Hewot as his voice rose over the sounds of the wagon bouncing on the uneven road. "Wonder how the soil will be for a garden?" the horseman asked.

"We'll find a good spot soon," the German assured him, pointing to an especially lush patch of ground near the stream. "I can feel it in my bones." He shifted his massive buttocks on the unyielding plank seat. "And I can feel it in my rear end, I can!" The men laughed, appreciating the raw beauty of the brightly painted hills but searching ahead for an indication of soil good enough for the farm they would develop.

The Englishman kept alert as he rode slightly ahead of the wagon, watching for rattlesnakes and for badger holes. Some red adobe banks they were traveling along sloped downward to pathetic looking creek beds that hadn't carried much water for quite a while, though the tufts of grass indicated there had been adequate spring rains to start those small bits of vegetation.

The road turned sharply to the east, rounding a steep, rocky bluff and winding up a narrow canyon lined with grass-covered hills blocking the view to the north and to the south. It was becoming a warm day and the men began to smell their own sweat mingled with that of their horses.

"I'll find a place to rest a bit," Hewot offered, motioning towards the creek that flowed steadily beside the road. "Horses can get a drink, too. I need to get rid of some of this dirt," and he wrinkled his nose. Meyer agreed with a broad smile as he nodded his massive head and pinched his forefinger and thumb over his large nostrils. Another hundred yards and the narrow canyon opened up.

The men pulled their animals up short as they took in the panorama before them. From their places on the narrow military road, they could see the bunch-grass-covered valley, green from spring rains. An occasional outcropping of basalt rocks broke the smoothness of the low weathered hills that bordered the valley's four sides. Behind them, far to the west, they could see the blue tips of distant mountains. A small willow-lined creek they'd followed since turning from Bridge Creek ran

Site of the Meyer homestead. The scattered rocks are all that remain of
the Meyer Fort House. The old locust trees were planted by Meyer.

through the center of the broad basin with a floor so flat it looked as if
some ancient hand had scraped the bottom smooth.

The men sat quietly, turning to take in the view on all sides. Perhaps a mile long, maybe a little less, and maybe half as wide, the terrain showed promise of a garden spot without too much work. With the
gentle slope of the land to the west following the path of the waterway, it
would be easy to set up an irrigation system for their plants. The hills to
the north and to the south formed natural barriers from cold winds that
could freeze plants late in the spring and early in the fall. The site seemed
custom-made for raising crops.

The horses began to stomp impatiently, pulling at their bits, wanting
to move towards the creek. Each man hesitated to look at the other, hoping to see approval on his partner's face but fearing rejection of the site.
Slowly, out of the corners of their eyes, and then full face, they looked at
each other questioningly.

"This is it!" they exclaimed in unison, and both began to laugh, the usually taciturn Hewot throwing his head back as he gave out a throaty bellow of approval.

"Ja! This is it!" Meyer thundered. "Mein Gott! This is it!"

"You know you'll be the first to settle between the Des Chutes River and Canyon Creek, don't you?" the clerk had asked Meyer as he inquired about the availability of his 160 acres. "Everyone has to register with me and I'd know any different." His self-importance made little impression on Meyer, who had thanked him and abruptly left the office. He had business to tend to. Hewot had opted to remain at their homestead site, just in case another settler chanced by and decided the spot would be ideal for his venture in the unmarked, unsettled land.

Meyer had no trouble finding a satisfactory team of horses, one with a reddish brown coat, the other a tan, to pull a new, large wagon. He'd left the smaller wagon and his first team of horses with Hewot, borrowing his partner's saddle horse for the trip. The men had decided it would be prudent to have two teams so they could alternate horses and their mule and work from daylight until dark. All five animals could pull a plow when it was time to establish the fields. Oxen would be best, but the new pair of horses would make the trip from The Dalles to their property faster and they'd best hurry with the initial work so they could get their seeds planted and take advantage of what they hoped would be a long growing season.

"You're one motley looking group, you are," Meyer assured one of the newly acquired horses as he put a collar around her neck. The traces that had come with the team were made of good leather and should last well, as would the girth complete with a harness saddle. Meyer had spent more than he'd wanted to on the harness, but good leather meant he'd not be making repairs soon.

The round trip of just over 200 miles took him eight days to make as he'd had to spend a few days to buy the wagon and some lumber to help in the building of their cabin. He'd also stopped to buy a few months' supply of flour, coffee, and tobacco and other staples. Satisfied with his purchases, he headed back up the military road to the chosen parcel of 160 acres. Soon as the government surveyed the land, they could file a legal claim for their homestead, but it might be several years yet before the surveyors reached the remote area.[1]

Like Biffle, neither Hewot nor Meyer was a carpenter and they knew they'd live in the first cabin they built just until they could build the bigger fort-house they intended to use as an overnight stop for travelers on the military road. The fifteen-foot-square cabin, though, was needed to meet the requirements of the Homestead Act, and it would be good to have a shelter, no matter how humble.

Two days after Meyer pulled his heavily loaded wagon up to the camp site where Hewot waited for his return, the men finished framing the one window that was required for their homestead cabin and they were done.

Early in the evening as the sun's last rays played their light show on the tops of the hills surrounding their little valley, the men sat on the large flat-topped rocks they'd rolled against their cabin to use as seats, just as Biffle had done. While he was in The Dalles, Meyer had replenished their supply of whiskey and they each had a healthy portion of the fiery liquor in their tin cups set on the makeshift table beside their rock seats.

Hewot took a sack of tobacco and a small packet of cigarette papers from his shirt pocket and, licking the tip of his index finger, pulled out a thin paper and began to roll a cigarette. Meyer filled the bowl of his blackened pipe with tobacco from the pouch he carried in his shirt pocket, packed the tobacco firmly into the bowl, and lighted it with the match Hewot shared.

---

1 Meyer filed on his 160 acres in '84. BLM Government Land Office Records. http://www. glorecords.blm.gov.landpatents.surveys

This was a good ending to their day, sitting beside their cabin, sharing a drink, and taking in the scene before them. As they leaned against their cabin wall, the partners gestured to the east and to the west, indicating where they would plant a field of wheat there, a root garden here, the corn over in another place. Pointing with their fingers in the air, they planned the route of their irrigation ditches, allowing for the pull of gravity to do its work and carry the depleted flow of water back to the original stream.

Hewot rubbed his aching shoulder muscles as he surveyed the broad floor of the valley. "Ja. It's work, all right," the German agreed, watching his friend work his muscles. "But, we'll do our job and make us a farm and then, someday, we'll leave it all behind and someone else will take advantage of our sore backs and put in their time. Then, they'll move on. And, over and over," and Meyer grinned at his friend.

The partners sat quietly for a time, bodies relaxed and eyes constantly perusing the landscape. Meyer stuck a sausage-like finger into his bulbous nose almost absent-mindedly, twisting his hand slowly back and forth. "Findin' any gold, Prospector?" Hewot asked as he watched his friend at work. All he got was a wry grin in response as Meyer continued his efforts. "Wouldn't do fer some lady to be sittin' here, now would it?" the Englishman goaded the German, and the partners sat companionably while Meyer completed his task, both men occasionally and openly relieving themselves of gas. For sure, a lady would inhibit their lifestyle, both men agreed good-naturedly.

The show of light on the hilltop to the north claimed the attention of the two men sitting on their rock chairs. As the sun lowered itself in the western sky, they saw the colors on the grass-covered face of the hillside change from brown to yellow to orange to red to violet, and finally to dark brown as the light faded from their valley. The two friends and partners would never tire of the evening light show on their homestead; nightly, they renewed their feeling that life was going to be good for them in their little valley.

The men developed their morning ritual, Hewot watering the horses and mule and Meyer cooking breakfast, neither man speaking until they had finished their breakfast and downed their first cups of coffee. Then they began planning their day as they drank a second cup of coffee together.

Meyer would continue pulling sage and Hewot would dig the bunch grass on the floor of the valley surrounding their shack. They figured they would be able to clear an average of about an acre and a half a day. They wanted to get four or five acres cleared and tilled before they started planting their garden, which they needed to get in as soon as they could as the soil felt warm enough for seeds to grow well. Too, they'd have to devise a system for irrigating before sowing the seeds they'd brought with them. Once the garden was under control, they could begin their permanent fort-house.

While Meyer worked at loading the sage onto a wagon to haul off the garden site, Hewot harnessed up the mule and took over the pulling of the sage. The men seldom planned breaks during the day, reserving their resting for the times a passerby would stop to visit with them. Neither the homesteaders nor their visitors tarried long during working hours; they either had miles to travel or acres to clear and they all wanted to make the most of the daylight hours before darkness overtook them.

One day a traveler on the military road neared Hewot working in the field he was developing, a cloud of white powdery alkaline dust boiling up behind the plow as the sharp blades dug deeply through a streak of the dusty bleached soil. The traveler's eyes widened as he discovered an apparition thoroughly covered from head to toe with the white dirt, guiding the horse and plow. Hewot pulled the horse up short, removed his hat, and beat it on his leg, attempting to clean it of the alkali. He grinned ironically as he noticed the surprised look on the horseman's face.

"Alkali," he said shortly. Not getting a response, he added, "Frank." Another pause. "Hewot," he finished.

"Pleased ta meetcha, Alkali Frank Hewot," the stranger grinned, reaching out to shake the hand Hewot extended. The introduction was repeated to Meyer, and from that day on, his partner was known as "Alkali Frank Hewot."

Some days, they had just one or two interruptions; other days, they seemed to be able to only work an hour or so before stopping to share a cup of the coffee they kept simmering on the stove all day, the brew growing stronger and blacker as the day wore along. With each session of sharing the coffee, Meyer replenished the water in the pot and added a suitable amount of coffee grounds. By the end of the day, the coffee was strong enough to make the hair on his chest stand straight out, Meyer declared, and he often shared a cold sourdough biscuit with his companions to use as a buffer for the strong black liquid.

"That John Deere, he's one smart man," commented Hewot as he looked at the new steel plow the partners had brought to their farm with them. The inventor had developed the implement in '37 by taking a saw blade and working it into the shape of a plow. The new invention had a self-polishing blade and a curved iron plate called a moldboard. A bonus was that the new device pulled easier than any other plow so far invented, and the John Deere implement was being used all over America.[2]

By the '60s, an optional seat could be added to the plow so that farmers could plow while sitting down, though Meyer and Hewot chose not to. Instead, Hewot guided their mule while Meyer walked alongside to steer the plow and to use his massive strength to push it deeply into the topsoil and to keep the blade cleared.

The progress over the ground was satisfying despite the jolting and

---

2 Pioneer Resources and Webliography. "Plowing." 2//9/2011. http://www.campsilos.org/mod2/teachers.

pitching as the steel blades cut through the topsoil and struck an occasional stone in the rich silt. They found they could easily turn about an acre or more of ground a day, the rich earth in their valley having few rocks.

Plowing the virgin soil was a back-breaking chore for the men and they took turns, spelling each other often during the day. As they hooked their John Deere plow to their mule's harness, they wished they had a slow, dependable ox to use while plowing. The mule tended to be a bit long-legged once she got started, but she was steadier and sturdier than their horses.

Meyer had picked up handful after handful of the rich soil in the floodplain, checking it, feeling it in his hand, smelling the freshness of the dark earth. With enough water, a man could grow just about anything he'd ever want or need in this little valley. The water would be vital, though. They'd have to lay out their irrigation system soon.

The men plowed their five acres one direction, then a second time across the furrows, breaking the sod into even finer clumps. The third time over the soil the plow fairly skimmed over the broken ground as it followed the course of the initial ground breaking. The ease in which the plow sliced through the twice-broken ground made the men lengthen their strides and break out in a heavy sweat as they tried to keep up with their mule. The $10 he'd spent on the farm implement had been worth every last red cent, Meyer told Hewot.

Meyer used a flat hoe to chop the few remaining clods into small pieces. His partner followed behind, raking the ground into rows running horizontally across the gentle slope to the creek to help prevent erosion. The small ditches, or furrows, they dug in the middle of the raked ground would serve two purposes: to carry water from the creek down the rows where it would seep out to irrigate the plants, and to help slow the rain water to prevent soil from washing across the garden during rain storms.

The men dammed up their spring-fed creek with boulders as large as they could wrestle and pry into place, leaving a substantial part of the creek to continue on its course and provide water to those who might settle below their farm. They made the dam fairly watertight by forcing the sagebrush they had pulled and bits of bunch-grass roots and mud into the gaps, pounding them into place with the flat of their shovels.

A large ditch was dug to the area of their garden, with smaller channels directed towards each row in the cultivated soil. They kept the water flowing from the creek in a small but steady stream, running it down the rows before planting, adjusting the height in one place, the level of the row in another, letting gravity carry the water, until they saw that their irrigating could be accomplished with very little effort on their part.

Beans and corn; carrots and cabbage; turnips and lettuce; tomatoes and squash; cucumbers and onions; potatoes and peas; melons and pumpkins. The garden grew in size each day as Meyer and Hewot stooped and planted, straightened their backs and rubbed them, wiped the sweat from their sun-darkened faces with their handkerchiefs, and then bent to resume sowing the vegetables.

Within a week after planting the first of their tiny seeds, green began to show in their garden and the men sat on Meyer's latest carpentry effort, a crudely built bench placed against their cabin wall, and assured passersby that they could count on vegetables by the end of the summer. The fertile soil and the always flowing water nearby, helped by the hot summer sun, would all ensure a good crop.

"Lettuce and radishes in a month," Meyer promised expectant travelers hungry for fresh vegetables.

Less than a week after they had examined the new shoots of vegetables poking through the rich loam of their garden, the partners experienced their first flashflood. The day had grown increasingly hot, the oppressive heat seeming to press down upon them as thunderclouds built rapidly in the south, the heavy black clouds rising ominously into the sky. The sound of thunder could be heard at a distance, then closer and closer. Their valley grew eerily quiet just before heavy winds began, followed by almost simultaneous lightning strikes and thunder claps and then torrential downpour.

The men watched helplessly from the window and the open door of their cabin as rivulets formed in their garden ditches, then widened and rushed from their bounds, washing madly across row after row of the young vegetable plants. The heavy rain lasted only ten minutes or so. Then, the tempest blown quickly and forcefully to the north, the thunderstorm left the little valley as abruptly as it had arrived, marking its progress with the sound of thunder fading into the distance.

The men surveyed the damage, following the path of the water through their garden by the small plants strewn about. Sighing, they knelt in the muddy ground and began gathering what they could to replant in the soggy soil.

"Looks like we'll be repairing the dam, it does," Meyer complained, pointing to their dam that had been washed badly during the flood. "Looks like the creek is deeper than it was, too. It's a regular gulch now. Meyer's Gulch, ja?" He shrugged his broad shoulders in acceptance of Mother Nature's handiwork.

"And just tell me how to tell a turnip from a rutabaga by looking at their roots," Hewot asked disgustedly, holding up two scraggly inch-long plants for inspection by the master gardener. Then, overcome at the enormity of the task of replanting their garden, the men plopped down in the mud and looked at each other's straggly wet hair and the pathetic looking plants, and they began to laugh hysterically as they sat in the midst of the mud in their scattered crop.

Once their garden was re-established, the men staked out nearby areas for their orchard and for a grain field where they planned to grow wheat, which would be ground into flour, and oats, which could be made into a cereal to be fed to travelers or as feed for their work animals.

After planting their grain field, Meyer took a trip to The Dalles to purchase some of the lumber they would need for building a large fort-house to be used not only as a stage station but also as a haven from the supposed "marauding Indians" that were so active in the area, though he had yet to hear of such an incident nearby. He figured they could buy the remainder of what they would need from the loads of lumber being pulled past their holdings, heading for the gold field. He padded out his load of lumber with the makings of a farm.

As Meyer drew the wagon up near their home site, Hewot saw two bony milk cows tagging along reluctantly at the ends of their long lead ropes, and he could hear the cacophony of angry animals coming from the back of the wagon. The milk cows were obviously not happy, their feet tender from the long trek, which had taken an impatient Meyer an extra day because of his new acquisitions. The German had made the dairy animals some leather boots, which he had tied over each hoof. Regardless of the extra protection, the cows, heavy with calves, had slowed him down even more than he'd anticipated.

"Good cheeses!" Meyer beamed. "Milk for the porridge," and he gestured to the two cows. "And eggs for the breakfast." He reached into the back of the wagon and lifted out a large chicken coop full of squawking, very unhappy hens and one indignant rooster with bedraggled tail feathers.

Hewot had smelled the pigs before he heard their unhappy squeals, and he watched as his partner reached again into the back of his wagon and, from beside the high stack of lumber, pulled out a large crate with a huge white boar and two brown sows crammed tightly inside. The German seemed to hardly strain as he slid the heavy wooden box to the ground.

"And bacon and sausages for the eggs! Now we are a farm!" Meyer beamed.

At the end of each day spent working their farm, the partners made at least one trip to a nearby rocky hillside, looking for large yellowish-brown sandstone rocks, with an occasional patch of dusty-red, to be shaped roughly into rectangular building blocks. After knocking off unwanted protrusions and giving the small boulders sides flat enough for adding to a wall, the two men lifted the heavy pieces into the wagon. Pausing long enough to wipe the sweat from their faces and to take a drink from the stream, they then took the weighty load home and added the rocks to the growing wall of the fort-house they were constructing. The men were grateful for the late afternoon breezes that blew up their valley; it was a welcome relief from the sometimes oppressive summer heat of their homestead site.

The rock building would be roughly twenty-five feet by fifty feet, the walls about ten feet high. With the varying sizes of the rocks making the walls two-feet-thick in places, the shelter would offer good protection for surrounding settlers from the Indian attacks that were feared more with each passing day. As a bonus, the walls would keep the interior cooler in the summer and warmer in the winter than would the crudely built cabin they had erected.

There was no shortage of travelers to help the two men with the construction of the fort-house. Meyer and Hewot often waited for the sound of an approaching traveler and then hurried to their work site to ask for help with an especially heavy rock to be placed high on the wall. Word spread fast and passersby soon knew they could work for an hour or two and then would be treated to a portion of Meyer's seemingly never-ending supply of whiskey and a bowl of the hearty soups he kept constantly simmering on the back of his wood stove. The whiskey cost $1.50 a bottle in The Dalles and the cost of the potatoes and onions in the stew, boiled with the venison Hewot brought to the house, was very little. The partners figured the whiskey and stew were pretty cheap wages to pay for the help in building what would be known as the Meyer Fort-House.

Upon completion of the stage stop fort-house late in the fall of '63, the refreshment was still free to neighbors. Strangers or travelers, however, would visit a bit and then would reach into their pockets to pay the German for their food and drink, dropping a coin or two in the empty tin saleratus can kept on the dining table for that purpose. Business was lively for Meyer and Hewot as travelers were plentiful on the military road and the few neighbors in the area had found a local gathering place where good conversation, good food, and good drink were abundant.

The two settlers found they eagerly anticipated an approaching horse or wagon. They never knew what interesting character might drive up to their homestead, but that a unique individual would soon be sitting at their table, sharing a cup of whiskey and a story, was a sure thing. Only those folks willing to take a risk and break free from their roles in their former lives would venture to this area, and only those with an independent spirit would remain to help develop the fledgling region. Meyer and Hewot looked forward to visiting with those folks.

Chapter 3
1864 — Gold Fever Builds

It was in early summer of '64 that Christian Meyer, returning from a trip to The Dalles with a wagon piled with provisions, saw James Biffle sitting on his horse near the juncture of the military road and the small trail the squatter had worn on his trips to and from his home some ten miles to the northeast. Meyer knew his nearest neighbor was lonely, and he couldn't fault the fellow for riding down to look for a passerby on the road, hoping to break his loneliness with a visit. Although Biffle had squatted on his homestead sometime in '62, the year before Meyer and Hewot had arrived, the men seldom saw each other.

"It's a warm one for June," Meyer announced in greeting as he reined in his team and looped the guide lines around a wooden peg near the stiff board seat he'd been sitting on for almost three days. He'd be glad to get home, but he'd also welcome a short break from the jolting wagon. And, it was always a treat to be able to share news he'd heard in The Dalles and along the road from other travelers.

Biffle dismounted, dropping his reins to the ground to allow his horse to wander a bit and crop at the sparse grass near the road. The hills had been green and lush with bunch grass during the spring rains, but as soon as the heat had begun in May, the countryside had turned dry and brown seemingly overnight. The two men reached for their over-sized handkerchiefs simultaneously and wiped the sweat from their weathered faces, blew a bit of dust and mucus from their noses, and returned the cloths to their hip pockets.

"Load of supplies for your stop?" Biffle asked his neighbor as he looked at the well-packed wagon, though he knew that it was.

"Ja. Ja. Those gold-diggers and those soldiers, they eat a lot!" the big German chuckled. "Frank, he stay home to cook for them, get their money!" Meyer gestured towards his home site. "Dug enough for gold in California. Pays more to feed the miners than to look for the gold." The stocky farmer hitched up his canvas overalls and poked a few times at the tail of his plaid flannel shirt, stuffing it into the waistband of his pants.

"Bought these in town," he said, looking at his overalls. "Overhalls cost a dollar and fifty now, they do. But, it's a good deal for me, with all of this," and he good-naturedly patted his enormous girth. "Not such a good deal for you, my friend!" and he looked at Biffle's slight build. "These would make two pairs for you, I think." The thin man smiled.

"Still got that cough?" Meyer asked, and the homesteader nodded. "Got just the ticket fer fixing it up," the German said with a grin and lumbered towards the back of the wagon where he dug through the load, located a wooden box with a lid, and opened it, bringing out a bottle filled with a light brown liquid.

"Dry. Turned hot in a hurry, didn't it?" Biffle replied, and he reached for the drink offered by his friend, taking a cautious sip before deciding it wasn't too bad, then enjoying a larger swill and handing the jug back to the big German farmer. Meyer wiped the mouth of the bottle with his hand, tipped it to his lips, and took a big swallow. He shook his head slightly at the bite of the drink, and rested the container on the side of his wagon, his huge hand dwarfing the glass bottle.

"Any news from the river?" Biffle asked. He'd not often taken time from building up his fields to travel to the military road or to the newly opened overnight rest stop operated by Meyer and Hewot, and visits were an occasion to catch up on the latest news.

"That Henry Wheeler. He got the stagecoach route now, making three trips a week from The Dalles to Canyon City. Or, from Canyon City to The Dalles. Depends on where you start!" Meyer grinned. "Gave it the name The Dalles-Canyon City Stage Line. Pretty fancy name, ja? Pretty fancy for me, too," and the German patted the deep pocket in his trousers, and the smile on his face widened. Wheeler had asked Meyer to pasture a team of horses to be swapped out for the ones driven from the previous stage stops further up and down the road in each direction, so Meyer was benefitting from Wheeler's efforts, too. No doubt of it. He'd picked a good location for his homestead.

"He'd better watch out for those Indians. Heard they like their horses. Remember that attack a few years ago, up close to Canyon City?" Biffle asked. "Shame 'bout them miners." The two men shook their heads, remembering.

The first signs of winter had just begun to show late in the fall of '62 and five miners on their way to the gold field had camped and had just crawled into their bedrolls for the night when they were ambushed by Indians. The attackers, very probably members of the Snake tribe, killed one of the men outright and seriously injured the remaining four.

The survivors had struggled on towards Canyon Creek but one of the young men, unable to continue, crawled into some bushes and died. Another made his way to a nearby ranch where he died the next day. The last two survivors made their way further east, but the oldest died soon of his wound from a poisoned arrow. The only survivor of the massacre never did regain his complete health. The area of this attack was subsequently named Murderers Creek.[1]

The often-repeated story of the attack occurring on The Dalles-Canyon City road had heightened awareness of the danger from the natives whose land the miners were invading. There had been an increase in the demand for protection along the military road but it was two years be-

---

1 Shaver et. al., p. 637

Camp Watson, 1865, artist rendition.
Used with permission by McLaren Stinchfield

fore the military camp, long promised, was slated for construction in the fall of '64. It would probably be completed during the winter.

The military camp would be near The Dalles-Canyon City Military Road and Meyer had heard it would probably be named Camp Watson in honor of Lieutenant Stephen Watson. The young officer, very popular among his men, had been killed during a skirmish with a band of Snake Indians on the Crooked River in May, just a month earlier.

"Wonder why it's taking so long to get a dad gummed fort built?" Biffle asked. "Indians have been a plague for the past two years, long as I've been here."

"Money." Meyer paused. "Money. Damned packers raised their price from fourteen cents per pound to twenty-two cents, to be paid in coin. Army couldn't pay the difference — or didn't want to.[2] And, the government, it's slow. Folks at Antone'll be glad to have some protection, even if it's not in their backyard. Our house will do for folks in this area. There'll be trouble soon. I can feel it in my bones." He offered the bottle to Biffle, who took a big swig.

---

2 Judith Keyes Kenny. "The Founding of Camp Watson." Oregon Historical Quarterly. Volume LVIII, Number 1. Portland, Oregon. 1957

"Been to Antone?" Biffle asked, wiping his mouth with the back of his hand, coughing and loudly blowing his nose into his soiled red handkerchief.

"Nah. No time. No time. Too much to do." Meyer answered. "The trees, they're showing good green. Most of them survived the winter, look good. Be good to get fruit in two, three years. I hear old George Jones is making himself a farm there, just north of Antone. Goin' to raise a few cows. Mine a little."

The two men continued to stand propped against the side of the wagon, visiting, sipping from the opened bottle of whiskey, Biffle hungry for the news Meyer carried. He learned of a couple of fellows named Edgar and Jones who had established an express serving the miners in Canyon City, traveling from the gold field to The Dalles. "I feed 'em sometimes." Meyer shared, "Water their horses."

Biffle said that he hoped Abraham Lincoln would be re-elected President, an occurrence he felt would be good for the country. Meyer agreed, and both men concurred the leader was going to have a tough time of it. "Better watch his back," Biffle commented, worried about the safety of the president who was causing such controversy with the conflict over slavery.

For a time, the men discussed the Battle of Gettysburg fought the year before and the ensuing battles between the Union and the Confederate armies. The struggle seemed a world away from where they stood in the late afternoon sun, though Meyer related how he'd given supper and a free drink to a one-armed Union soldier who had passed by his fort-house.

"He'd been at Gettysburg. A purely awful battle on July 3 last year. He described the rocky hill where one helluva fight took place and the nearby valley surrounding the small town. One woman killed. Makin' bread, and a sniper's stray bullet went through her kitchen window. 20,000 lost on each side." Meyer shook his head slowly at the enormity of the loss. "Lee's army escaped back into Virginia. There wasn't a winner that day, even if the Union did hold that hill against Pickett's charge." The two men stood silently for a time, each lost in remembrances of stories heard of the battle. "Lotta kids died that day. Lotta kids. Sixteen, seventeen years old. Pure shame." The men stood in silence for a moment.

"New state now. Nevadie," Meyer changed the subject. He'd also heard of a new activity, something called "roller skating," where folks would roll around in shoes that had wheels on them. "Break their necks, they will!" he chortled, and the men shook their heads in amazement that anyone would have time to spend playing like that let alone risk breaking their necks or an arm or a leg doing anything so silly.

Their shadows were showing long on the ground, the sun just about to sink behind the hills, before the men shook hands and parted. Meyer admonished his friend to not work so hard; he opined he looked a bit peaked and weary. The German had another hour of travel to reach his home; Biffle would take a few hours to reach the lonely cabin on his holdings.

Biffle wondered, as his horse picked his way steadily up the trail worn into a crumbly 'dobe bank, if the little spot of paradise he'd found was worth the sacrifices he'd made for his independence. A man could get pretty darned lonesome, homesteading by himself with next to nothing to live on. He was having a hard time paying his bills and hoped he'd get enough from the sale of his wheat crop to do some catching up with his creditors.

He'd been thinking of getting a few sheep. With two crops a year, the lamb and the wool, maybe he could get enough cash to pay his bills. He'd need to borrow even more money, though, if he were to expand. As his horse picked his way across the adobe hills, Biffle wondered if Myer would be good for a loan.

When he rounded the final hill before his homestead and saw the rims with their rosy glow from the last of the sunlight, the small wheat field on the bottom land a carpet of green below the towering basalt bluffs, his breath caught in his throat as it always did at the sight. He knew he'd made the right move.

The homesteader coughed deeply, the effort bending his body over in the saddle as he hawked and cleared his throat, spitting a huge glob of phlegm onto the ground, and then reached for his well-used handkerchief and blew his nose and wiped his watering eyes.

Meyer unloaded his wagon when he got home, deciding to call it a day after completing the trip from The Dalles. He usually went to replenish the stock for his stage stop once a month, though he'd found he could also buy some of the needed staples from the freighters constantly passing by on their way to the gold field. At times Hewot would reluctantly make the trip to The Dalles, though the Englishman preferred to stay home, tending the crops and the animals and making stew for the travelers, who found his offerings of food as thin as his conversations. The travelers missed Meyer when he was away.

"Got that big ditch dug, the one that carries water to help 'em with their mining," Hewot told Meyer as the men begin to catch up on the news. "South of Antone, in Spanish Gulch. S'posed to be five miles long.[3] They're finding a bit of gold. Be enough to bring some more folks to Francisco's town." Hewot sighed in contentment. He was glad to not be part of the group of miners digging in the dirt, looking for a few nuggets of gold, which they might never find. When he dug in the dirt, he planted seeds and could be certain of the outcome, despite a thunderstorm or two.

Located towards Canyon City on The Dalles-Canyon City Military Road, the small community built within an easy half-day's drive from Waterman's homestead was in an area that had been named Antone.

The small settlement, never a town, nestled at the foot of the Ochoco

---

3 Jack Steiwer. "Communities Past and Present," in Glimpses of Wheeler County's Past. F. Smith Fussner, ed. Portland, Oregon: Binford & Mort. 1975

Antone area looking to the north.
The Ochoco Mountains are in the background.

Mountains about 30 miles southeast of Meyer's Gulch, and was located on the Military Road on Rock Creek in '62. This was the area where two packers, of Mexican or Spanish descent, worked a pocket of promising ore near the military trail. Antone Francisco gave his first name to the area[4], showing his pride in his Portuguese heritage. Rolling bunch-grass covered hills dotted with outcrops of basalt formed the basin surrounding Antone.

In 1904 the following news would be written about the Antone area: "The best placer claim is owned by Robert Cannon and Charles Johnson. In a ten weeks' run last Summer with four men they cleaned up $9,800. The gold is coarse and of fine quality. They took out several nuggets of from $50 to $100 and one piece of sixteen ounces, value $272."[5]

Many men dreamed of making their fortune in Spanish Gulch,

---

4 Bob Collins interview
5 Pacific Northwest Homestead, Inland Empire Edition. Salem, Oregon. November 10, 1904, p. 35

many men found just enough of value to inspire them to continue their efforts, and many men grew hungry and defeated and left their diggings for other endeavors. "…We are led to say that, while Wheeler county is the stockman's paradise, there are not a few of our hardy mining citizens, who while others sought their fortunes in Nome and Klondike, have been content to remain at home and are undoubtedly much better off by so doing."[6]

"Waterman stopped by yesterday," the Englishman continued. "Had a drink and said he had to hurry home. Was on his way home from The Dalles. Think he's doing okay. Another independent soul for the country," and the partners grinned at each other.

"Hmmm," grunted the German. He'd never admit aloud to anyone that he resented to a certain degree that Ezekiel Waterman had settled on his homestead in '62,[7] a year before Meyer had marked his own holdings. This made Waterman the old-timer, the German one of the newcomers.

Of course, Biffle had been the very first, having come earlier in the year than Waterman, but Meyer had a feeling that the likeable homesteader wouldn't be able to hold on to his land much longer; that perpetual cough of his was sounding worse. And he also had a feeling that Waterman wouldn't last long, either. His premonitions proved correct: By 1870 both Waterman and Biffle would be gone and Meyer would have the honor of being the earliest of the permanent settlers, an honor he would prize but did not wish for if it came about because of bad luck for some other fellow.

"Sorry I missed Waterman. Quite a gentleman, he is. And, his stage stop doesn't bother us much. Folks know where to get a good stew and a good drink," and the German smiled smugly, then saluted Hewot with

---

6 Ibid.
7 Ralph Waterman in The History of Wheeler County, Oregon. McLaren & Janet Stinchfield, eds. Dallas, Texas: Taylor Publishing Co., 1983, p. 234

his glass and downed a large gulp. "We'll be hearing more about him, I'm sure. He's full of energy, that one."

"Had a new machine with him. Called it a seed planter," Hewot volunteered.

"Gold and cows," Meyer commented, referring to the Waterman and Antone areas. "Something this farmer doesn't need to worry about. Don't know about 'em, don't need to know about 'em." He rapped his pipe against the side of the table, knocking the remaining tobacco from the bowl, his signal that it was time to bed down for the night. Tomorrow would come early in Meyer's Gulch and the big German needed to rest up for whatever might arise in his valley with the dawning of a new day.

Chapter 4
1862 — Ezekiel Waterman

Ezekial Waterman had been on his way to his holdings north of Antone when he pulled a team of horses up beside Meyer's stage stop, the wagon bed filled with a new horse-drawn seed planter, which he had proudly showed to Hewot. Hewot and Meyer had broadcast their fields by hand; Waterman's fields were too vast for such a task.

As he showed off the farm equipment, Waterman had explained how the seed disk would spin by the rotation of the wheels on the machine. The grain would be broadcast on top of the ground and would have to be harrowed to prevent the ever-present blackbirds and grouse from eating the seed. The constant wind, too, would do its damage to uncovered seed. It would be important to finish the seeding while the ground still held the spring moisture, and the crop would have to be in early enough to mature before the weather turned cool in the fall.

"Plan to get the crop seeded earlier next year. April, May. Off to a late start this year, but oughta be time for a good crop," Waterman had explained.

"We heard about that new fort up your way," Hewot remarked, as they sat outside the stage stop. "Is it near your place?"

"New fort will be south of our holdings," Waterman replied. "Less'n ten miles." He'd shifted his slight body on the hard bench, needing to get back onto his wagon again, yet hesitating to finish the journey. His son, John, would be unhappy at the news he was carrying.

"Can't get that fort built fast enough," his host had commented, filling Waterman's glass with whiskey and topping off his own tin cup. Both men kept eyeing the hills surrounding Meyer's holdings, watching for Indians.

Waterman drove east from Meyer's Gulch, heading to his holdings on what folks were calling Waterman Flat. As he rode through a narrow rock-lined canyon with scarring on the rock walls a reminder of past floods, Waterman had no doubt there would be another flashflood. He supposed he'd be safe today; the sky was clear blue and there was no indication of a storm in the making.

"Not much of an area for settling here," the homesteader thought. "Only a fool would take a certain chance of getting flooded out, that's for sure.

"And, folks probably think I'm an old fool to start farming up new ground at my age, I imagine," and Waterman grinned wryly to himself. "Funny, 50 doesn't seem as old as it did ten years ago. Still and all, there's good money to be made supplying the miners with beef. Doesn't take a young man to raise beef."

Making his way upstream near the waterway, Waterman followed the military road, letting his horses set their own speed as he kept an eye peeled for Indians. There were narrow strips of fertile soil on either side of the creek with only one small draw leading away from the stream and up between hills rising from the level of the waterway. With the large boulders on either side of the creek and steep walls providing no easy way out, the canyon would be a likely place for an Indian attack.

His deeply set eyes roamed over the passing landscape carefully, looking for any sign of movement, and he reached for his rifle and checked to see that it was loaded and the safety off, ready for use at a moment's notice. He knew a solitary man would be easy pickings but he'd needed to make a quick trip to The Dalles to take care of business and he knew a man who travels fastest travels alone.

Waterman had already been fairly long in the tooth when he started his homestead venture. His dark hair showed streaks of gray as did the chin beard he kept neatly trimmed. In '62, many men his age were beginning to think of retiring to their rocking chairs as their bodies had been pretty well worn out by years of hard work.

Men who knew him admired Waterman's stamina. Part of that energy might have been brought about by a desire to work hard enough so that when he lay down to rest at night, his body would quickly give way to sleep and he wouldn't have to think about his son Oscar's death in a mining accident in California a few years before. Ezekiel had buried Oscar in California and in '58 had moved with his wife, Mary Straud, and their son, John, to the Willamette Valley.[1]

Ezekiel and John had made a trip to eastern Oregon early in '62, scouting the country for a likely place to settle, and had chosen a spot near the military road. Ezekiel had been the first white man to take up squatters' rights in the area north of Antone's holdings. Mary remained in the Willamette Valley; there were no women in the new territory and she preferred the security of the city. Never a strong woman, Oscar's death was affecting her health.

Waterman thought of the home in Jefferson, near the town of Salem in the western part of the Oregon Territory, that he'd left when he had headed east with John and a herd of cattle. He wasn't sure he'd make his fortune from miners traveling to the diggings in Canyon City, but it was new territory and the challenge of opening up new ground appealed to him. Focusing on his new enterprise would give him something to fuss about other than his son's death. Hard work tended to exhaust his body and his mind to the point of his being able to sleep when he lay down at night, and hard work was what he had.

Ezekiel and seventeen-year-old John had driven the cattle along

---

1 Waterman in History of Wheeler County, p. 234

the military road until about half a mile past the summit of the mountain they'd climbed. They'd just left the narrow canyon behind when they turned north and pushed their herd another five miles or so before reaching their selected holdings on a large, fairly flat area made up of rolling bunch-grass-covered hills.

Their 160-acre homestead was in the midst of a meadow several miles square. In all directions, no matter where he looked, Waterman could see rounded mountains, growing bluer as they grew more distant. Not many trees were in sight closer by, but the blueness of the distant rises indicated the growth of evergreens not ten miles from their home site. They would need the timber for their home and their outbuildings.

Waterman had built a crude cabin of square-hewn logs harvested from the nearby forest. He didn't suppose Mary would approve of the humble dwelling, but the cabin provided shelter from the elements and the men didn't spend many waking hours there, anyway. It was a place to cook simple meals and to sleep, and nothing more was needed than the small twelve-by-sixteen-foot hut.

Greener patches of grass on the rolling hills nearby indicated springs that were plentiful enough to provide water for their beef animals. The

Waterman's cabin.
Used with permission by McLaren Stinchfield

men dug out some of the springs, forming depressions large enough in the sod to hold water for their cattle. Several small brooks ran from the springs into a larger willow-lined stream that would run all year; the Watermans referred to the stream as Willow Creek. Deer and antelope could be seen frequently, grazing on the hillsides and drinking from Willow Creek or from the springs that dotted the terrain. Grouse were plentiful and the calls of blackbirds and meadowlarks were commonly heard.

After their first crops the previous year, the men had found out that the Waterman Flat area was proving to be especially suitable for growing vegetables. It was on this fertile soil that, with the help of men traveling the military road on the way to the gold field needing a grub stake, they had established gardens to supply food to the miners passing nearby. Ezekiel and John had dug a series of ditches leading from the springs and the small creeks to their gardens and found there was more than plenty of water for their vegetables.

Unfortunately, however, there wasn't a source of water nearby large enough to irrigate other crops to any extent and, with the rainfall being that of semi-desert country, all working of the soil had to be done with that in mind. With a bit of research, Waterman learned of the crops that would be successful on his dry-land farm, and he'd rely on those varieties for his homestead.

Waterman gave a nod of approval as he rounded the last rise near the wagon trail leading to his cabin and pulled his horses to a stop. He rested on the rounded top of a grassy knoll, the land stretching out below him on all sides. To the south rose the grayed-blueness of the Ochoco Mountains; to the north more curved landmarks with no name known to Waterman. The rolling bunch-grass-covered acres seemed quietly expectant, awaiting the feel of plows to turn them into productive land.

He sat quietly, absently stroking his beard as he surveyed his acreage, breathing the fresh air deeply into his body weary from the trip. The men had been busy while he was gone, the newly turned soil looking dark in the fading light, and there were two of John Deere's apparatuses still working the soil for the new field that would be planted soon.

Two men were working in the last light of the day, one following behind the plow to steer it, the other driving the team of oxen. Waterman could see a third man, perched on the seat of a disk pulled by a team of horses, following the plow at a distance and breaking the plow-turned sod into even smaller clods of dirt that could be seeded.

As Waterman sat watching from his vantage point, the men working the plow pulled back on the leather straps leading to the team of oxen, stopping the animals for the night. They unhooked the plow, leaving it where they would begin work at daylight the next morning, and began to lead their oxen to the house pasture for the night. The worker driving the disk his team pulled his horses to a stop near the abandoned plow, unhooked his machine, and joined the procession to the house.

Ezekiel supposed John had been able to get hired help by offering food and a bed in exchange for a few days of work. There seemed to be no shortage of hungry men traveling by on their way to the gold field, and some of them were good workers and would delay their trek to the diggings and stay until the crops were planted, harvested, and in the barn or in the stacks. There was plenty of room for the workers in the hastily built barn; the cabin barely held the small platform bed John had built for himself and his father. Some men had spent a night or two with the Watermans and had moved on down the road, deciding the lure of gold was stronger than their desire to break new farm ground.

"Is there a keeper among those fellows?" Ezekiel asked John, nodding towards the three men who sat at the table outside their small cabin. His son looked at him, an unspoken question in his eyes, as the two men stood at the small cast-iron cook stove dishing up a plate of warmed- up beans.

"Mother wants us to go home," Waterman explained, showing his son the letter he'd picked up in The Dalles. "I wrote and told her we would. At least for a while. She won't come here, and maybe we can get something going there, hold on to this for now. With a good man here we can depend on, we can leave this, go to Jefferson and get something going, and come back once in a while to keep an eye on things."

John knew without asking that his father had already made up his mind, and, likewise, Ezekiel knew without asking that his son didn't want to leave what they'd begun. John's quietness and his downturned mouth as they lined out a foreman and a hay crew the next few days belied his assurances that leaving the homestead was fine with him if Mother wanted him. Both men knew Mary needed them, and so they prepared to journey to the Willamette Valley to spend time with her while they could.

The planting crew began to sow the wheat and barley seed Waterman had brought in the wagon with his new seeder. One man drove the two horses pulling the seed planter and another followed, driving a second pair of horses pulling a disk to cover the broadcasted seed. The men seeded forty acres into wheat and another forty acres into barley. With luck, harvest would be good that fall; in the meantime, there was nothing to be done with the fields except hope for enough moisture to sprout the seeds and enough warmth for the crops to grow well.

John returned to the ranch with his father for their first harvest in September. The summer had been ideal for growing the grains, the weather being fairly warm and the rains seeming to fall just when moisture was needed. The men knew they were lucky; Mother Nature's whims weren't always so beneficial to farmers.

Haying was a back-breaking chore, and Waterman had traveled to Canyon City and recruited several strong-backed hungry miners to help with the crops. From early morning, when the light was barely bright enough to see what they were doing, the men would begin, bending to grab a bunch of wheat or barley, and then cutting the hay stems with sharpened scythes. Setting the scythe on the ground, and with a quick movement of their free hand, they'd wrap a few stalks of the grain around the bundle and secure the loose end by tucking it behind the coils around the stalks.

The bundles of grain were gathered together a dozen or so at a time and then stood on end where they'd been cut, forming a teepee-shaped shock open in the center to allow air through. With the green grain standing upright, the sun helped dry the harvest and the fields turned a light golden brown as the wheat and barley dried. After about a week, when John was satisfied with the dryness of the grains, the men loaded the shocks into wagons and hauled them to an area near the barn where they were stacked, the harvest of wheat in one pile and the barley in another.

Waterman had helped one of the workers build a wooden floor near the barn and the hay crew hauled armfuls of wheat to the platform. There they stomped on the grain, doing war dances, big smiles on their faces, and gyrating around on the slick shocks until the grain heads were separated from the stalks. The men also beat the stalks with large sticks, alternating between beating and stomping to separate the grain from the chaff. The dancing slowed as the day wore on and the novelty wore off. By the end of the day the smiles were gone and the exhausted men were merely stomping on the shocks.

"Whyn't we use horses for this?" a disgruntled miner asked, wiping sweat and chaff from his forehead and cheeks with his handkerchief.

"Next time," John agreed. "I plan to alter the platform so they can walk around on it. For now, we've got to get this done and you're doin' fine."

"Sure, 'n' we'll have horse poop all over our oats for breakfast," commented a second miner wryly, shuffling his feet on the oat stalks as he talked.

Harvest time — unidentified crew.
Courtesy of the Fossil Museum

"Nah. We won't feed 'em 'til night," John explained. "They can do their business at night. On top of that, horses don't pee while they're walkin'. Secret is to keep them movin' once they're on the platform."

The two miners kept stomping and one enthusiastically mimed popping an imaginary whip over the back of a phantom horse. "Bring on them horses!" he chortled.

Placing handfuls of the hay onto a large screened tray, they tossed the chaff into the air, allowing the afternoon winds to blow the dried stalks and chaff to one side while the heavier grain kernels collected on the screen. They dumped the grain into large sacks and raked the stalks and chaff into piles near the barn. Nothing would be wasted: the grain and the stalks and chaff would be used as feed for the stock that winter, and a small part of it would be sold. A dozen or so baskets full of the grain would be lugged to the barn where John had set up a hand-cranked grinder and ground wheat for the coarse flour that would be used for bread.

Their first grain harvest had been a success and the men figured they'd harvested an average of forty-four bushels per acre. Ezekiel chose one of the men from among his haying crew to carry on the farming for him while he was gone. After leaving instructions with the miner-turned-farmer, the Watermans reluctantly returned to the Willamette Valley and Mary. It had been two years since they'd built their homestead cabin and broken the first ground for their gardens and their grain fields and they regretted leaving their farm when there was still so much work to be done.

The Waterman men opened a mercantile business in the city of Jefferson late in '64, becoming partners in the venture. Ezekiel returned to Waterman Flat often to supervise the men he hired to work his farm land while he was gone. Mary's health continued to decline and she died in '66.[2] Ezekiel later married Nancy Smith, and then he returned to the land in eastern Oregon, living near Camp Watson for six years before selling his property to a newcomer, John Fopiano. Waterman moved to The Dalles, leaving behind both the land he had helped to develop and a large part of his passion. Once relocated, he went into the loan office business, a successful business venture, and purchased several ranches in that area[3] before his death in '03.

John worked with his father for a time and then entered the pharmaceutical business on his own, continuing in that line of work for two years. It would be four years after leaving the homestead on Waterman Flat before he would return, and great changes were made in the area during his absence.

Typical of many of the early settlements in the area, the Waterman community first served as a stage stop. George McKay originally laid out the town site on land he owned. The hotel he built was a two-story structure with sixteen bedrooms, two parlors, a dining room, and a

2 Ibid., p. 234
3 Ibid.

Barn and stable at Waterman Flat. Courtesy of Betty Potter

kitchen. Travelers could put up their horses in the livery stable near the hotel and, eventually, post an occasional letter in the new post office.

McKay visited with a customer over a late dinner one night, discussing the 3,700 acres of land he owned. Altogether, McKay ran 680 head of grade Shorthorn cattle, seventy-five horses, and fifteen well-bred hogs.[4] The cattle provided the beef that was served in his dining room, and the hogs, the bacon. Taking care of his holdings was a full-time job, and with the additional burden of managing his hotel, McKay felt he needed to sell his farms.

McKay's holdings were divided into seven parcels and, in 1904, the year after Waterman's death, the tracts, all with tillable land, were advertised for sale. These holdings became known as the Iremonger, the Pine Park, the Jeville, the Colby, the Darrier, the Smith, and the Tubs Springs ranches, named for the families who lived on them.

Meyer's friend Waterman had chosen well when he pounded in the stakes around his farm tract and picked the site for his homestead cabin.

4 Pacific Northwest Homestead, p. 55

Although he didn't remain in Wheeler County for much more than half a dozen years, he left behind a community with his name and the beginning of a productive ranching area.

When he waved a last good-bye to his friend as he drove out of sight down the dusty military road, heading for The Dalles, Meyer sighed. It seemed to the German he was always making new friends, but sometimes one stood out among the others as being a kindred spirit in the development of the area. Waterman had been such a friend.

Chapter 5
1865 — Henry Wheeler, Sutton, Burnt Ranch

The year 1865 was a very profitable one for Meyer and Hewot. Their garden expanded and their fruit trees grew sturdy from the nutrients in the fertile soil and the plentiful water from the little creek running past the orchard. Travelers flowed by daily, a great many more heading east towards the gold field than west to The Dalles. Camp Watson had been finished in January and the soldiers, led by Captain Henry Small, made frequent trips past the farm in what was now known as Meyer's Gulch, on patrol to look for signs of Indian uprisings and to purchase fresh vegetables. The German's reputation was growing along with his garden and his orchard.

Meyer shared his friend's pride when Henry Wheeler had been awarded The Dalles-Canyon City postal contract by the government. Wheeler would be paid the handsome sum of $12,000 per year, a substantial amount in the early settlers' eyes. The stage was to make three trips each week and mail was carried for the first time that spring of '65, though Wheeler had begun his passenger stage in May of '64.[1] Wheeler also handled the Wells Fargo Express Company's business for them, his piercingly dark eyes closely watching the letters entrusted to him.

Wheeler, his thick white hair standing tall on top of his head and his long but neatly trimmed beard thick with dust, pulled up his sweating and exhausted four-horse team one day, unharnessing them from

---

1 Shaver et al., p. 638

his mail stage while Meyer and Hewot helped him swap them for a fresh team from the holding pen. Wheeler had to change his horses eight times during the journey, which meant a steady business for the stops that were set up along his route. The German kept a wary eye out for signs of any "thieving and marauding" Indians lurking near his holdings; he didn't want to lose any horses on his watch.

Wheeler charged passengers $40 for a one-way trip, and his stage was often filled to capacity on each trip to and from the gold field. He could haul eleven passengers by cramming them tightly onto the hard seats inside the stagecoach, its stiff springs unmercifully jarring the travelers' eye teeth almost to the point of falling out. The stage could travel about 110 miles each day, Wheeler boasted, making the trip from Canyon City to The Dalles. He didn't add, however, that the trip would be a very bumpy and miserable two-day ride.

Making the contracted three trips a week meant Wheeler could only pause briefly at each of the many stage stops along his route if he were to keep his schedule. His horses were always more than ready to be unharnessed and traded for the fresh team Meyer and Hewot had cared for until Wheeler's return trip.

The German and his partner opened their stage station to the weary travelers, giving them food and drink and a short breather from their journey while Wheeler fussed that it was time to load up and get going because he had a schedule to keep. The occasional female passenger hurried out to the small privy to relieve herself while the men rushed to the sheltering walls of the barn, all anxious for that small respite before gobbling down a quick meal and hurrying back to their places on the stage.

From their farm in Meyer's Gulch, it was about 110 uncomfortable miles to The Dalles and 80 miles on the same kind of road to Canyon City, making their stop somewhat close to the middle of the run. The two men shook their heads in commiseration when the dust from

Henry Wheeler.
From History of Central Oregon

Wheeler's stage left the stop behind; they were glad to be hoeing in their garden and their grain fields, free from the jouncing, miserable trip the passengers were making.

In was in April of '65 the news of President Lincoln's assassination and of the abolishment of slavery spread rapidly along the military road. Early settlers felt their isolation keenly at times and eagerly waited for travelers to bring them news of the world outside their environs. The unofficial "Military Road Newspaper" was their sole source of current events and both Meyer and Hewot had a tendency to draw out their visitors' stops until they had gleaned every bit of information they could from the passersby.

Some travelers heading west on the stage road brought news of both E. B. Allen and S. G. Coleman establishing stock ranches near Waterman Flat. A nearer neighbor was J. N. Clark, who settled at the mouth of

Bridge Creek only about ten miles northwest of Meyer's holdings. Too, early in '65, Al Sutton had located on the north side of the mountain that lay just north of the well-established garden and orchard kept by Meyer.

"Alfred 'Call me Al' Sutton," was the way he'd introduced himself to Meyer and Hewot. He was one of the men's closest neighbors, although he lived fifteen or so miles to the north, across the river from Biffle. An infrequent visitor, seldom leaving his home nestled in the river basin, Sutton soon began to extend his holdings to include a substantial amount of land from the John Day River to as much as fourteen miles to the north.

He borrowed Biffle's name for his fields and began calling his ranch the "Big Bottom" ranch. His fields soon surpassed those of his neighbor, creating a broad expanse of green next to the river. Sutton referred to the high rock-topped mountain to the south of the John Day River as "my mountain," and the landmark was soon called Sutton Mountain.

The settler had come a long ways from being a tow-boy on the Erie Canal for several years and he shared his pride in his accomplishment with Meyer and Hewot over a drink one early evening. He had worked his way west while employed by the government in the freighting business, Al explained, and through hard work and sacrifice, he had finally been able to fulfill his dreams of owning land in the central part of the new state.

"Fella by the name of Clarno, old J. W., settled about thirty miles or so that way," Sutton told Meyer, pointing to the northwest. "Got himself about 800 acres on the river, staked it out a few weeks ago. Said he wanted to get into the cattle business, maybe get about 200 head or so."

"Wonder what breed he'll get?" asked the German, filling his visitor's coffee cup to the brim, thereby ensuring at least a few more minutes of visiting time as he knew his frugal guest wouldn't waste his drink.

"Maybe Hereford. Maybe Shorthorn. Usual breeds. And, of course, he's planning to get that many horses, too. 200 or so." Sutton shook his head. "Seems like a lot of horseflesh for that much area, if he's going to have cows, too."

"Army'll buy lotta the horses," Meyer declared, "but there's a lotta rock in that area, lotta up and down country, if I remember right. Hope it works out for him." His guest nodded in agreement, holding his heavy cup and sipping his still-hot coffee, his free hand hovering close to cover the top should Meyer attempt to fill it again; he had work to get done today. This sitting around and visiting leisurely was enjoyable, but it didn't get the fields planted; he had a ranch to build.

Sometimes, the news arrived dramatically and in a cloud of dust.

In August of '66 Meyer and Hewot had just about finished weeding for the day, their backs aching from stooping and hoeing for close to ten hours in the garden, now grown to more than the original five acres, when they heard a rapidly approaching horse. Looking up, they saw a foam-covered horse staggering up the road from the northwest. The rider was bent low over the saddle, turning to look behind him as if the hounds of hell were right at his heels. He was whipping the animal viciously, trying to get more speed out of the exhausted mount.

The messenger began blurting out his news before he'd left the saddle. There had been an attack earlier that day on James Clark's ranch at the mouth of Bridge Creek by a renegade band of Indians, led by Chief Paulina. Clark's wife had traveled to the Willamette Valley to visit her family and had left her husband to prepare for the cold weather they knew would soon arrive. Clark and his brother-in-law, George Masterson, had crossed the John Day River and proceeded to cut up driftwood to add to their winter's supply of firewood.

As the men were working, they looked to the south to see Indians racing towards the ranch house on the opposite bank. Clark and Masterson had left their rifles at home and, unhitching their horses from their harnesses, leaped up on the bare backs and headed towards the house, hoping to get to their rifles before the natives reached the structure. Soon realizing the Indians would arrive at the house before they could, they changed course and headed up Bridge Creek; but the renegades had spotted them and began pursuing them.

Masterson's mount was a workhorse, built for labor but not for speed, and he was soon exhausted. "Save yourself!" Masterson had screamed at Clark. "Keep going!" Clark knew he had no choice; his horse couldn't carry two men and keep up the speed he needed to outrun the Indians closing in on them. With a look begging forgiveness from Masterson, Clark whipped his horse to an even faster speed and continued up the creek.

Masterson vaulted from his workhorse and slapped him on the rump, sending him thundering after Clark. Then he dashed into the brush bordering the creek, stumbling down the waterway for a distance until he found a hole overhung with brush. It was in this shelter that he hid from the Indians, his body shaking violently from a combination of fear and cold. He could hear his pursuers from time to time, searching the willows lining the creek near him, but finally their voices grew fainter as they moved away from his hiding place.

Failing to find him, the Indians returned to the ranch. They cut open featherbeds and pillows and scattered the feathers around on the ground, taking the ticking with them. They also took other items valuable to them and then set the ranch house on fire. The ranch would be known from that time on as Burnt Ranch. A post office would be established at that location in '68 and it, too, would bear the name Burnt Ranch until it was closed in '82.

Clark, meanwhile, continued his ride to the nearest ranch, which was about eight miles distant. There he found some packers who joined him as he returned to look for his friend. Masterson, after hearing their calls and realizing the riders were his friends, left his hiding place, thoroughly

The Elzy Stephens family purchased part of the Burnt Ranch in 1902
and they lived there until 1912. The picture shows his family.
The house was built to replace the one burned by the Indians.
Used with permission by McLaren Stinchfield

chilled and relieved to see his rescuers. Upon reaching the home site, the men found the house burned to the ground and the Indians gone.

The wild-eyed rider bearing the news continuously scanned the area around the stage stop the whole while he was sharing the news. He sat on a bench, exhausted from the ride and from the sheer fright of the incident. His horse had not fared well, either. His sides heaved in and out and he stood on still-wobbling legs, head hanging low while the foaming sweat slowly subsided. It would take several days for the fatigued animal to recover from the ride; his rider would never recover from the sight of the charred remains of Clark's home and from his fear of the Indians.

"We've got to be on the lookout," Hewot cautioned Meyer, and he motioned to their rifles propped against the thick rock walls of their fort and patted the loaded .44 Colt Dragoon revolver lying on the window ledge. "Better keep these in the fields with us."

About a month later, on September 7, Meyer and Hewot were resting their elbows on their large table set up outside the stage stop, enjoying the cool afternoon breezes and a drink of whiskey. They admired the neatly weeded rows of the garden and the young fruit trees, the afternoon sun lighting up the rounded hills that lined their flat-bottomed valley.

"I'm dog tired and peacock proud, I am," remarked Meyer, surveying the results of their hard labor for the past few years. "From where we sit, we can see what we've done and hear about what is going on around us. It's a good location. We can watch our country grow along with us."

"Lots of folks moving in," Hewot commented, frowning. "Wonder how many are living close now?" Meyer shrugged; he enjoyed meeting folks and welcomed new settlers.

The partners continued sipping their whiskey and swapping stories, when they heard the pounding of hooves. Startled, they looked up to see two men riding swiftly around the rocky point just east of Meyer's farm. They were riding bareback, leaning over and clinging desperately to their horses' manes, their legs clamped tightly to the mounts' foam-covered sides.

It was Wheeler and his Wells Fargo messenger, H. C. Paige. Wheeler had dark blood slowly seeping from a wound in both cheeks and falling onto his shirt front and he staggered as he half dismounted, half fell from his lathered coach horse. Before they got their shaking legs solidly on the ground, the men began to blurt out their news.

The incident Paige reported as Hewot cleaned the jagged bullet wounds in the mail contractor's cheeks would ensure Henry Wheeler a place in local history. He and Paige had been the only people on the coach when they had topped a rise in the road not ten miles northeast of Meyer's farm. They came upon a group of Indians, maybe as close as ten feet from the lead horses before they saw each other. The braves were as surprised as the two mail carriers were at the encounter.

Paige carried a Henry rifle and Wheeler grabbed the pistol he packed and the two men got six shots off at what may have been fifteen or twenty Indians before the shocked braves responded with shots at the stagecoach men. The Indians scattered and Wheeler turned the coach around to head back down the road towards Meyer's fort-house.

The road was rough and Paige insisted they stop the mail stage, cut the lead horses loose, and escape on them. Wheeler refused to stop and in desperation, his companion jumped off the seat of the coach, forcing Wheeler to make the stop. While Paige opened fire on the Indians, Wheeler cut the lead horses loose. A bullet from the first round of shots fired by the Indians hit Wheeler in the mouth, shattering several of his teeth and exiting out of his cheek in front of his right ear. [2]

The two terrified men had hurried from the scene of the attack and raced down the road to Meyer's farm. There they spent a few hours while Hewot finished cleaning the wound, picking bits of teeth from Wheeler's mouth and cleaning the open mess as best he could. Meyer applied liberal doses of whiskey both to the inside and the outside of Wheeler's mouth and face, unsure of what else to do.

The burning alcohol would act as a good antiseptic and the slug or two of whiskey the mail carrier gulped down would also act as a tranquilizer. Meyer, Hewot, and Paige commiserated with Wheeler by taking their own liberal drinks of the alcohol; no need for any of them to suffer from a bad case of nerves.

While Meyer remained at his fort-house with his loaded .58 Springfield rifle in his hands, a substantial supply of ammo next to him on a table, Wheeler and Paige cautiously returned to the scene of the attack, with Hewot accompanying them. The attackers had left, having taken leather from the stage top and all else that was precious to them, including the two wheel horses. They had left behind ten thousand dollars in greenbacks and three hundred dollars in coins, as well as other valuables that didn't appeal to them.

---

2 Ibid.

A group of cavalrymen led by Captain Small arrived on the scene, and they constantly swept the landscape with their eyes as they talked, looking for signs of the Snake braves who had made the attack, their rifles cocked and ready to fire. That the Indians would attack again soon, they felt there was no doubt. The job of the soldiers was to patrol the military road in the area, stopping by to warn settlers of impending danger. Wheeler's brush with the Indians was the first incident on the road for quite some time and the cavalrymen were ready for action.

Wheeler, Paige, and Hewot, accompanied by the cavalry, returned to Meyer's fort-house where the mail carrier could rest for the night. While Hewot mended the harness so Wheeler could resume his run early the next day and get the medical care he needed in The Dalles, the group of men passed around the bottle offered them by Meyer, many of the soldiers young and their hands shaking. When Hewot's dog gave an alarmed bark as he rounded the house and saw the cavalrymen, the soldiers jumped in such unison they would have done any drill sergeant proud.

Prior to the loss of the two horses, Wheeler had already lost eighty-seven of his stage stock and his business was suffering financially. Soon after the attack when he was wounded and escaped with his life, Wheeler told Meyer he was going to give up his mail contract.

"I just can't afford to keep going," he explained, absent-mindedly hitching his belt up another notch. "Too, I've run the stage line four years, from '64 to '68, and carried the mail from '65 to '68. Time for a change."

The particulars of Wheeler's wound from his attackers were repeated over and over, and each teller of the tale added embellishments of his own. Even Wheeler, in later years, would give a bit of a different twist to the tale each time he told it, but the gist of the incident became a treasured and often repeated story in the history of the county.

The flow of settlers into the region was increasing and their arrival was noted and discussed by Meyer with his many visitors. The German seemed to have a mind like a steel trap and could quote the names of people and the places and dates of their settling in without hesitation.

From the time he'd first pulled his weary team up and staked them near Bridge Creek in '63 until the time of his death forty years later, the big farmer would see an area devoid of inhabitants grow from one crudely built stage stop to a county populated with over two thousand residents. The farmer in Meyer's Gulch, however, had no cause for worrying about his competition; his reputation for producing nothing but the best of vegetables and fruits ensured a steady and profitable stream of customers to his farm.

"The neighbors are fightin' again," Hewot commented wryly to Meyer as they loaded a wagon of limestone to strengthen a wall on their rock fort.

"Ja, it's their legs again," the German laughed, and Hewot joined in. "That boundary markin' isn't a woman's job, for sure!"

The influx of settlers in the region had increased rapidly with many early settlers simply squatting on their claims, staking off an area of roughly 160 acres until the land could be surveyed by a licensed surveyor. This establishing of property lines was a time for the men to take long strides, with an acre being roughly 200 feet to a side and a man's average step said to be about three feet.

"Settin' out a boundary is for sure not a woman's job," Hewot agreed, nodding his head. Meyer and Hewot listened as many of their visitors voiced their complaints about boundaries over and over. The two men who had set up their stakes around Meyer's Gulch were relieved they had been the first in the area and therefore fairly secure in their holdings.

In '67, Al Sutton was designated postmaster of the first post office in what would become Wheeler County. The service meant visitors for Sutton and he welcomed the folks who arrived to pick up their mail and share news of the settlers moving into the area. Meyer wished his neighbor well, but he missed Sutton's infrequent but welcomed visits to the stage stop in Meyer's Gulch.

Sutton's post office was established on what was being called the Sutton Ranch. The northern portion of his ranch, part of which he purchased from the homesteader J. K. Rowe, was covered with large areas of rich soil deposited by the river in the flood plain, broadened with each spring flood. Because of the large areas of fertile loam on both sides of the river, Sutton called his ranch and the surrounding flat area in the large valley the "Big Bottom," echoing Biffle's term for his land.

Sutton had new neighbors, Robert Sedman and Jake Smith, who had moved to the area near Biffle's homestead. The two men planned to raise stock on the bunch grass that grew abundantly in the valley on the John Day River. Sutton carefully watched the men; there seemed to be plenty of land and grass for everyone, but those folks had a lot of stock and the grass only grew just so fast. He hoped they'd keep an eye on the grazing, Sutton confided to Meyer.

It was in this same year that travelers on the military road brought news to the settlers that Chief Paulina had been killed and that gold had been discovered in Wyoming, diverting some of the miners from Canyon City to the new diggings. In '67, a new state, Nebraska, was formed and, locally, a fellow by the name of I. N. Sargent had built himself a home right smack dab in the middle of a flood plain on the main route traveled to and from the gold mine in Canyon City, where the town of Mitchell would eventually be located.

Sargent's house was only five miles or so southeast of where Meyer and Hewot had settled; perhaps they could pick his brain when they met him to see why he'd build in such an unlikely place where scarring of old floods, "bad ones," Hewot declared, could be seen on the rocky walls of the narrow canyon. Unfortunately, they would all find out in '84 just how those old marks had been made.

The newest book discussed among the readers traveling the road was Mark Twain's Jumping Frog of Calaveras County, though few of the settlers had time to worry about jumping frogs let alone read about them. If he did have time, Meyer told Hewot, he couldn't read English anyway, so the book would do him absolutely no good; no, he'd take that statement back. He could read the labels on his whiskey bottles and the names on the tins used to hold groceries.

Meyer heard that among those who were said to have come to the Mitchell area in '68 were H. C. Hal, Mr. Marshall, and Wick Cusick, but as they'd not stopped at the fort-house for some good food and some good advice, the German felt that perhaps they were of no consequence. Settling on Gird's Creek about ten miles southeast from where Richmond is now located was J. P. Brown, and he brought his family with him, an unusual event as most men came to first establish their holdings and then to send for their families.[3]

"Now here is a man that will go far," Meyer decided silently to himself as he answered the questions Brown asked him about how to best make a profit from his homestead. The farmer took his newly made friend out to his orchard and dug up half a dozen seedling apple trees. He handed the young plants to the new settler, instructing him on how to wrap the roots of the small saplings along with some of the rich orchard soil in canvas to prevent them from drying out.

Long after the clatter of Brown's wagon could no longer be heard on the military road leading to the east, Meyer and the men sharing his whiskey and pots of stew talked often of Sarah Brown, the only woman they knew of living in the country early in '68. "I saw her, I did," Meyer

---

3 Ibid., p. 640

could boast proudly, making the event seem as important as seeing the Queen of England. "They stopped by, heading for their land. Independent woman, she is."

Sarah had traveled with her husband across the plains to Oregon in '54 with two small daughters. Their daughter, Jessie, was born in March of '69 on their Gird's Creek homestead and was presumed to be the first child born in that particular part of the developing county. Two more children, Henry and Effie, would also be born on the farm. Sarah was known for her nursing skills and, after setting the broken arm of an Indian, the family claimed that they never had any problems with the natives.[4] Hearing this statement, Meyer remarked to Hewot with a smile that, as far as he'd heard, neither had anyone else.

The Brown family planted Meyer's fruit trees near the creek running through their land, little suspecting that some of their trees from that orchard would still be seen a hundred years later. In '77 Meyer heard that the family had moved a few miles east and filed another claim and built another cabin. "I hope they took some starts of their apple trees, I do," Meyer commented. "Those're good apples."

Then, after the Indian uprising, known as the Bannock War of '78, the Browns moved about half a mile to a creek that became known as Shoofly Creek. The name supposedly came about because Brown, the first "pesky" sheepman in the area, could not be "shooed" out by the cattlemen.[5]

"I think they are shooing themselves, I do!" laughed Meyer when he heard of the Brown family's third move in ten years.

William Saltman also arrived in '68 at his location on Burnt Ranch, where he raised stock and helped to supply the steady stream of travelers on the military road with whatever he could spare for their needs. Meyer wasn't sure Saltman would do much good; the new settler hadn't

---

4 Jessie Butler Sharp, "Jonathan and Sarah Duty Brown" in *History of Wheeler County*, p. 53
5 Ibid.

A load of lumber headed for Sutton's ranch and for the Prairie Ranch.
Courtesy of the Fossil museum

stopped by the German's home to ask for advice and the fellow just might not understand what it would take to be a success in the newly developing country.

Travelers who did stop by Meyer's holdings to visit a while brought news of the election of Ulysses S. Grant to the office of President in '68. The former store clerk was known for his common sense and his talent for military strategy [6] and, as a leader of the Union army during the Civil War, he had gained popular support among many of the travelers on the military road. Meyer allowed that Grant would do just fine for the country. As for himself, he'd do his part by advising folks in his immediate area.

Meyer traveled to Sutton's new home one Sunday, taking a rare break from his farm. As he returned home, jouncing along in his buggy on the crude road, the wooden seat uncomfortably hard and the ride jarring every bone in his body, he mulled over his visit with Sutton.

Biffle had approached Sutton for a loan, and was able to borrow enough to purchase a small band of sheep. He had trailed close to 750 head of sheep from Crook County to his Big Bottom holdings, bringing a herder with him. When it was time to shear, Biffle knew he could

6 Dr. Phillip Bacon. *The United States, Its History and Neighbors. Orlando, Florida: Harcourt Brace Jovanovich, Inc. 1991. p. 435*

depend on Sedman and Smith to help him. That's what neighbors did in this new country, and as Biffle's health continued to deteriorate, his friends aided him more and more. Meyer never failed to take a bottle of whiskey to his friend for use in treating his incessant cough.

Chapter 6
1868 — Samuel Carroll

S ettlers continued to arrive in the area, most of them stopping by the fort-house at least long enough to rest their teams and to water their stock and to get advice from Meyer and to meet his new bride, Anna. Late in '68, three wagons piled high with household goods and the bobbing heads of so many children that Hewot couldn't get a count on them, pulled up to the fort-house. Three sore-footed milk cows, their calves milling around the wagon, stopped and began to pick at the few bunches of grass still left near the well-traveled road.

"Name's Carroll," the driver of the lead wagon offered. "Samuel Carroll. Margarette,"[1] he said, nodding at the weary-looking woman slouched beside him on the plank seat of the wagon. He gestured with a work-hardened hand towards the young woman in the wagon nearest him. "Daughter Nancy," he said briefly. "Looking for my holdings," and he thrust his hand out to Meyer. The German enfolded the smaller man's hand in his own and took the crudely drawn map the traveler held out to him.

"Back down there," Meyer said, gesturing to the northwest. "'Bout a mile or so. You drove right through it. Creek runs right through it — Bridge Creek. Good spot. Stop and have a bite to eat, rest a spell, and Hewot will take you down to show you where the place is. Abandoned claim, but ought to work out for you, I s'pose."

---

1 The spelling of Samuel's wife is noted as both Margaret and Margarette in resource books. The latter spelling is used here, however, as that is the spelling on the grave marker in the Carroll Cemetery near the Painted Hills Park.

The youngsters in the wagons were passed down to him and the German placed them on the ground, four variously sized bodies beginning to dart around the wagon like a little flock of quail chicks. Two more children had been tagging along behind the milk cows, willow switches in hand to drive the animals.

As the men began visiting in the midst of the energetic youngsters, Meyer finally decided Carroll was a man of fair intelligence; the help from the large number of children in the family would come in handy while Carroll was establishing his holdings. Five more youngsters would be born to the Carroll family while they were on the Painted Hills claim. Each time he heard of a new birth, Meyer would declare, "Ja! That Carroll, he's a smart man!"

But now, Meyer shook his head, overcome by the presence of so many little people. It would be good to have help building up a homestead, he guessed, but he wasn't sure it was necessary to have quite that much help. That active brood would devour half of anything that fellow could grow.

Hewot, inside the house, dumped a few dippers full of hot water from the large pan simmering on the side of the stove into the stew pot bubbling away on the back of the range. He reached into the potato bin for another half dozen spuds and began to peel the shriveled tubers. That Meyer; Hewot knew that he and his partner would always find a way to have enough for whoever stopped by, but another dozen or so hungry folks was stretching it some. Muttering to himself, he began pulling bowls from the cupboard to set on the table.

Seventeen-year-old Nancy sat watching as Father helped Mother down from the wagon seat, catching her as she stumbled slightly when her feet touched the ground. Nancy, tired from her ride on the jouncing, hard, unforgiving board where she had spent the past five days, took inventory of her surroundings. The big rock building they had stopped beside must be about fifty feet long, she guessed, and maybe thirty feet wide. That it was a place where travelers stopped often was evident from the large dusty area formed from countless hooves trampling the area that surrounded the fort. Wearily, she crawled down from her bench, wanting to rest, yet eager to just keep going and get to the family's destination before relaxing.

The Carroll family had come from Linn County near the town of Lebanon, Father told the German. He planned to build a home close to the well-traveled military road for his family with lumber freighted from The Dalles, figuring he could make money by also accommodating the steady stream of travelers. He also had intentions of establishing a toll-road, keeping a section in good repair so he could charge freighters for their use of the thoroughfare.

Nancy heard Meyer saying he knew that he could continue to sell all the vegetables and fruit his own farm would produce and he wouldn't begrudge the competition; his established customers were well-satisfied with his crops, he explained proudly.

"And the travelers seem to like my sourdough biscuits," Hewot, told himself with a satisfied smile on his face, listening to the conversation through the open window in the kitchen. He bent over the bread board to knead the dough ready for rolling out and began cutting rounds using an old peach can with both ends removed. "And, my noodles," and he glanced at the drying strips of dough hanging from the four long willow switches suspended from the ceiling. He flipped a dish towel towards the pasta, shooing away the flies that walked along the drying noodles and occasionally leaving a fly speck behind. "It's a good thing I add pepper to the pot," he grinned to himself.

The Carroll family, every last able-bodied man, woman, and child, set to work establishing their homestead the day they pulled up their wagons on the pre-empted claim not five miles northwest from Meyer's holdings. By the time winter reached Bridge Creek, the family had built the large home that would also serve as a stopping place for traffic on the toll-road they would maintain.

Samuel had chosen to build near the creek, and the house was nestled under a long rim that would soon be known as the Carroll Rim. A steep yellowish tan clay bank, some hundred feet tall, rose sharply to meet the rock ledge on top of the long rim that stretched for about a quarter of a mile. The valley where the Carroll homestead was located was fairly flat, the floor gently sloping to the creek. The parcel of land was thick with sage and rabbit brush, indicating the area would be ideal for crops grown on the rich loam that had been deposited by Bridge Creek through the years.

Red adobe hills streaked with light tan and greyed-green ribbons were scattered along the sides of the valley floor. Where the rains had washed the unfruitful soil there was very sparse vegetation, but Carroll could see that his holdings were well-located. There was plenty of rich soil and the stream flowing through his land would provide the necessary irrigation for his crops and water for his family and for the livestock.

As soon as they began to build their home, Samuel had dug a well, only to discover the water, though cool and clear, had an alkaline taste that was hard to drink. Margarette solved that problem by adding vinegar and sugar to the water, making the water somewhat drinkable.[2]

The family worked during the winter days when the weather allowed, clearing land to be planted to crops in the spring. They utilized every bit of tillable land they could find on their 160 acres, hoping to grow large vegetable crops as well as grains for themselves and for their stock. In addition to the vegetable gardens, Samuel planned to plant cane for sugar and molasses.

---

2 George Cecil Carroll, grandson of Samuel. Written statement.

Their new home was large, but quarters were close for the energetic Carroll brood. Often, during the winter months when the closeness of the rooms seemed to set off frayed tempers, the bickering boys were sent to the barn to fork manure from the stalls to the pile outside that would be transferred to the fields in the spring. Margarette could always use help tending the youngest of her children and there were socks to mend, clothes to launder, and any other number of chores for squabbling girls. Nancy, being the oldest child, was often put in charge of her younger siblings often as her mother's baby was due soon and Margarette needed to rest regularly.

Deer brought in for meat were skinned and the hides were tanned to be used for making moccasins and leather thongs for shoe strings. Later, the family would trade with friendly Indians, usually the Warm Springs and Umatilla tribes, for moccasins.[3]

The story of the Indian attack on Wheeler was one of the first stories Meyer had shared with Carroll, so the homesteader and his family gladly helped volunteer soldiers construct a small fort made of limestone blocks mined from a nearby quarry.[4] Ft. Seward, as it was called, was large enough to hold their extended family and a few neighbors. It was located on the east side of the property Carroll claimed, opposite what would in later years become the entrance to the Painted Hills Park.

As always when an occasion arose that could lend to a history lesson, Samuel shared with his children that the fort was named Ft. Seward for William Henry Seward, former governor of New York, U.S. Senator, and the U. S. Secretary of State under Presidents Lincoln and Johnson. Seward had helped engineer the purchase of Alaska, a move that was not favored by all and an effort that was labeled "Seward's Folly".

Seward was "one of those spirits who will sometimes go ahead of

3 Ibid.
4 George Cecil Carroll

public opinion instead of tamely following its footprints," claimed a contemporary of the well-known statesman.[5] His courage seemed to be the epitome of those settlers who were moving into the unsettled areas near Meyer's holdings, and those pioneers felt the fort was suitably named.

An additional historical tidbit Carroll shared with his family and his neighbors was the fact that Seward and his son and several other members of his household were seriously wounded by an associate of John Wilkes Booth at the same time Lincoln was assassinated. This knowledge solidified the appropriateness of the naming of Ft. Seward in the Carroll family's minds.

As soon as the spring rains subsided somewhat, Carroll and his family began to improve the section of The Dalles-Canyon City road that they would maintain and for which they would charge a fee. Work progressed slowly. Early in the morning Samuel and his sons, each armed with a shovel or a pick, would walk to the point where they had finished working the previous day. Loose rocks were rolled off the road bed and those bigger stones imbedded in the packed soil were dug out. When rain poured down, Samuel knew the next wagon passing by would leave ruts deep in the mud that would need to be evened out as soon as the soil had dried enough.

In places, where possible, the road was widened to accommodate two wagons passing. The Carroll segment of the military highway was about five miles long and ended at the mouth of Meyer's Gulch. Every hard rain left behind damage to the road surface and on occasion, when newly exposed boulders were obviously too large to dig out, the Carroll men built a detour around the obstacle. In exchange for their daily maintenance, Samuel's family charged the freighters twenty-five cents for each wagon and for each of their horses.

---

5 http://en.wikipedia.org/wiki/William_H_Seward. 4/13/11

While Samuel and his sons worked on road improvements and crop planting, Margarette and Nancy kept the cook stove burning and pots of beans and stew simmering. They baked bread daily and cut huge roasts of venison from the carcasses hanging in the barn. If they were to charge twenty-five cents for each meal, the food had to be plentiful and it had to be always prepared. Travelers had miles to go in either direction before they reached their destination in The Dalles or in Canyon City, and they couldn't tarry long at the Carroll way station.

Samuel returned from a visit to Meyer's one day to find his oldest son, John, very upset. "That man just drove by and never stopped, Father!" John complained, gesturing down the road at an empty wagon going out of sight to the north. "The pole was up, too." He pointed to the pole held across the road by two upright posts on either side, signaling to passersby to stop to pay a toll. "I waved at him and he just drove his horses around the post and whipped them so they would go faster!"

"That's okay, Son," Samuel told him. "He has to come past again." He knew the driver to be a regular who freighted goods from The Dalles to the gold field. He'd be back in a few days and Carroll would be ready for him. He hitched a horse to a wagon, put an axe in the bed, and told John to hop in.

Not a week later, as he was working in his field near the road, Samuel saw the dust from an overloaded wagon pulled by four slowly moving horses. From a distance he recognized the freighter who had refused to stop for his oldest son. He called John and the two of them hurried to a narrow place in the road where there was a slight rise in the passage that would cause the heavily loaded wagon to slow considerably. Carroll leaned down and picked up the long and substantial pole he and John had hacked out of a large pine tree a few days previously.

As the freighter approached the two men, Carroll thrust the pole between the spokes of the rear wheel, locking it up and effectively stopping the freighter and his wagon.[6]

"Toll's twenty-five cents for the wagon and for each horse," Carroll said. "And the same charge for the last time you forgot to pay it." Scowling, the freighter reached into his pocket for some coins.

"Just give it to my toll collector here," Samuel said, pointing to a grinning John. The freighter never forgot to pay after that episode.

The Carroll baby, George W., was born in '69 and is believed to have been the first white child born in the Bridge Creek area.[7] As there were no doctors nearby, Samuel assisted in the birth, as he had for his first seven children. The baby boy died a year later and was buried in the Carroll Cemetery where, later, five generations of the family would be included in those buried. At the time of his death, Samuel was in bed, very ill with diphtheria, and could not bury his little boy. Instead, his son George Cecil, six years old, had to bury his little brother; neighbors were scared of contacting his father's illness and would not help.[8]

Samuel and Margarette added four more youngsters to their family home on Bridge Creek, making a total of twelve children born to the couple. Their last child born was named George Ben Franklin.

In the late '70s, Carroll began running a small band of sheep, and he hired a herder to take them to the summer pasture in the Blue Mountains near Summit Prairie.[9] He was busy working his gardens and fields and, though the sheep were a necessary addition to his operation, Carroll simply didn't have the time to care for them along with keeping his farm worked.

On Summit Prairie, about ten miles directly south of the new town

---

6 George Cecil Carroll
7 Mrs. Glenn Helms, *History of Wheeler County, Oregon, p. 61*
8 George Cecil Carroll
9 George Cecil Carroll

Early 1900s shearing crew; people and place unidentified.
Courtesy of the Fossil Museum

of Mitchell, Carroll established two camps known as Big and Little Carroll camps.[10] Nancy's husband, Sam Wilson, helped to shear the sheep on the prairie[11] and on his trips between his father-in-law's homestead and the summer range he kept an eye out for renegade Indians.

Wilson took vegetables and staples to the sheep camp on the prairie and helped to doctor any sheep that might need it. When it was time to shear in the spring, he joined the herder and a shearing crew, shearing the sheep with hand clippers. The process was slow and sometimes took as long as two weeks, depending upon how many men could be rounded up to help.

Arriving at sheep camp early one evening, Samuel Carroll found his camp tender jabbering away in excitement. The Chinese gold miner, down on his luck, had been willing to work for his room and board.

10 Ibid.
11 Ibid.

Communication with the sheep herder was hard for Carroll but not impossible when the two men talked slowly to each other.

This was not one of those times for deliberate speaking, Carroll was to find. His herder had been seeing a bear near the camp and the beast had wandered closer to the camp every day; the young man was certain the bear was going to eat him. Samuel dismissed the threat, assuring his herder the bear wouldn't bother him, but in the event that he came close, he guaranteed, the beast could be scared off by the man's waving an axe and screaming.

That night, as the men lay sleeping, they woke to the sounds of the bear in the sheep herd. The Chinese herder hurried out of the tent to the wood pile and grabbed an axe stuck into a block of firewood. Waving his weapon and shouting loudly, he ran to protect his sheep from the bear. The beast took a swipe at the screaming man, killing him with one blow. Carroll wrapped the bloodied body in a blanket and the herder was buried at the mouth of a canyon a short distance from the Carroll place on Bridge Creek.[12]

Sam Wilson returned to his home one day after being at the sheep camp for a week. With him he brought a freshly butchered sheep; the mutton would be a welcome change from their usual diet of venison. Along with the mutton was a large deerskin bag Wilson had stuffed full of tallow from the butchered sheep, which he proudly gave to Nancy. She put the globs of fat in a pan and placed it in the oven to melt the grease. The resulting tallow was mainly used for making candles and soap, although some of the rendered sheep fat was set aside in a cracked bowl on the kitchen shelf for use as a salve for chapped hands or lips.

In the summer of '78, the herder for the Carrolls was at camp on Summit Prairie when he got word that the Bannock Indians were on the

---

12 Ibid.

warpath. Jumping on his horse, he raced to the Carrolls' limestone fort for protection. There he found that the Indians had slaughtered mules left at Ft. Seward by soldiers. The Indian scare soon subsided, and the herder and Samuel Carroll returned to the band that had been abandoned the month before. There they discovered the faithful sheep dog still on watch; only a few head of sheep had wandered off during the herder's long absence.[13]

In '80, Carroll set out the first orchard on Bridge Creek. That same year, he donated land and helped to build the first schoolhouse in the area.[14] The sizes of the vegetable gardens had increased and so had the families. The children grew well on their farm produce and on the deer meat that was readily available in the nearby hills.

Nancy and Sam Wilson had built a house just north of Nancy's parents and by '84, they had five children. The oldest, a girl named Julia Belle, was joined by her brothers Clyde and Autie and the twins, Maggie and George, born in '80. The children could often be seen tagging along behind their father, aunts, or uncles or their Grandpa Samuel. Nancy had been seventeen when the Carroll family had arrived at the site of their new homestead in '68 and now, at the ripe old age of thirty-three, she was the mother of five healthy children.

The children kept her more than busy; merely feeding and clothing them was just a small part of her daily chores. The older children, Julia, Clyde, and Autie, tried to keep the younger toddlers from falling into Bridge Creek or stumbling into piles of prickly pear cactus. An occasional rattlesnake would cause a lot of excitement until it could be killed, and the family was constantly on the lookout for hostile Indians.

In early June, Sam planned to go to the Carroll camp to shear sheep and Nancy asked him to help her make some whitewash for the house

13 Ibid.
14 Mrs. Glenn Helms, *History of Wheeler County.* p. 61

before he went. The couple gathered their brood, hooked their horse to their wagon, and drove to the fort-house. There were several large pieces of the light brown limestone left from the building of Ft. Seward, and Sam began to break up those stones. As the larger stones became smaller, Nancy found several large, flat basalt rocks and placed them on the ground near the wagon.

Each of the three older children found hard rocks and began to pound the soft stones into smaller and then even smaller pieces. The resulting coarsely ground soft stone was scooped up with their hands and placed into buckets to be hauled home.

"We're truly blessed, aren't we?" Nancy said softly to Sam, putting an arm around him and turning his body slightly so he could share the sight of their oldest children working industriously away at their job.

"We are at that," he responded, giving her a hug and a quick kiss on the top of her head. He and Nancy both chuckled softly as Clyde tossed a small piece of rock onto the top of Julia's head and she swatted at it, thinking the pebble had been an annoying insect. Clyde grinned mischievously at his parents. "And, they are normal children, that's for sure," Sam said.

The parents stood for a minute longer, enjoying their family and each other, their eyes taking in the greenness of the fields and the gardens they were growing. Above the light chatter of their children and the soft thudding of their rocks as they pounded the limestone, they could hear the soft cooing of a pair of camouflaged mourning doves. A swallow zipped along over the course of the wandering Bridge Creek, in search of his afternoon meal of water insects.

They could see Margarette hanging a wash on the clothesline near her kitchen door, her stooped body grown rounder and slower through the years of birthing a dozen children and providing for their daily needs. Samuel Carroll was probably working in a field, though they couldn't see him; he would appear soon as a wagon was approaching from the north and that would be a fee for him to collect and another hungry mouth for her mother to feed.

Sam and Nancy returned to their task. There were a few more chores to be done before Sam left his family for a week of shearing sheep on Summit Prairie.

At their house, Nancy and Sam mixed the ground limestone with salt and added hot water until the mix was the consistency Nancy wanted to use for painting the house. She was tempted to add beet juice to the mix to make a pink shade, but she didn't reckon Sam would like a pink house, and she smiled to herself at the thought. They left the mixture to set until the next day when it would be applied to the inside of the cabin. The day seemed unnaturally warm and Nancy hoped the next day would be, too, as the heat would make the whitewash dry faster.

The afternoon heat reflected from the Carroll Rim onto Sam and Nancy's little home by Bridge Creek. The daily afternoon breezes that would soon be blowing up the creek had yet to start when Sam began to pack up his bedroll and saddlebags full of food for the herder. It would take a good four hours to ride to the camp because Sam knew he'd stop for a quick visit with Meyer as he passed by his neighbor's home. Too, he planned to stop by Mitchell to pick up some flour and coffee for the sheep herder.

He gave each of his five children hugs as they clamored around him, each child waiting for a turn with their father. The four-year-old twins raised up their arms to be held, their faces showing the happiness they felt from the attention they were getting. They knew they were too big to be held like small children, but they also knew their father had a tender spot for the babies of the family.

Ten-year-old Julia, his oldest child and already doing most of a woman's work each day as she helped her mother, held back as her younger siblings vied for Sam's attention. Maggie's fly-away brown hair blew into her eyes and she gathered it back with one hand as her other squeezed her dad's leg. Autie and Clyde solemnly shook hands, manfully declaring they would help Mother while Father was off shearing in the mountains. Giving Nancy one last hug, Sam reluctantly mounted his horse and headed for Summit Prairie.

The camp tender was glad to see Sam ride up; there were half a dozen men gathered around the evening fire and the food supply was getting a little low. After a round or two of the bottle of moonshine Meyer had insisted Sam take to sheep camp, the group of sheepmen was contentedly sharing stories along with the drink.

There was a lull in the conversation, broken by a not-too-discreet belch and the breaking of wind. "Definitely not a camp for women," Sam thought. In the distance they could hear a coyote's plaintiff howl, the soughing of the wind in the pine and fir trees. Nearby, an owl hooted.

"I hear an owl calling someone's name," commented one of the men lying prone near the warmth of the fire, propped up on one elbow as he picked at his teeth with a pine needle. "Hope it's not mine."

"Nor mine," added another, "though when it's my time, I figure it'll be my time." The men were thinking of the Indian story claiming that before a person died, an owl would call his name. Whenever Sam heard an owl calling in the night, he would wonder half-jokingly what soul would soon be winging its way to heaven.

"Hopefully, not mine tonight," he thought. "I have sheep to shear in the morning." In the distance, another owl took up the call, then another, until there were four owls calling back and forth in the trees near Carroll Camp at the head of Bridge Creek.

"The story's pure myth," Sam reminded himself as he turned over under his bedroll and tucked his wool blanket a little tighter. The night seemed uncommonly cool.

Sam was shearing sheep at the camp on Summit Prairie as the day of June 2 dawned, hotter than usual in the morning. Nancy sighed as she helped Julia wash the breakfast dishes and start a pot of beans for lunch. She envied her husband's being in the mountains where it would undoubtedly be cooler, knowing she could look forward to fretful children during the heat of the day. Perhaps she could pacify the twins by placing a wash pan in the creek and tying it with a rope to the fence post, making a makeshift boat for them to play in.

Nancy finished the morning work in the kitchen and began whitewashing the house. On a trip out to the creek for water, she noticed threatening greenish-gray clouds balling up, rising in heavy columns as they joined together. By early afternoon, she could hear the loud booming of thunder to the southeast, and the sky darkened. Outside, the countryside had grown quiet and ominous and Nancy could feel anxiety growing deep inside her body. The water in Bridge Creek seemed to be rising, so she let out some of the water from the irrigation ditch. The diverted water appeared to be on the verge of overflowing its banks due to the uncommon amount of water flowing into it from the main waterway, and Nancy guessed there had been heavy rains further up the creek.

Heavy thunderclouds had gathered quickly in the oppressive midday heat, rising tall and threateningly in the southern sky. Bent over a kicking ewe, working his hand shears quickly to clip off the heavy wool on her belly, Sam was startled when the first loud clap of thunder seemed to boom directly overhead, signaling the beginning of the storm. The deluge started without further warning where the crew was working, and Sam and the men stopped shearing and dashed to the shelter of a large pine tree nearby.

The lightning streaks gained in size and duration, snaking unceasingly out of the darkened sky and grinding into the earth, striking trees and starting small fires that were soon quenched by the falling deluge.

The earsplitting roar of thunder pounded through the bodies of the men huddled under the tree and soon the branches gave them no shelter as the pouring rain penetrated the boughs. The air was filled with the smell of burnt timber and of rain-drenched soil and meadow grass. Small rivulets formed, and then grew in size as the rain continued to fall.

Sam and the men watched the trickles become small creeks, which grew wider and wider as they gushed across the meadow. A herder dashed into the storm and was joined by a shearer and then another as the men opened the gate to the sheep pen, driving the frightened animals out of the enclosure and onto higher ground as the water reached their corral.

Sam ran from the pine tree to help the men with the sheep, when he stopped suddenly, looking at the churning, rushing water running where a few minutes before there had been grassy meadow. A thought struck him like a bolt of lightning: this same water that would soon fill Bridge Creek and overflow the banks would also rush down towards his home and his family.

He dashed to the corral, grabbed his mount's bridle from the pole fence, and threw a rein around his saddle horse's neck, jerking the frightened animal's head down to put the bit in his mouth. He took no time for a saddle, vaulting onto his horse's back and slashing him with the reins almost simultaneously, heading off the high prairie and towards his home northwest of Mitchell. The trip would take him a couple of hours riding at breakneck speed, no matter what shortcuts he might take. The route of the storm would be widespread and would be more direct than his course and as he whipped his horse unmercifully, Sam doubted he could reach his family before the flood waters.

The thunderstorm drew nearer the little house on Bridge Creek, deafening thunder claps and bolts of lightning scaring the children and Nancy equally. She wished Sam were home. Torrential rain pounded the roof of the Wilson home and when Nancy looked out the door, the creek had risen to the level of the house. Looking south, she saw a wall of roiling caramel-colored water advancing towards the house, small trees and sagebrush tumbling in the turbulent stream.

Screaming, Nancy ordered her children to run for the hills. They would have to cross the flooding irrigation ditch, but the highest ground was there across that waterway and Bridge Creek was rising rapidly.

"Then Ma commenced praying for help," wrote ten-year-old Julia, remembering the flash flood.

"Autia[15] said to Ma, "If we can get to the hill we will be all right," and Ma said, "we can't do that."

"Then Autia commenced getting us across the ditch. He fell in with Clyde and Ma helped him out. He had us all across but Ma and Maggie and had gone back for them when the water was up to his neck.

"That was the last time I ever saw any of them.

I then ran for the hills.

"The last word I heard them say was: Autia said, "If we can get to the hills we will be all right."

"Ma said, "We will never get there."

Maggie said, "Oh! We can't live any longer, can we?"

"George was standing by the ditch crying."[16]

Nancy, chest deep in water, reached for George standing by the rushing flood, his arms stretched towards her, the lightening striking nearby and the roar of the thunder terrifying the little boy. She could see his round baby-face contorted with terror and knew he was crying, but she couldn't hear him above the roar of the deepening water and the grinding and clashing of the boulders tumbling down the engorged creek. She tried to move through the rushing water, her long skirt whipping

---

15 Julie spelled the name "Autia"; it is spelled "Autie" on his grave marker in the family cemetery.
16 Ibid. *p. 243*

around her legs from the surging of the flood waters, her feet slipping on the stones churning under her feet. The brown torrent was rushing into her home and it seemed to her the house was beginning to move off the foundation. Just a few more feet and she could reach her son. She reached towards his outstretched arms and grabbed his tiny hand in hers and never saw the trunk of the flood-tossed juniper tree that hit her on the back of her head.

Sam clung tightly with his knees to his horse's wet back, whipping the tired animal with the loose ends of the reins. Focused on his family, he rode south and west of Mitchell, heading north to his homestead, seeking the most direct route. He forced his horse down the slippery bank of Nelson Creek, through rushing muddy waters in the bottom of the draw and up the other side, his horse slipping in the water-logged soil time after time.

The rain slackened somewhat but still drenched his shirt, plastering it to his back as he came to Gable Creek. The roiling flood waters in the deep canyon below created a deafening roar as he guided his tired mount down the muddy, slippery hillside, through the churning water, and up the far side of the ravine, making his way home to his family.

A sickening foreboding wrenched his stomach as he saw the destruction from the flash-flood becoming worse the further he rode. Every small gully he crossed was running deep with floodwaters, sometimes reaching his horse's belly as he forced the frightened animal through the raging streams. A board from some homesteader's destroyed home, part of a chicken coop, a deer drowned by the powerful flood, uprooted trees and sagebrush, huge boulders all tumbled their way down the streams, pushed by the powerful torrent.

Sam's horse was struggling to keep moving forward as he gamely stumbled onward, his breath coming in loud wheezes, the spray from his foam-covered chest flinging backwards. When Sam reached his home-stead, there was no house. He could only find a sobbing ten-year-old Julia crouched into a ball on a nearby hillside with her arms around the family dog, watching the receding flood waters in hopes of seeing her mother and her brothers and her sister. Sam held his hysterical daughter's head tightly against his chest, placing his hand over her ear to deaden the sound of the lessening flood waters still pounding against huge boulders and washing tumbling debris down the flooding course. Sam was powerless to do anything but watch the flooding Bridge Creek slacken off, leaving behind an awesome path of destruction.

The next day, Julia and Sam were reunited with Clyde, the only other survivor of the family. Clyde had spent the night huddled on the hillside above the Wilson home. The bodies of Nancy, Autie, and Maggie were found. Nancy's body had been swept away and deposited almost fourteen miles from her home. George's tiny body was never recovered.

Nancy and her two children were buried in the family cemetery near Nancy's little brother, George W., the small graveyard not too far from the debris left by the flashflood. Large boulders with splintered juniper and pine trees jammed among the rocks were unpleasant testimony to the powerfulness of the waters that had claimed the lives of four of the Carroll family.

Grandma Margarette stood with her arm around little Julia as her family was buried. Temporary markers, four slabs of limestone that read "Nancy Wilson," "Autie Wilson," "Maggie Wilson", and "George Wilson" were grim reminders of the destructiveness of the flashfloods that would strike the area near Mitchell again and again in the future. The unanswered question was when.

"Sometimes it's a hell of a price a man has to pay for where he lives," Meyer told Samuel Carroll, who had just seen his daughter and two

The Carroll cemetery on Samuel Carroll's homestead. In the background is the Carroll Rim. The road into the Painted Hills Park marks the site of the old Sam Wilson home where Nancy and the three children lost their lives.

grandchildren laid to rest in the graveyard established in the clay soil and a slab placed for the missing grandson, the painted hills a backdrop for the new cemetery on the Wilson farm.

The two friends eyed Sam Wilson, overcome with his grief as the graves of his wife and two children were filled in with the blood-red adobe. The big German clumsily put a huge work-roughened hand on Carroll's shoulder and gave it a gentle squeeze.

"It's a tough and demanding country, all right." Carroll choked up, nodding his head in agreement. "Damn tough." He stood watching his son-in-law and his two grandchildren grieve and he clenched his square jaw tightly and swallowed hard, fighting back his own tears as he hugged his wife more firmly, and the gathering mourned together.

Chapter 7
1869 — Jerome Parsons's Twickenham

The opening of the Suez Canal in 1869 also marked the opening of the areas near the present day towns of Fossil and Spray. In '69, when the threat of Indian hostilities was deemed to have become non-existent in the area, Camp Watson was decommissioned. Meyer and Hewot felt a bit uneasy about no cavalrymen patrolling the road; however, earlier assurances of safety from the military had already opened up settlement in the locale.

Those seeking land began to move into areas where acreage was still readily available, lured to the region by reports of fertile land and lush grass for stock. "Everyone wants to raise stock, it seems," Hewot commented. "I wonder how long all this grass is going to last? Lotta grass, but lotta stock comin' in, too."

Popular areas for settlement in the area that would become Wheeler County were Biffle's Twickenham; Richmond and the surrounding area known as the Shoofly Country that traded in that small town; Waterman Flat; Bridge Creek; Caleb Basin; the "Haystack Country," which included the future town of Spray and the land from Kimberly to Service Creek; Mitchell; Fossil; and the Upper Butte Creek area.

Hearing of the settlers moving to the areas nearby interested Meyer and he never tired of sitting at the huge table he and Hewot had set up outside the door of their limestone fort-house, their favorite chairs facing the military road on the south side of their home. Passersby knew they'd be hailed to stop for a visit and a drink from the ever-present bottle of whiskey or the moonshine made from Meyer's grains. If it were anywhere close to mealtime, they would be offered a meal. For those who were "strangers" there was always the well-used saleratus can sitting on the table where a donation could be made for food and drink; for neighbors, the fee was the sharing of a story about the developing region and the characters who were settling in.

"Heard a good story the other day about one of those folks moving in with stock," Meyer laughed, entertaining Hewot and the visitor sitting at his table, its edges worn smooth from elbows rubbing against the soft pine wood. "That Parsons fellow, moved into Biffle's valley and wants to raise cattle and horses. The one that's building that ferry at the mouth of that creek running down from the north. Can tell a good story, that's for sure. Quite a fellow, he is. Five minutes with him and I figured out he could charm the sage right off a bush. Told a story about Indians … and a few more." The German chuckled and nodded his head. "Ja! Always a few more."

"I was riding one hell of a fine hot-blooded mare last year and managed to outrun the Indians long enough to reach my cabin, unsaddle and unbridle my horse, and fort up in the cabin where I kept them off," Parsons's story had begun. "The next morning when I ventured out, I saw the mare standing high on a rocky point nearby. I gave her no more thought, but noticed on the following morning that she was still in the exact same spot. Went to investigate only to find she had become so overheated during the chase that she had petrified. Well, I bred her to a petrified stallion and this spring she had a petrified colt."[1]

Jerome Parsons's listener had kept a straight face, nodding in agreement that Jerome's mare was a very fine horse, indeed. Meyer's willing-

---

1 Bob Huntington interview, 2010

ness to let his host dominate the conversation encouraged the settler to continue his stories. Not that he needed much encouragement. His neighbors already had learned that if there was anything Parsons enjoyed more than his three hearty meals a day, it was telling his tales to anyone who would listen.

"I was born in Virginia in '35," Parsons had offered, unbuttoning the top button of his pants and settling comfortably back into his hand-carved pine chair, settling in for a storytelling session. "Son of descendants of prominent colonial families. Verrrry prominent," he stressed, leaning back in the substantial seat he'd placed outside his cabin made largely of river rock with a bit of rough-cut and unpainted pine boards added for stability. He hooked his thumbs behind his wide suspenders. "Crossed the plains in '57 and arrived in the Sacramento Valley with five cents."

He had reached into his deep pants pocket and pulled out a well-used handkerchief, the stub of a pencil, a small ball of string, a few scraps of very crumpled paper, and a lint-covered nickel. "There it is," he announced, blowing the lint off the coin. "Keep it in my pocket to remind me just how broke a man can get.

"Anyway, spent two years there in Sacramento as a horseshoer and got kicked by a vicious brute. Purely mean. Put me in the hospital for thirteen months. Then, in '61, when I was just twenty-six years old, I headed for the Willamette Valley and in '66 … well, here I am."

"Isaac Holmes, he claimed a large — very large — level tract on this north bank of the river down there," and Parsons gestured broadly, showing the scope of his holdings in the center of the valley. He nodded his head in pride at the substantial size of his holdings, which was 320 acres, half a section, and the size of plot many of the locals had filed claim to. "Left his holdings. Abandoned them. When I came down from Umatilla County, I set up squatter's rights on the land."

Parsons had gone on to tell of fighting in the Rogue River Indian war and in the Cow Creek fight. He had been in an Indian war in 1846, and reported that he'd had many fights with the "savages" in various places.[2]

"Had an encounter with Indians chasing me. They chased me out onto the edge of a high cliff. I went over the edge but hung by my spurs. This fooled the Indians and they left, probably thinking I fell to my death. I hung there for two days trying to figure a way to get back up. Finally, I just climbed up my leg."[3] Parsons had lowered his head, surveying the well-worn toe of his shoe, and then peered up at Meyer from under his eyebrows and stroked his short white beard, thinking perhaps even he couldn't believe the story himself.

Meyer's face had remained impassive. He'd heard of Parsons's ire being aroused when someone voiced doubt about his stories. Besides, the German was enjoying a rare Sunday afternoon away from never-ending weeding and irrigating, not to mention the tin cup full of moonshine he'd not made himself…and, it wasn't bad at all, he opined, sipping the fiery liquid slowly and licking his lips after each drink. He settled back in a chair shaded by the rock walls of the homesteader's unique dwelling, as original as Parsons himself, and listened to his host's stories, knowing he'd be repeating them soon to his own audience.

Jerome Parsons had settled on an area near the John Day River that was reasonably level. The flow of traffic through the valley had created passable roads leading both into and out of the area, no matter what route was traveled. There was the first road built into the bottom land, leading from Bridge Creek and running past Biffle's homestead. "That's the first fellow to settle in this country," Parsons would repeat often, gesturing across the river and to the southwest. "Got himself a good little place started there."

The road continued past Biffle's cabin and followed the river until it

---

2 Shaver et al., p. 691
3 Bob Huntington interview, 2010

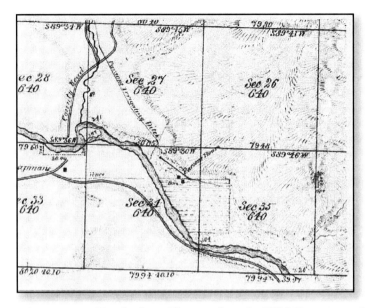

Parsons's property in Twickenham. The map, from the BLM Government land records, was recorded in 1870. Note the break in the county road; this was the site of Parsons's ferry. Rowe Creek is just to the east of the road.

reached Gird's Creek on the east end of the valley, then turned sharply south as it followed the creek flowing through a steep basalt rock lined valley. The rough and winding roadway followed the stream sharply up-hill until it met a thoroughfare some eight miles distant. Taking a right turn onto the road would lead the traveler past the Meyers' Gulch road; a left turn would end up at the route passing through the northern part of the newly settled area.

The third access passed just west of Parsons's holdings, following the creek running into the river from the north, and it was at the mouth of the small waterway that the entrepreneur established his ferry to connect the northern route with the southern. The northern end of this route ended at a well-traveled road running east and west some fifteen miles north of Biffle's valley.

Twickenham Ferry - Early 1900s

Parsons kept an eye on the routes leading past his homestead as he set about developing the community by the John Day River. The first line of business was to build a flat-bottomed ferry; folks had to get across the waterway and he may as well help them out and profit from their need while he was assisting them, he reasoned. Too, the crossing took long enough for him to jaw a while with his customers. Good way to keep up with the settlement of the country and to get to know the neighbors, offer advice when he could.

Parsons propped up two thirty-foot long planks, each one eighteen inches wide and four-inches thick, with rocks to hold them on edge during construction. Then he nailed cross pieces on either end between the side boards, each about fifteen feet long, making a rectangular shape for the bottom. Across those, he nailed sturdy eighteen-foot-long broad planks for the floor of the watercraft. Finally, Parsons erected a pole fence on either side of the ferry, ran a cable from the conveyance to a sturdy post on either side of the river, and he was in business.

If he saw a rider or a wagon approaching his homestead, the entrepreneur seemed to always have business to tend to close to the road.

And, there was always time for a story or two if the traveler didn't have to cross on the ferry right away.

"Soon's I get this ditch dug another twenty feet or so, I need a break," he would begin, wiping his forehead with his soiled handkerchief and readjusting his tattered wide-brimmed hat. "Pot of beans on the stove, venison hanging. Sure would be glad to share with you, soon's I get this done," Parsons would tell the passerby, and, bending over his shovel, he'd sink it deeply into the soft dirt. "Light a spell and rest a bit until I'm done here. Then we'll go get us something to eat." He always seemed to have a spare shovel handy and a tale or two to share — and a reputation for making use of the strong backs that passed by his holdings.

One of the tales Jerome told often was about running out of hay to feed his livestock. This tale he made no bones about: the story was told purely for entertainment. He said that he had hay on the south side of the river and was going to attempt to swim the cattle over. First, however, he rode down to the river to see how high it was and to check for ice flows. There he discovered a very large hollow juniper tree that had drifted down during high water and lodged in such a manner as to bridge the river.

"I got my cattle and drove them into the hollow log," Jerome declared with a big grin on his face, his deeply set eyes twinkling. "Once I got them all in and started, I jumped my horse up on top of the log and trotted him to the other end so I could count the cattle out. After the count, I found I was six head short. Upon walking back through the log, I discovered that the six head had gotten side-tracked into a hollow limb." Parsons would slap his leg and roar in laughter, and his guest would join in.

Another time Jerome told of quite an ordeal in the river. It seems he was prying on a pump pipe with a one-hundred-pound crowbar when he fell in over his head, still gripping the crowbar. Not wanting to lose

Jerome Parsons — master storyteller and early pioneer.
Courtesy of the Fossil museum

the crowbar and being unable to swim with it, he decided to just walk out to shallower water. This he finally accomplished, though he came out two miles down the river.

Jerome also told of losing his grandfather's watch while fording the river. He found the watch two years later and it hadn't lost a minute. The current had kept it wound, acting on the winding stem much as on a water wheel.[4] The lower the afternoon sun and the level of the moonshine in Parsons's bottle, the higher the enjoyment for the host and his audience, and his tales became part of the legends of Twickenham.

"Hmpff. Well," Parsons muttered when he heard of another ferry being put into place less than a mile to the east of his enterprise, and his fingers vigorously smoothed his mustache. He worked off his frustra-

4 Bob Huntington interview, 2010

tion by shoveling a little faster and a little further on his ditch, then re-signed himself to the reality of free enterprise coming to his valley. He'd still keep busy transporting folks across the John Day, he reckoned, and the few coins he collected for each trip would come in handy.

With irrigation, the rich bottom land on Jerome's holdings would soon be growing abundant crops, including the vegetables, grains, and fruits that were so essential to the settlers. First, though, he had to till the soil and that would take a lot of hard work.

"Folks are sure good to help out a neighbor," he'd comment after he had fed generous helpings of brown beans and fried venison to a visitor. The lucky dinner guest that got the back-strap, rolled in flour and fried in bacon grease, figured he'd been more than well-paid for his time. Usually the food was served after the guest had spent an hour or more helping Jerome dig on the trench that would carry his water from the creek run-ning into the valley from the north. Then, while the meat was frying and the beans heating on the wood cook-stove, Parsons would launch into another of his stories, perhaps telling about one of his hunting ventures.

"I was out hunting with my two dogs (as fierce a pair of dogs as you'll ever see) foraging out ahead of me, when all of a sudden here came my dogs ky-yiing, tails between their legs, running right by me and on toward home. I figured as how it had to be a grizzly or something worse to give them such a scare. I cautiously proceeded in the direction from which the dogs had come. Nearing a deep canyon, I heard a noise that sounded like some huge beast on the rampage. Cautiously, I peered down into the canyon to find that it was only a large log so crooked it couldn't lie still. It would roll down one side of the canyon and up the other, then back. It had been doing this so long it was almost worn in two."[5]

Parsons slowly built up his holdings, in between visiting with folks

---

5 Ibid.

who passed by and often stopped to do some "neighboring" for him. He'd been aided in his undertaking with some cattle owned by his uncle Jerome Harper of San Francisco[6] and that gave him an added incentive to succeed with the stock raising. His herd was soon known as one of the finest in the area surrounding his valley. His 150 head of Durham and Hereford cattle and his 75 head of horses[7] took a fair amount of grazing land. Given there were no fences on the rangeland in '66, Jerome made use of his neighbor's generosity and moved the stock around as the need arose.

Parsons would soon realize, as many of the local stockmen shortly did, that the luxurious grass they found wouldn't last long with the intense grazing demanded by the large numbers of animals brought into the country. For many, good stewardship of the land would be a lesson learned too slowly.

To passersby, the valley was a beautiful sight, bordered as it was to the north by the picturesque rimrocks, to the south by the rock-topped steep rolling hills, with the backbone of the river flowing through the native pasture lands lush with abundant bunch-grass. Those hardy settlers, the ones who planned to work the land for their livelihood, knew they'd tax their minds and bodies and pocketbooks before they could succeed.

Appreciating the beauty of the river basin or having the capital to begin their venture wouldn't see the pioneers' plans to fruition. It would take both tough minds and tough bodies to conquer the tough land.

"A man might have the "wanta" ta get started, but the body has ta have the "gonna" if he's goin' ta succeed," Parsons advised.

"Biffle's down," a sober looking Meyer told Parsons one day. "Hadn't seen him for a while so I come to check on him." The German knew, without asking, that the neighbors would join together in caring for their fragile friend, who had long appeared to be terminally ill.

---

6 Ed F. Horn letter, November 26, 1940
7 W. G. Trill in *Pacific Northwest Homestead*, p. 55

Perhaps, some of the neighbors speculated, had Biffle traveled to The Dalles, he may have been able to receive treatment that would have prolonged his life. The determined homesteader, however, maintained his independence and remained in his valley where he had found his liberty. He could no longer physically work the holdings on which he had never filed claim, and he had relinquished the land over to a newcomer, James Dedman.

As long as he could shuffle out the door of his crudely built homesteader's cabin to sit on the wooden chair that had long since replaced his seat of sandstone, Biffle enjoyed the first warm rays of the sun striking his home each morning. There he remained most of the day, watching the play of the light across his fields and the distant hills and the rimrocks, satisfied with the greenness of his newly planted Liberty Bottom, the field he'd added to the Big Bottom.

And always, as the last rays of the day's light sun began their final show across the face of the basalt border to the north of his valley, the frail pioneer drew strength from his mother's tattered Bible as he gently smoothed the worn black cover with his shaky, gnarled hands. There was no need to open the book to the place marked with the worn wallpaper marker; he'd read the words of her favorite Psalm so many times he knew them by heart, and he drew his strength by repeating the words in his mind as he absorbed the strength of the rimrocks.

When he became too weak to sit upright for long periods of time, his lounge was covered with a straw mattress and moved outside where the failing homesteader could recline in comfort. Biffle propped himself up with two pillows so he could continue to keep an observant eye on his neighbors toiling in their valley bordered by the rimrocks to the north and the tall, rock-topped hills to the south.

The gaunt homesteader could see an occasional rider passing on the road to the north of the John Day River and those who traveled near

Biffle's cabin would stop to inquire about his health and to offer help. He was grateful for his newest neighbors, the Dedman family, who seemed to always be nearby to watch over him, though that precluded his previously customary morning reveries as he relieved himself while surveying his valley.

"Too dad-burned many folks anymore," he complained to Dedman one day when that neighbor hung the door on Biffle's newly built outhouse. Dedman, one of those "many folks," grinned and nodded in agreement. His family was moving onto Biffle's homestead, and the privy had been constructed at the request of the women in the family.

Parsons was given the task of building the casket for James Biffle, that first settler in Wheeler County, who died October 11, 1870, after spending eight years on his homestead. For this undertaking, as well as for assisting in Biffle's sickness, Parsons charged the sum of $25.00. A. H. Gates charged $25.00 for attorney fees in handling the estate, Wm. Monroe charged $39.00 for appraisal fees and taking charge of the sale of Biffle's property, and J. S. Dedman received $50.00 for his part in "... attendance in last sickness and other services."[8]

Among the items listed in Biffle's estate were the following:

- One Dog Muzzle $1.00
- One prs overhalls $1.50
- Two prs socks $1.50
- Two Bot. whiskey $3.00
- 1 Prs Gloves $2.00
- 1 Pair New Boots $6.50
- One lounge $3.00
- One Straw Mattress $1.50
- Two Pillows $1.00

---

8 O. W. Weaver, administrator for the Estate of J. C. Biffle, "deceased." February 12, 1871

- 22 lbs of Beef $2.20
- 1 lb Tobacco $1.00
- 2 Box Pills. 2 Bot whiskey $3.50
- 1,210 feet of lumber . . . . $36.30[9]

The value of Biffle's estate was listed as $2,103.79. His ranch, with improvements, was assessed at $800.00, and B. D. Butler helped list the assets of the deceased, to include the following:

734 sheep, $1.62 head $1,189.62
Four mules $200.00
Three calves $18.00
Two turkeys $3.00
22 chickens, $5.00 per doz . . . . $ 9.15
Half stack of oats $26.25
Half stack of straw $5.00
Two stacks of hay $69.00
Half stack of wheat $13.50
Lot of Ruta Bagas . . . . $20.00[10]

Included among his personal effects that were sold at auction was a "sett teeth gold" for $5.00 that were sold to Chapman, who also bought the straw mattress for $1.50. A "lot of old clothes" were sold to Mr. Monroe for $4.00. A pair of drawers listed for $2.00 never sold.

Perhaps the possessions Biffle would have hated to be sold the most were his well-trained shepherd dog and his four mules. Mr. Chapman paid $12.50 for "One half Undivided interest in Dog." Biffle's mule, Eliza, sold for $65, her team mate, Patsy, for $55, and the pair of mules, Jack and Jinni, for $40 each. Biffle, his faithful shepherd dog, and those

9 Ibid.
10 Ibid.

mules had spent many days together, doing much to begin the settlement of Biffle's beloved valley and of Wheeler County.[11]

Although the area hadn't been surveyed by the government yet, those who moved into it established the boundaries of their holdings, and Parsons was often present to ensure their boundaries were fair. He liked to return the favor of their hard work to his neighbors, and to keep his own boundaries intact.

Included in the list of early settlers arriving in Parsons's area in 1870 was James S. Dedman and Jerome was quick to find out the history of the family that moved onto Biffle's homestead. Like many of the earlier settlers, Parsons sometimes quizzed his friends about their families, learning particulars that made the absent members seem like close relatives, despite the fact they had never met. Occasionally, after an initial inquiry, Parsons surmised it was best that he ask no more questions about a man's background.

At the outbreak of the Civil War, Dedman had been the owner of an iron foundry in his home state of Tennessee. "The Confederate Government had confiscated his foundry to make munitions and placed him in charge of it. As the war progressed and things went badly for the South, they moved the operation farther and farther south to keep it working and out of the hands of the North."[12]

At the end of the war, the Dedman family was in Texas and had lost a great deal of their assets, so Dedman determined to get a fresh start in the Oregon Country. With him were his two sons and two daughters. Joseph Kitchen Rowe, engaged to Dedman's daughter Martha (Mattie), joined the family in the move. Dedman's wife remained in the South and planned to follow later when the family was relocated.[13] Unfortunately, she never made the trip.

---

11 Ibid.
12 Glenn Cooper, grandson of Joseph Rowe; letter to Ruth Wilson December 6, 1967
13 Ibid.

When the Dedman family arrived in Portland, having come the way of the Isthmus of Panama by train and boarding a ship on the West Coast, they found the city to be a "very small town" and determined it was not large enough to support an iron foundry. They heard about the John Day River country having native bunch grass growing "belly deep to a horse" and the men rode to investigate. Satisfied with what they found, they returned to Portland and made arrangements to move[14] and Parsons quickly notified folks in the area that there would soon be new neighbors in the vicinity of Biffle's homestead.

"Dedman told me the family had found Portland to be a 'very small town,' and I'm wondering just what he's thinking about the size of this place?" Parsons shook his head in puzzlement as he shared the information with his neighbor.

The family traveled to The Dalles by river steamer and "...set out with their ox-drawn wagons, laden with provisions and the necessities of home-making, for their destination one hundred miles away. They settled near a place now known as Twickenham, building log cabins across the John Day River from the settlement. The country had not been surveyed yet, and they established squatter's rights, which would entitle them to homesteading privileges at a later date."[15]

Perhaps Parsons was feeling a twinge of guilt as he thought of what his own reaction would be if he were to be invaded by a group of intruders who simply moved in and took over his land with no or very little compensation. At any rate, he encouraged James Dedman to build a fort-house, located near Biffle's homestead, to serve the area in the event of an Indian attack on the settlers, and Dedman agreed the fort would be a good idea. It had only been four years since Wheeler had been shot by the braves attacking his mail stage, and the square logs of the Dedman home offered protection to settlers in the valley and nearby areas, though it was never used.

"Martha (Mattie) Virginia Dedman and Joseph Rowe were married January 6, 1870. Grandfather Rowe came clear to The Dalles to obtain the license, and he took a minister back to the settlement with him to perform the service."[16] Joseph reported to the folks in the valley that while he was securing his marriage license, he'd heard the population of the United States had reached 39 million. The settlers just could not grasp the concept of that number of people; they surmised — and hoped — not many of those folks would come to the area where they were settling, though Parsons opined a few more neighbors would do the settlement good.

Joseph Rowe moved his bride to his land claim on the stream to the north that flowed into the John Day River running through Parsons's valley and the little waterway became known as Rowe Creek. There Mattie learned the hardships of frontier life for the women. She and her sister had been reared in the South where they had slaves to do all the work, including cooking, laundering, sewing, and gardening.

Life on the ranch on Rowe Creek was a definite change for the young bride. She learned the requisite sourdough recipes used by the early settlers as well as how to make her family's clothing by hand, ripping apart well-worn clothing to use as patterns for new garments.

"The family grew and the ranching prospered, at least mildly. Grandfather Rowe planted a family orchard and garden and grew some hay for their saddle horses, oxen and milk cows. The beef cattle lived on the range, winter and summer. Grandmother made butter which was salted down in wooden casks, stored in the spring-house, and brought to The Dalles and sold to the merchants on Grandfather's semi-annual trips for provisions."[17]

---

16 Ibid.
17 Ibid.

Dedman Fort House - 1925

The fort house was located in southwest Twickenham.
Courtesy of the Keyes Kenny collection

Joseph Rowe remained in the area until he began to feel his children weren't getting a proper education. In '81, at a time when he and Mattie were considering what would be best for their children, he received a letter from his brother in Baltimore. "Preserving food in metal cans was a brand new thing, and his brother wanted him to return to Baltimore and join him in a canning venture."[18] This request made up Joseph's mind as to what would be best for his family.

He sold his cattle, his buildings, and his improvements to Al Sutton and started his journey to Baltimore. The Rowes reached The Dalles and, upon hearing of a lethal disease raging in Portland, they chose to stay in the area for a time. The children began school there and Rowe bought a 47-acre place near town.[19]

Robert, Martha's brother, remained in the area of the Dedman forthouse and married a woman named Jane Williams. She had formerly been married to H. B. Williams and was the mother of four children.

18 Ibid.
19 Ibid.

Robert and Jane had two daughters, Opal Dedman Waters and Gracie Dedman Mabe. The young couple lived for some time on Rowe Creek before they moved to the Shoofly neighborhood, and Parsons found time to visit the family to see if they needed any advice, timing his arrival to coincide with mealtime complete with Jane's sourdough biscuits.

Robert sold a couple of pieces of land to Rod Mabe when Rod and Gracie were married in '98. The newlyweds bought some of the field owned by the homesteader Trent and they built an Aladdin home, ordering it from Sears and Roebuck and having it shipped by wagon to their land. To build their new home which was located on a hill above the Waldron school house, about one mile from the main road, they nailed the numbered pieces together.[20] Building a home in this manner would have been welcomed by the Dedman and Rowe families; they had resorted to cutting down trees some distance north from their home site, hewing the logs and cutting notches, and putting their homes together with chinking to stop the drafts.

"Kids have it easy nowadays," grumbled Parsons when he heard of the Mabes' Sears and Roebuck home, remembering the work he and his neighbors had gone through to build the Parsons's home. The building effort had taken numerous pots of beans, several venison, and countless "Parsons stories" to complete.

One of Parsons's haphazard efforts had been the addition of rounded river rock to the sides of his cabin. His fireplace had been built of the same type of stone and he mixed adobe mud with chopped straw and small sticks as mortar between the rocks.[21] Though he soon came to the conclusion that rounded rocks don't stack well, he determinedly clung to his method of masonry like a cocklebur clings to woolen stockings, and river rocks it was.

---

20 Fred Dunn interview, 2011
21 Bob Huntington interview. Bob is an old-timer from the Twickenham area and remembers seeing the results of Parson's masonry efforts.

In the same year as Biffle's death and the Dedman family's arrival, Parsons married Josephine Writsman, who had crossed the plains in '45 with her parents. Jerome and Josephine had four children: Frankie, Stella, Guy, and Cleve. Like any children, the Parsons's brood grew well in all kinds of dirt, and the soil on their parents' farm seemed to agree with them. As soon as they could wield a hoe, they helped in the large garden, working under their father's guidance.

> "One of the most developed small ranches in the Twickenham district is that owned by J. H. Parsons, consisting of 320 acres of land. On this place he raises sweet potatoes and all kinds of garden truck. Wheat has yielded 60 bushels per acre on the place. He has a 40-acre field of alfalfa, which yields four crops with irrigation, and the average yield is five tons per acre. He has a fine orchard of 100 trees, and next year expects to compete at the Lewis and Clark Fair at Portland, Oregon, especially on peaches. A walnut tree growing on the place is 20 inches in diameter and 50 feet high. This is also a stock ranch, and Mr. Parsons has 150 head of cattle — Durhams and Herefords — 75 horses and 20 Poland China hogs."[22]

Parsons and Josephine acted as the "first family" of the valley and often entertained visitors in their home near the John Day River. Parsons helped with preparations for the gatherings by sitting in the shade and sharing stories to keep the visitors out of Josephine's way so she could get her work done.

In February of '79, Henry Heidtmann and Winifred Metcalfe were

---

22 W.G. Trill in *Pacific Northwest Homestead*, p. 55
23 Viola Parker Engelman et al., in *History of Wheeler County*, p. 109

married at the Parsons's home. Henry had come from Germany when he was fifteen; his parents had sent him to this country to prevent him from having to serve in the German army. He took up land just east of Rowe Creek north of Parsons's holdings on what would be later known as the Zack Keys ranch. There he raised horses, which he drove to Canada for sale.[23]

"That Henry, he's a worker," Parsons admitted. "I'm not sure the German understands everything, though. He likes me to help him when I can spare time from my own work. Uncle Sam's trying to be official now, survey the land here, and now that Heidtmann's the county surveyor, layin' out those property boundaries, I know he'd like the help." The German surveyor undoubtedly was kept honest with Parsons's guidance.

With his strong will, Jerome was sure to lock horns with Anthony 'Pike' Helms, another early settler with similar independent traits. Helms had been born in Missouri in '42, and served in the army during the Civil War until he mustered out in '65. Pike married Mary Paul that same year and the couple moved to Oregon in '75. He arrived in the Waldron area with his wife and five children and lived in Waldron for twenty years where he was the proprietor of the first post office and store in that area.[24]

Helms sold his property in Waldron to John Butler and lived for six years in Parsons's valley. He then moved to the town of Mitchell and established the *Mitchell Sentinel and published that paper until his death in 1923*.[25] While living close to Parsons, the two men had a meeting of the wills quite often.

"Damned Yankees," Parsons would thunder, his eyes sparkling in anger. "Always did think they were better than folks from the South. Might

---

23 Viola Parker Engelman et al., in *History of Wheeler County*, p. 109
24 Shaver et al., p. 664
25 Dick Helms and Jessie Butler Sharp in History of Wheeler County, p. 109

Anthony "Pike" Helms
Used with permission from McLaren Stinchfield

have won the war, but — hmpff! If only they knew!" and he would shake his head in despair and scowl at anyone listening. No matter that Helms was strongly civic minded and spent countless hours helping neighbors with the development of the newly settled area. And, no matter that Parsons had similar qualities. The men just could not, would not agree.

With two such strong-willed men heatedly discussing what the name for the settlement alongside the John Day River should be, there appeared to be no immediate and satisfactory solution to the discussion. A municipality must have a name, so the new western stage stop was called Contention and a post office was established July 8, 1886, with Edward Horn as the first postmaster.[26]

"You suppose this will be the end of contention in Contention?" the good postmaster asked wryly, watching Parsons as he ambled out the door of the post office, a self-satisfied smile on his face, having posted a letter bearing one of the first of the postmarks with the small community's name inked on the envelope.

---

26 Ed F. Horn letter

A mail contract was signed between J. H. Boomer of the county of San Francisco, California, and W. E. Helms of Waldron in Crook County, Oregon, on May 16, 1891. Helms sub-contracted the route from Waldron through Contention and to Fossil. Running the route for him would be E. N. Brown and H. C. McEachism. The men would make the trip three times a week for $880 "per annum" from November 1, 1892 — June 30, 1894.[27]

Jerome's daughter, Frankie, apparently inherited some of her father's strong will. She objected to the name 'Contention' for her family's home, arguing that it was undignified. Her father operated the ferry near the eastern end of the small settlement, and the lady crossed the John Day on his transport often. The popular song *Twickenham Ferry,* which had been written as a poem by young Theophile Marzials about a small suburb of London, came to mind one day as she crossed the waterway.

Frankie insisted the name of the newly established settlement be changed to Twickenham, a name which was pronounced by the British as "Twik-num." Apparently Parsons's daughter was more charismatic in her approach to the strong-willed Helms than her father, and the lady got her way. On June 6, 1896, the Twickenham post office was established with Anthony Helms as the postmaster.[28]

Twickenham boasted of a livery stable, a store, a hotel, and a post office by 1900, and vied for the county seat of Wheeler County, which had been formed the year before. The contest between the small town and the nearby town of Fossil to the north caused much friction between the two contesting communities, and led to the publishing of the following article in the *Fossil Journal,* which was published in that town in 1900:

> A few days ago two wayfaring men crossed Twicken-
> ham Ferry. When the would-be county seat site was

27 Contract between J. H. Boomer and W. E. Helms; copy provided by Glenna Potter Lange
28 Grace Younce et al., in *History of Wheeler County*, p. 13

pointed out to them, they took a long look at Parsons' undulating bottom; then one remarked after taking a mouthful of water and squirting it out, 'It's a pretty good looking spot for a county seat and only seems to lack two things — good society and drinking water.' With a far-away look in his weary eyes, the other way-farer made his soft reply, 'That's all hell lacks.'[29]

Parsons was not impressed.

One of the earlier settlers in Twickenham whom Parsons advised was A. S. McAllister. The gentleman owned 2,160 acres of land to the west of Parsons's and also a homestead of 160 acres, including part of that settled by Biffle. The holdings, known as the "Twickenham Stock Farm," included 480 acres of bottom land, and the greater part of that was perfectly level. McAllister raised barley, alfalfa, and rye on the fertile soil and used the hay for his 100 head of cattle and 100 head of horses. At one time, he raised 6,000 head of sheep but sold those and concentrated on his cattle, which were principally Shorthorns[30].

McAllister also found coal on his ranch, including a large area of the bituminous mineral on the north side of the river. By 1904, a company was being formed to develop the coal fields, and the local inhabitants were hopeful that the town of Twickenham would expand rapidly to accommodate the workers in the coal field. It was "an assured fact that as soon as the mines are in operation a railroad will be constructed to one of the nearest rail points to afford facilities for the shipment of coal."[31] Reality set in when the coal was found to be of a poor quality and full of too much ash; there would be no fortunes made on coal in Jerome's settlement, nor would there be a railroad linking the river valley with the outside world.

---

29 F. Smith Fussner in *Glimpses of Wheeler County's Past*, p. 58
30 A. S. MacAllister in *Pacific Northwest Homestead*, p. 3
31 Ibid.

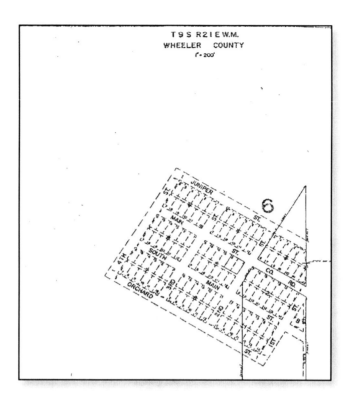

Plat of Twickenham

When McAllister had the ranch, the report was "There is a good house, barn, granary, cow-barn and wagon shed, and there is also an outdoor cellar covered with earth and rock. A windmill supplies the house with running water... ... water is piped to three corrals. The well is 12 feet deep only, but furnishes an abundance of clear, cold water the year 'round."[32] Also noted was the fact that there were black willows and cottonwoods near the river that provided shelter for the livestock.

Parsons liked to tell of an experience with his huge hunting hounds. It seems he had them going from Fossil to Twickenham over Dry Hollow grade. Jerome noted on arriving home that his dogs were missing.

32 Ibid.

He went back and found them high-centered on a curve they were too big to navigate.

Parsons repeatedly told of an interesting experience with a cougar. It seems that Jerome dressed in his Sunday best suit and struck out for Fossil a courting. Just above the Neilson orchard (on Rowe Creek) he met an old she-cougar. Now, he could see that he couldn't get by her and that she was on the peck. Well, Jerome didn't have even a pocket knife for a weapon. Right quickly he peeled off his suit and tore into her bare-handed. He managed to choke her with nary a scratch. But, Parsons said, "It's a good thing I took off my suit or it would have been torn to shreds."[33]

Parsons was telling a story one day about when he was driving a freight wagon coming up Pine Creek to the head of Dry Hollow. "Rain?" he said, "My God, it was a raining." The harness got wet and stretched and Parsons thought "Where are my wagons?" He tied his horses to a tree, spread out his bedroll, and got comfortable for the night. The next morning, he got up and there were his wagons. The leather had dried and pulled the wagons right up there.[34]

In Parsons's later years, he did have a very real painful experience. He was feeding hay into an old stationary thresher when his hand became entangled in the Chinaman, a part of the machinery that, through a chopping motion, helped force the hay into the separator. It mangled Jerome's hand pretty bad. He tore up an old shirt, bound it up, and kept on trying to work until the foreman made him quit and took him to the doctor.[35]

The post office in Twickenham was discontinued in February of 1917[36], and Parsons's community dwindled as technology replaced much of the manpower that was needed on the ranches and farms in the

---

33 Bob Huntington interview
34 Richard Mortimore interview, 2010
35 Bob Huntington interview
36 Grace Younce et al., in *History of Wheeler County*, p. 13

valley. Parsons, however, left behind some of his legacy when he — undoubtedly — furnished the following information:

> Jerome H. Parsons has passed a career well worthy the pen of the historian, and in it all he has displayed the same fortitude and bravery, coupled with wisdom, that characterized his ancestors when they assisted to open the new world for settlement and later fought its battles. Starting in life when very young, thrown on his own resources from the first, and having been on the frontier all his life, he has acquired that ruggedness and stability that characterize men of force and strong nerve. He bears many scars of battle with the Indians and on many a field he has shown his true grit and bravery. When young, he was not favored with an opportunity to attend school, and consequently reached manhood without being able to read or write. Seeing the mistake, Mr. Parsons applied himself and soon was well trained in these things. He is a close observer and is a well-informed man.[37]

Of all the residents to ever live in the area, Jerome Parsons undoubtedly had the biggest and widest known reputation of being able to embellish events until they could not be recognized by those who had been in attendance. Woe upon anyone who accused him of stretching the truth!

Parsons's infamous temper was still talked about a hundred years later, and an old-timer recalled why. "Parsons was the original mayor of Twickenham, I think. He had some dandy stories. But, don't call him a liar! Hardy over at Condon had a paper and he put in there that Condon had two bigger liars than Wheeler County, so Wheeler County editor,

---

37 Shaver et al., p. 691

Fitzsimmons, he put in his paper that Wheeler County had three bigger liars. He challenged Gilliam County to name theirs. Which they did. They named two liars. Now, Wheeler County said that James Conger was one of the liars and old Parsons was the other two! He (Parsons) rode his horse to town and beat hell out of the editor! So I heard."[38]

Parsons was to learn, as many of the earlier settlers did, that the grass that was knee-high to a good saddle horse could not long sustain the large numbers of stock that were initially brought in.

> Jerome Parsons settled there (Contention) about 1876 (and) before that time he was employed by his Uncle Jerome Harper of San Francisco in buying cattle and driving them to Calgradanada he married my ant Josephine Writsman his uncle gave him a small start of cattle and he settled on the river later when the range began to fail he moved his stock to the Malheur range.[39]

This letter placed Jerome Parsons's arrival in Twickenham seven years after other sources state his arrival. There may have been disagreement as to the date of his arrival in the area, but there appeared to be no dispute among the newcomers to his valley that Parsons had a gift for telling a good story and that he and his story-telling would be missed when he decided to move on.

Packing the last of his tack onto the top of an already overloaded freight wagon, Parsons gave his son Cleve orders to keep an eye on the load; if anything tumbled off, he was to stop and pick it up. His older son, Guy, was given the task of driving the buckboard that carried his mother and his two sisters, Frankie and Stella.

---

38 Bob Huntington interview
39 Ed F. Horn letter. (Horn's date for Parsons's arrival conflicts with that noted in the History of Central Oregon. In his letter, Horn commented: "I am not very good on dates.")

Parsons remained for several minutes beside his home after his family started slowly down Juniper Street and through the small settlement to cross the John Day River on his competition's ferry just out of town at the eastern end of the valley. The owner of the ferry declared there was no charge for the Parsons family that day. Cleve touched the brim of his hat, thanking his neighbor, and then turned south and up Gird's Creek.

Parsons sat on his horse, taking a last look at his fields on the banks of the John Day, noting with satisfaction the forty-acre field of alfalfa he'd planted, the large garden area his family had worked while the man of the family was about his civic duties, and the home he and Josephine had made together. The fruit orchard with close to 100 trees would give the next family a bit of an income, and Parsons hoped all the time and effort he'd taken to dig the ditch from Rowe's Creek would serve the next family well.

The fifty-foot-tall walnut tree with a diameter of twenty inches — Parsons had measured it himself — was empty of the turkey buzzards that had taken to roosting there at twilight just as the sun sank behind the red hills to the west. "The buzzards are coming in for the night; time for dinner, Josephine," he had joked one evening, and his children had echoed his refrain almost nightly thereafter.

"The buzzards always come home to roost, don't they, Papa?" Stella had commented one night, watching the large black birds with their singularly ugly red heads glide gracefully onto their favorite perches in the walnut tree. Parsons had watched the flock settling in for the evening, thinking there was more than birds coming home to roost. He knew he and his neighbors were using the countryside to the point of abuse, and the overuse was already beginning to show, the overgrazing and the drier than normal seasons threatening the originally abundant grasses. He was afraid they were already paying for their misuse of the land, and he thought of the popular phrase, "The chickens always come home to roost."

"Yep, Stella, the buzzards always come home to roost," he muttered quietly to himself, and he wondered if they'd find another friendly family of feathered friends on the Malheur range. With a loud sigh, Parsons turned his horse to the east down Juniper Street, turned south onto Third Street, and then reined east into Main Street to follow the route his family had taken.

Just past the livery stable to his left and the post office to his right, he saw Harry Reed sitting in his chair beside his Riverside House hotel located on the corner of First and Main streets, slurping coffee from a large, thick white mug. Parsons pulled his horse up beside the hotel, planning to visit a while. For once, he had nothing to say. He sat for a minute, the two men eyeing each other silently. Then, with a slight gesture of farewell with his hand, a nod of his head, Parsons turned his horse away and left his Twickenham behind.

As he left the little valley which he had helped develop, Parsons was trailing a group of horses which had grown to far more than the 75 head in the original herd. Traveling up the narrow rocky basalt canyon to the

The Twickenham Riverside House, once operated by "Pike" Helms; he
and his wife are standing in the gate. This is one of the last buildings.
Parsons saw as he left his Twickenham. From the Keyes Kenny collection

south for a few miles, he instructed one of his helpers to cut out a dozen or so horses from the bunch and to drive them up a side draw for a ways.

"Better make that fifteen or twenty head. Naaah…maybe a few more. Someone's going to need a good mount soon, and I'd like to accommodate them," he grinned wryly. Earlier settlers who had already moved from the area had left behind some of their horses. Parsons's contribution to the growing number of animals in the herd was to inspire the name Horse Mountain that was given to the elevation southeast of Twickenham.

Malheur's gain was Twickenham's loss, but Jerome Parsons would leave behind his stories — and several wild horses — as a reminder of his passing through Wheeler County.

Chapter 8
1869 — T. B. Hoover and Fossil

By 1869, the steady flow of traffic on the road past Meyer and Hewot's holdings lessened as other roads were built in the area to serve homesteaders who continued to move into the region.

"It's getting so it's hard to keep track of everybody moving in," Meyer complained one afternoon. "Settle here, settle there. We're getting so settled, no place to set a setting hen," but he brightened considerably each time a passing wagon or horseman slowed and pulled up to his front yard.

As the coins clinked into the saleratus can, folks gathered around the table at Meyer's Gulch heard of settlers, including Louis Manning, William Bigham, Horace Parker, Al Straw, J. W. Chambers, and T. B. Hoover, arriving in an area just about thirty miles straight north of the stage stop in '69.[1] All of these early settlers were establishing boundaries around their holdings and planned to raise stock as well as the necessary gardens for themselves and for their families.

"Never met T. B.," Meyer commented one day. "Never met him, but s'pose he's a busy fella, tryin' to develop a city away over there," and he gestured to the northwest. The German would hear of T. B. Hoover a bit at a time through the years as he visited with folks who stopped by, giving him news of the small town Hoover had named Fossil.

Thomas Benton Hoover was the son-in-law of J. W. Chambers who, in the 1830s, at the age of fifteen, had told his family he was headed for the romantic Oregon country. J. W. sowed his wild oats among moun-

---

1 Shaver et al., p. 640

tain men, Indians, and French voyageurs, keeping his family somewhat informed of his whereabouts with an occasional letter home. When he returned to his family home in Missouri, his father sat him down and had a talk with his son.

What J. W. needed was the settling influence of a wife, his father decided, and his choice of a woman for his son was the widow Scoggin and her five children. If that didn't settle his son, it would at least gentle him down, Thomas Chambers thought. J. W. went along with his father's choice, which slowed him down somewhat but didn't quench his adventuresome spirit.[2]

The Chambers families joined the wagon train of '44 and headed from the East for the Oregon territory along with several families who would eventually settle in the country near Meyer's Gulch. The Reverend James Cave, William Gage, Cornelius Gilliam, Jacob Hoover, Alexander McQuinn, and their families were in the group of emigrants that moved westward with Thomas and J. W. Chambers.[3]

The journey was not an easy one, though they benefitted from the trials of the first such immigration the year before. The wagon train of '44 stopped in The Dalles for a time, and that is where Mary Jane Chambers was born, joining her five half-brothers and -sisters.[4]

J. W. had returned to western Oregon and had settled on 640 acres on the Tualatin River, but occasionally his restless spirit led him to check out the land in the central part of the state. There he found the proverbial grass that was as high as the belly of a horse in the area he would call Butte Creek, east of where Fossil would be situated. Chambers also found virgin timber for building homes and plentiful water and natural meadows for raising livestock,[5] and he filed claims on the land in '64.

2 William J. Bowerman in *History of Wheeler County*, p. 63
3 Stephenie Flora, http://www.oregonpioneers.com/1844.htm
4 William J. Bowerman in *History of Wheeler County*, p. 63
5 Ibid.

In '70, after his children had grown and his daughter, Mary Ann, had married Thomas Benton Hoover and the couple had two children, J. W. moved to the central Oregon land he had explored forty years before, leaving the widow Scoggin behind. She had already experienced more than her fill of adventure, she informed J. W., and only one of her children accompanied her husband on the move to the new land. The family settled on what would be called Hoover Creek, and there J. W. made four claims for his family: one each for himself; his son-in-law, Thomas Benton Hoover; Woodson Scoggin; and William Bigham.[6]

"It's prime land for stock growing," J. W. had told his family and friends. His son-in-law, T. B., agreed. The abundant bunch grass lent to perfect conditions for the grazing of the livestock that would form the mainstay of the family ranch. Too, there was abundant forest land nearby from which to build homes.

"Just think of it as an adventure," T. B. advised his wife, Mary Ann, as she jiggled two-year-old William on her lap, trying to get him to stop fussing. "Annie can go with me," and he picked up the small four-year-old girl, setting her on the saddle in front of him. He cradled her against his lean body, his light hair short and neatly combed despite the breezes that constantly blew.

"Adventure? Adventure? It's an adventure all right," Mary Ann thought, remembering the words T. B. had uttered with a grin before riding away with their small daughter. She smoothed her long, dark hair and she and her little son continued jouncing along on the wagon seat, following the rough trail that would take them to their new home.

"Following Indian trails. Washing diapers in creeks, if we can find them when we camp at night. Picking blood-sucking ticks off little Annie all day long and watching out for rattle-snakes. Burning meat on an

6 Ibid.

Mary Jane and T. B. Hoover
Used with permission from McLaren Stinchfield

open flame — after we gather the sticks for the fire. Bouncing along on a
hard old wagon seat or walking and tripping over rocks and sticks. Getting hot and tired and cranky right along with the children. Adventure?
Thomas Benton Hoover, if I didn't love you, I'd have stayed in the Tualatin Valley with the widow Scoggin. Adventure? Sure it is."

The couple, with their two children, had traveled by boat from Port
land to The Dalles, and now they were heading overland to their new
home. There were no roads at that time, and the Hoovers had to follow Indian trails, driving their cattle and horses through the thick brush
and rocky gullies. It would take three rough, exhausting weeks to reach
their destination in April of '70. Mary Jane was more than ready to crawl
down out of their uncomfortable wagon as it pulled up beside the flowing spring where they would build their home.[7]

T. B. and the men worked long hours each day to build four substantial
cabins that first year. Trees had to be cut down and shaped into the rough
logs that would form the walls of the new homes, which would be a far cry

---

7 Descendants of Thomas B. and Mary Jane Hoover, *History of Wheeler County*. p.113

from what Mary Jane had been used to. She tried to keep her inquisitive children from underfoot as the men worked to finish their building.[8]

Setting up housekeeping in a small log cabin, with part of one wall left unchinked with mud to accommodate rifles in the event of an Indian attack, was a challenge for Mary Jane. "The holes in the walls are big enough to throw a cat through," she complained to T. B., who grinned and kept forcing thick clay between the logs not only to cut down on the flow of wind from the outside but also to help keep crawling creatures from entering the small log home.

In between cooking and washing and caring for the children, Mary Jane began to make the cabin a home for her family. The few necessities the family possessed didn't lend to any frills, but she hoarded every scrap of fabric left from the clothing she sewed, and she pieced together warm and colorful "crazy quilts" that brightened up the beds. Not a scrap of fabric was wasted but was sewn onto the previous piece, regardless of shape or color, resulting in a random pattern that was none-the-less both attractive and practical.

When T. B.'s denim jeans wore thin, Mary Jane would take them apart and cut smaller sizes of jeans for her son, keeping the scraps of fabric to be used later for other projects. Rags left from overalls far past the stage of patching the patches that covered the original patches went into the rag box. When the box was full, the rags were torn into narrow strips, sewn together, and crocheted into warm rugs for the cold pine-board floors.

What Mary Jane missed more than any of the conveniences she had left behind was the company of another woman. She was the only white woman in the area surrounding her new home for her first two years on the homestead and she missed female companionship. Almost daily, she visited with William Bigham and Woodson Scoggin as the men worked together with T. B. building their new homes and helping each other

8 Ibid.

develop their holdings. Regardless of how hard she tried, however, the discussions of house building and of developing springs and of potential fields and of increasing the herd of cattle couldn't interest Mary Jane as much as would one simple visit with another woman to discuss children and cooking and gardens.

When, after two years with no woman to talk with, a couple stopped for the night and Mary Jane was able to visit with the woman, she cried for joy. Mary Jane's tiny newborn baby, Harriet, was the object of much of the discussion; finally Mary Jane could talk "woman talk" to her heart's content, and the two women chatted all night. The next morning she carefully brushed her hair and pinned it neatly on top of her head, checking her efforts in the small mirror she had hung on the wall. She wasn't trying to impress visitors, she told herself, but she could take pride in her appearance and she knew T. B. was proud of her neatness.

T. B. seemed to have more relatives than a nine-year-old jackrabbit, and his kin began to move to the area. Marriages would add to the lineage in leaps and bounds. Some of the earlier residents connected to T. B. by marriage were the Bowerman, the Reinhart, the Chambers, the Kelsay, the Scoggin, the Reisacher, the Steiwer, and the Edwards families.[9] Mary Jane would get to know them well and welcomed them as a significant part of her life in the rapidly developing area.

"This looks like a good place to build a town. If we don't get one started, someone else will," T. B. told Mary Jane one night as she sat at their table taking advantage of the fading light showing through the cabin window. Mary Jane's never-empty hands plied a needle to mend yet another three-cornered tear in little Annie's dress.

"That child," she sighed, holding up the torn garment and showing T. B. the numerous rips in the muslin fabric. "She just insists on trying

---

9 Ibid.

to keep up with William, even if that means crawling through the berry bushes on her hands and knees."

Her husband nodded absently, not focused on his wife's mending but rather on the building of a community. "There's a good, flat spot down there a bit," and he gestured vaguely to the south. "Let's take a picnic lunch down there tomorrow and check it out. What do you say?"

"Are there bramble bushes down there?" Mary Jane asked. T. B. nodded; his daughter would always find something to discover, he figured, as she followed her father while he was exploring the surrounding area.

He saw potential for the region evolving and petitioned for a road to be constructed from the area of his holdings to The Dalles.[10] The trip between his property and the city where the family went for supplies was rough and it was a major task seldom taken by the pioneers. T. B. was successful in his bid, the road was carved out of the wilderness, and more settlers began to arrive in the region.

While walking with her children, Mary Jane and her offspring often found the fossilized remains of ancient animals and plants. Though Annie didn't appear as interested as little William, the two children lugged an array of the petrified relics to their home.

"Fossils, Father," Annie would explain proudly, holding up her latest finds for her father to inspect. Her little brother, Will, would shove her aside to show the bigger and better fossil he'd found. Because of the large number of petrified remains of extinct animals and vegetation to be found near his home, T. B. felt the name Fossil for the post office he wanted to open would be appropriate. Like the name Big Bottom that Biffle had given to his land, the name in no way resembled the inhabitants of the little settlement that was soon to develop nearby.

On February 28, 1876, T. B. succeeded in getting a post office estab-

10 Ibid.

T. B. and Mary Jane Hoover's homestead and the site of Fossil's first post office.
Courtesy of the Fossil museum

lished in the log cabin on his ranch. He was, naturally, the postmaster, and Mary Jane was appointed the deputy postmistress.[11]

"It's not much more than a title," she told T. B. modestly of her position, but she was nonetheless pleased to have a part in the post office and that significant step towards establishing a new settlement. Each morning, after the breakfast dishes were done and T. B. had left for whatever work he had planned, Mary Jane would carefully comb her hair and put a clean apron over her dress. She was always ready for the occasional neighbors who might show up to collect their mail in the "post office" housed in the small and crudely built, but neat, homestead cabin.

A year later, Mary Jane helped bury her father, J. W. Chambers, on a dry hillside above her home, his grave surrounded by a picket fence. Always an avid horseman and spirited adventurer, he loved to race his horses against Indians passing through the homesteaders' valley. There were always unbroken and half-broken horses presenting him with a challenge and he was thrown from one of those broncs and broke his

11 Ibid.

neck in July of '77. The adventurer who had led countless settlers to the area died at the age of 60.

In '81, Hoover chose a site at the juncture of Butte and Cottonwood creeks for the location of the town of Fossil.[12] The new settlement would nestle in a broad valley surrounded by the rounded grass-covered hills that had lured the large number of new settlers to the area. There weren't many large trees in the immediate valley for building purposes, but not much more than a dozen miles to the east there was an abundant supply.

"It's looking good," T. B. told Mary Jane after he'd seen the plat the Thompson brothers, George H. and W. S., had made for the town site for Fossil.[13] T. B. would later be called by some the "Father of Fossil," and his efforts to build up the small city began to take up much of his time. His wife maintained their home, keeping the household running efficiently while her husband began spending longer and longer days away from his family.

Mary Jane was helped in part by drifters passing through the town who were directed to her home for a good home-cooked meal free of charge. Instead of expecting them to pay for the food, she gladly put them to work chopping wood for the kitchen stove, which required small pieces of firewood. The heat stoves which were located in the other rooms in the house could use larger pieces, but the always-burning cook stove took a great deal of wood to produce the large amount of food Mary Jane cooked each day.

By the time Fossil was platted in '81, Mary Jane had fifteen-year-old Annie and nine-year-old Harriet to help her with her daily work. While William, a sturdy thirteen-year-old boy, could usually be seen tagging along with T.B., the older girls helped care for six-year-old Mary and little Elizabeth, an energetic, inquisitive three-year-old.

"I am so thankful to have women friends to talk with," Mary Jane

---

12 Shaver et al., *An Illustrated History of Central Oregon*, p. 649
13 Ibid.

Thomas Watson, early businessman
Courtesy of the Fossil museum

confided to a friend one day, remarking that although she missed the visitors that had come with her postmistress job, there were now plenty of women nearby for her to visit. "T. B. is so busy building up his town that it gets lonesome with just the children to chat with."

Her husband had established a store with Thomas Watson in '81 and moved the post office to the store. T. B. figured old Tom would be a good partner; he'd been born in December of '28 and had crossed the plains in '50 with his Grandpa Hamilton. At the age of 53, he'd surely be ready to settle in and would be a dependable partner.[14]

A small general merchandise store had been located near the town's site by the Thompson brothers in '79, and upon the platting of the new town, their business was moved close to Hoover's. The small community soon had two stores, a livery stable, a blacksmith shop, a public hall, and a hotel.[15]

---

14 Information on the back of Watson's photograph
15 Ibid.

Mary Jane no longer had to rely on T. B. or his friends to bring her supplies from The Dalles on those rare occasions they made the trip for provisions. She and her children could peruse the well-stocked shelves of the small businesses in Fossil and they could actually make choices now, though the variety of merchandise was limited mostly to the bare essentials of frontier life.

In '83 the first church was established in Fossil with the building of the Methodist church. This was also the year of the birth of a fifth daughter, Maud, for T. B. and Mary Jane. The Hoovers proudly attended the first Sunday service in the new building with their brood in tow, Mary Jane's dark brown hair, pinned perfectly in place, now showing a few streaks of white. She had brushed T. B.'s best coat clean for the occasion, and the Hoovers drew the eyes of many congregants.

Seventeen-year-old Annie wore her Sunday-best dress with pride,

The First Methodist Church, Fossil
Courtesy of the Fossil museum

knowing her first attempt at seamstress work had resulted in a stylish dress that would be worn for all important occasions until she outgrew it, if she did, or when it wore out. She was far past crawling through berry bushes in pursuit of bugs, but little five-year-old Elizabeth had taken over that role.

As the preacher droned on and on during the first services in the stuffy little church packed with parishioners squeezed tightly together on the newly made hard pew seats, Annie's little sister steered an unfortunate wood-beetle in a circle with the toe of her scuffed black shoe. The older girl nudged the younger one and mouthed the word, "Stop." Elizabeth glanced up questioningly, frowned, and then continued her herding.

Again, Annie prodded her little sister and again she mouthed, "Stop," whereupon Elizabeth lifted her shoe and stomped down hard on the unfortunate beetle, the sound echoing loudly during an inopportune pause in the preacher's exhortations.

"I thought she said 'stomp' so I stomped," explained a defiant Elizabeth to her father when she was later asked to explain her actions.

"You need to listen better next time," T. B. cautioned.

"She needs to move her mouth louder next time," retorted his younger daughter, and T. B. turned away before Elizabeth could see his smile. He'd better leave this type of counseling to Mary Jane, who seemed to handle such things better; he could see he didn't understand the workings of the mind of a five year old. His wife could focus on tending their family and he could concentrate on building his town.

The next year a drug store was opened in Fossil by A. B. Lamb and that gentleman was licensed to carry liquor, that most essential item in many a household's pharmaceutical supplies.[16] T. B. joined forces with Bert Kelsay in '85 to build the first general store in Fossil. The new building was located in the city center.

---

16 F. Smith Fussner in *Glimpses of Wheeler County's Past*, p. 30

The Kelsey home. Courtesy of the Fossil museum

Kelsay and his wife, Euphrasia Gillis, had owned much of the land where the new city was platted to be built, and the red-brick mill that was located on their property would later be used in building the county's courthouse in 1901. The Kelsays built their grand two-story home on land where the Fossil Motel now stands, but, unfortunately, the impressive home would burn to the ground in 1932.[17]

It was in '85 that the Baptist and Catholic churches were built[18], adding to the choices of churches for the citizens of the area to attend. "Wonder if those churches have beetles, too?" Elizabeth asked Annie, but the only answer she got was a frown; her older sister's mind was too preoccupied with her upcoming wedding to worry about insects encroaching upon the local churches.

Mary Jane spent several months preparing for her oldest daughter's marriage to Winlock Steiwer, known by his friends as "W. W." The wedding was held July 14, 1886[19], after much fussing and preparation by Mary Jane and Annie; T. B. wisely concentrated on matters out of the household during the frantic arrangements.

Winlock had first settled on Pine Creek to raise horses and cattle and later bought the Thompson Brothers' store. From the time he'd

17 Alma Jean Tipley & Edgar J. Kelsay in *History of Wheeler County*, p. 132
18 Jack Steiwer in *Glimpses of Wheeler County's Past, p. 30*
19 Jane Steiwer Campbell in *History of Wheeler County*, p. 216

The home of Winlock and Annie Steiwer.
Courtesy of the Fossil museum

moved into his business in '83, Annie had her eye on him, feeling the debonair young man possessed some of her own father's political drive, and indeed, he did.

Annie was able to entertain often during Winlock's terms as Gilliam County's first County Judge, his serving as a county commissioner and as a Fossil City Councilman, and his two terms in the Oregon Senate. T. B. and Mary Jane were proud of their new son-on-law's achievements, and were always available to give the newlyweds advice.

In 1886, the *Fossil Journal* was established and the first publication appeared in the new town.[20] Also putting in his first appearance was little Thomas B. Hoover, Jr. He was the seventh child to be born to T. B. and Mary Jane, and he would be the last.[21]

"Quit thumping on that table before I start thumping on you!" Mary Jane threatened her son Will as she sat on her settee, nursing little T. B. Her oldest son was constantly thumping anything in reach, often beating time to a tune bouncing around in his head and occasionally

20 Shaver et al., p. 649
21 Tom Hoover and Pat Frank in *History of Wheeler County*, p. 113

breaking into a song as he went about his day. "We'd better get that child involved in a band before he drives us crazy with his constant thumping," she told her husband.

In '87, the Fossil Band was formed with C. J. Quinn as leader of the musical group. The social group survived for many years, and young Will Hoover was among the musicians. He was the snare drummer in the town band and he also played the cornet. His tenor voice was said to be second to none and he sang and played his cornet in both the Methodist and the Baptist choirs.[22]

In '88, T. B. and Mary Jane proudly observed as their Annie's husband, Winlock, helped to establish a post office in the tiny settlement that would be named in his honor. In 1903, W. W. helped George Carpenter open the Bank of Fossil, which eventually sold to First National Bank in 1937.[23] While their civic duties grew and expanded, so did their family; Annie and Winlock provided Mary Jane and T. B. with five grandchildren: Leland, Mary (Seaton-Smith), Susan (Rinehart), Ruth (Latourette), and William H.

In '88, T. B. and Mary Jane proudly observed as their Annie's husband, Winlock, helped to establish a post office in the tiny settlement that would be named in his honor. In 1903, W. W. helped George Carpenter open the Bank of Fossil, which eventually sold to First National Bank in 1937.[24] While their civic duties grew and expanded, so did their family; Annie and Winlock provided Mary Jane and T. B. with five grandchildren: Leland, Mary (Seaton-Smith), Susan (Rinehart), Ruth (Latourette), and William H.

By the Journal's account, in '88, there were several businesses in the town and T. B. visited them all frequently, spreading words of encour-

22 Maud Hoover Edwards in *History of Wheeler County*, p. 116
23 Jane Steiwer Campbell in *History of Wheeler County*, p. 216
24 Jane Steiwer Campbell in *History of Wheeler County*, p. 216

Bank of Fossil. From left to right: Winlock Steiwer, Osco Parker, and George Carpenter. Late 1930s. Courtesy of the Fossil museum

agement and news of the growing town. "W. W. Steiwer & Company and Hoover & Watson were the two leading general stores. Patrick Potterton was handling a fine furniture store; Barney Gaffney had a harness and saddle store; A. B. Lamb a drug store; L. M. Rhodes a hair dressing parlor and notion store; G. B. Tedlowe conducted a saloon; Sam Danaldson (sic) and Lyman Morgan each were proprietors of livery stables; there was a hotel and a restaurant; J. H. Bowen handled a meat market; Mr. Duncan had a blacksmith shop; N. C. Engberg was a jeweler; and among professional men were H. H. Hendricks, an attorney; H. S. Goddard, physician; W. W. Kennedy, civil engineer, and Prof. S. Goodnight who was in charge of the town schools."[25]

By '89, it was evident the citizens of the growing town could no longer rely on individual springs and wells, so the Fossil Water Company was organized, incorporated by the ever energetic and civic minded

---

25 Shaver et al., in *History of Central Oregon*, p. 649

Fossil Flouring Mill
Courtesy of the Fossil museum

T. B. Hoover. He was aided by A. B. Lamb, P. Potterton, W. W. Steiwer, and S. G. Hawson. A gravity flow system was developed with the water coming from a spring about two and one half miles southeast of the town. The initial reservoir had a 150,000 gallon capacity and the system was built at a cost of $15,000.[26]

With an abundant water supply, the town ladies began to discuss the possibility of indoor plumbing, though many of the city fathers drug their feet. "Who'd want a crapper in the house?" grumbled many a husband who thought the very idea of such a contraption was utterly ridiculous, not to mention the thought of the amount of work required to install such a luxury. However, the notion had taken root and in the early 1900s, goaded by the women, men began to install the indoor facilities in an occasional home, though backyard privies were still in use for several more decades.

"Kinda hard to prank an indoor privy," Will Hoover grinned to his little brother, Tom. "Those were the good old days!" and he related to his wide-eyed little brother the practice of enlisting the help of a friend

---

26 Ibid., p. 650

Fossil in 1901
Courtesy of the Fossil museum

or two and stealing quietly into the backyard of some cranky old gal in the middle of the night, and moving the privy back a few feet.

"Father woulda tanned your hide but good!" exclaimed Tom.

"Sure, he would have, if he'd known. Can you imagine Miss High and Mighty telling anyone she'd fallen into the privy hole?" Will grinned, referring to one of his least favorite of town ladies whose pig-like nose seemed permanently elevated. "We knew we were pretty safe," and he continued embellishing his tales of the good old days as he and his brother sat waiting for T. B. to return from his rounds about town.

Fossil was incorporated in '91 and Mary Jane and her seven children proudly watched as T. B. was sworn in as the first mayor of the new town, though that honor meant he would spend even more time away from home and Mary Jane would continue her task of keeping the family home running smoothly. Serving with T. B. on the town council were W. W. Steiwer, Bert Kelsay, P. Potterton, and C. W. Halsey. Their first recorder was C. W. Hall, who shortly resigned, and James Stewart took his place. Treasurer was J. H. Putnam, and marshal was F. M. Judd, who soon handed in his resignation and was replaced by L. T. Morgan.[27] The undertaking for the first set of officials was enormous, but the officials who had been chosen were up to the task. "We've got a good team," T. B. remarked with pride as the small town of Fossil developed its city government.

In '92, fire struck the new town when flames were discovered outside the livery stable occupied by Charles Branson, and William Cunningham immediately gave the alarm. Mary Jane gathered her brood in the yard, a horse hooked to a buggy ready to leave their home if fire threatened the structure. Where T. B. was, she had no idea; she might have known he was out saving his town.

"Mayor Hoover mounted a fast horse and searched out points where the cinders were igniting and directed their extinguishment."[28] The blaze had spread fast and many buildings caught fire from the sparks, but the flames were quickly extinguished by the volunteers and by 4:00 in the afternoon, only two hours after the fire had been discovered, the town was safe from its first disaster.[29]

T. B. served as Fossil's mayor for four years, retiring in '95. The Father of Fossil died in '96[30], and the minutes of the Fossil Band read: "Our band loses an esteemed and honored member and the community a respected citizen.[31]" T. B.'s oldest son, Will, who had been only two years old when the family moved to the area, took over his father's firm of T. B. Hoover and Son. Will was then twenty-eight years old.

While her husband had proposed and planned and politicked, Mary Jane had taken care of the home front. With seven children, that was not an easy task. Even with help from the older of her offspring, she had spent every waking minute cooking and cleaning and caring for her

---

27 Ibid., p. 651
28 Ibid., p.650
29 Ibid.
30 Descendants of Thomas B. and Mary Jane Hoover, *History of Wheeler County*, p. 113
31 Jack Steiwer, "Communities," in *Glimpses of Wheeler County's Past*, p. 32

brood, and she had taken them by the hand — and by the ear when necessary — and helped them grow into responsible young folks. Each milestone reached by her children and each bit of mischief they were involved in added another grey hair, she explained to T. B. with a smile, and her dark hair slowly turned white.

Mary Jane had sewed on buttons, made new garments and patched the old. She had directed the planting and the weeding and the harvesting of the large family garden. She had ensured that the chickens were fed, the eggs gathered, and the milk cows fed and milked and the pigs slopped. She had attended local events when women were welcomed and expected. Most importantly, she had lent an ear when T. B. raved about the wonderful new town or when he ranted about opposition to his plans. Always, she remembered that the man was the head of the family and that his wife was the secret behind his success.

Mary Jane would be remembered in '99 when the local ladies established the Native Daughters of Oregon, an organization that would include the "native daughters in Fossil." The group was named the Mary Jane Hoover in her honor as the first white lady settler in that part of the country and the driving force behind the first of the founding fathers.[32]

She was later honored in 1931 as Pioneer Queen by the Wheeler County Pioneer Association and a crown was placed on her silver-gray hair by little seven-year old Doris Prindle who would herself be queen of the Pioneer Picnic in 2011. H. H. Wheeler, his hair a bit whiter and his beard a little thinner than when he'd escaped the skirmish with the Indians along his stage route, had helped to organize the Pioneer Association in 1899. The Honorable Frank Davy of Salem had given a rousing speech and Wheeler had been elected president of that group, which met at Kelsay's Grove near Fossil. The group of 75 "old-timers"

32 Shaver et al., p. 647

had marched from the city to the grove, attended the festivities there, and marched back to the Donaldson Hotel to the accompaniment of Fossil's brass band.[33]

After lunch at the hotel, the group had again marched to their meeting place to elect officers. Wheeler was elected president; J. D. McFarland, secretary and historian; R. G. Robinson, vice-president; W. W. Steiwer, treasurer; and Thomas Watson, David Hamilton and P. E. McQuinn, directors. The group had agreed to meet annually and the formation of the association did much to tighten the bond among families of early settlers.[34]

Mary Jane would see many changes in her husband's town during her lifetime, and she often regretted that T. B. wasn't at her side — or, at least riding about his town — to enjoy seeing those changes with her. The Father of Fossil's right-hand lady died in September of 1934 at the age of 89.[35] T. B. had preceded her in death by thirty-eight years. Both had witnessed the birth of a town, the birth of a county, and, by this point in time, the birth of more relatives than a twenty-nine-year-old jackrabbit.

By the mid-1890s, early settlers in the area had begun to see the need for the formation of a county with regulations established by like-minded individuals. Initially, the Mitchell area was in Crook County, Spray and the Haystack and Spanish Gulch areas in Grant County, and Fossil in Gilliam. The county seat was located in The Dalles, around 150 miles from the Antone area on the military road. The trip was long and an expense to folks who had to do business there. Residents began to feel a necessity to become a more cohesive unit, with the local population having control of their daily lives rather than relying on distant and suspect outsiders.

It was towards the end of 1892 that a serious movement began to

---

33 F. Smith Fussner, *Glimpses of Wheeler County's Past*, p. 31
34 Ibid.
35 Descendants of Thomas B. and Mary Jane Hoover, *History of Wheeler County*, p. 113

form a county. In the *Antelope Herald* an article was published that stated that "We understand that a petition is being circulated in the Mitchell country, praying for the organization of a new county out of a part of Crook and a portion of Grant, thus entitling either Mitchell or Waldron to a county seat."[36]

By 1895, the movement gained momentum and a new county, to be named Sutton in honor of Al Sutton, was proposed to the Oregon State Legislature. This effort failed, but the idea did not.

It took a strong-minded individual from Tennessee in the form of R. A. 'Mose' Donnelly to introduce the legislation in 1899 that would succeed in the formation of the new county. Elected to the office of legislator by his peers, Donnelly presented the proposal in January of '99, but it failed in the first vote on January 26; however, a second vote by the legislature on January 30 passed the bill that was sent to the state Senate for final approval. There was much opposition from Gilliam County citizens, who objected to losing a part of their county, but a final vote was taken on February 16 and the bill passed. According to Donnelly, the baby was born. Proud of his part in the accomplishment during his term serving as a legislator, Donnelly preferred to be called "The Honorable R. N. Donnelly" from that time on.[37]

The new county was named for Henry Wheeler, the well-known stage line owner and operator who had survived the Indian attack on his stagecoach in 1866. His reputation had grown in stature with each telling of the incident, and the scar left from the bullet shot through his cheeks by one of the attacking braves had added to his growing fame and popularity. Wheeler had retired from operating his stage line and, after being a member of the Gilman and French cattle empire for a time, had purchased property on Gird's Creek. In a publication of the *Fossil Journal* said to be

36 Shaver et al., p. 642
37 Linda Gail Donnelly in *History of Wheeler County*, p. 75

published in about 1900, the journalist reported: *"Wheeler County is proud of its Godfather and H. H. Wheeler is proud of his Godchild."*[38]

An election to determine the location of the county seat was held on June 4, 1900. Spray, Twickenham, and Fossil were the areas competing for the honor and there was a great effort made on behalf of the community of Twickenham. Despite this political struggle, fueled greatly by Jerome Parsons's frequent and loud rantings, the tallied votes were Spray — 82 votes, Twickenham — 267, and Fossil — 436.[39]

When Fossil won the contest for county seat, E. M. Shutt, editor of the *Twickenham News,* wrote the following:

> Twickenham has fought and lost. So did Napoleon at Waterloo some time ago. But, while Napoleon soon died over it, the people of Twickenham still live, and, up to the time of going to press, were enjoying the best of health. Fossil won the county seat by a majority of 86 over all votes cast, which permanently decides the question. If it proves too (sic) have been an honest vote, and an honest count, let us be Americans enough to quietly abide by the will of majority, banish all bitter feelings against those who differed from us in the general welfare of the county.[40]

Parsons sputtered and fumed and resented that he wouldn't be in the center of the governing action that would make his ranch venture even more lucrative. He had to admit, however, that the voting had perhaps been as honest as it could be … just perhaps. He'd not been there to oversee the process.

---

38 F. Smith Fussner in *Glimpses of Wheeler County's Past*, p. 30
39 Shaver et al, p. 646
40 Ibid.

A newly built Wheeler County Courthouse, 1901
Courtesy of the Fossil museum

Interestingly, the worth of the taxable property in the proposed county in 1895 had been $432,431.[41] The value in 1899 was said to be one million dollars;[42] the publicity given during the birth of the county apparently added greatly to the value of the land. Upon formation, Wheeler County was found to be indebted as follows: to Grant county, $27,911.76; to Gilliam county, $5,985.74; and to Crook county $24.92. The total resources estimated for the county at its founding were $16,392.25.[43]

Bids were let in January of 1901 for the construction of the new county's courthouse and A. F. Peterson bid $9,025. His bid was the lowest, and he immediately began construction of the new brick structure. The new courthouse would be built on land donated by B. Kelsay.[44]

The three towns which conducted their business in the new county

41 Ibid., p.642
42 Ibid.
43 Ibid.
44 Ibid., p.646

were Fossil, which was incorporated in 1891; Mitchell, incorporated in 1893; and Spray, which would not be incorporated until 1958. Each community could boast of its own unique individuals, each could boast of its fine schools and churches, and each could boast of its potential for growth. Like any family unit, the individual parts of the whole retained their identity and there would at times be unpleasant rivalries between the three communities. Resembling the closeness of many of the families who made up the population of the county, however, when outside forces threatened the individuals, a strong bond was apparent and the young county's robust residents became stronger with each intrusion.

The town of Fossil continued to grow, and in 1900 the stage line from Fossil to Shaniko was developed, shortening the trip to Portland by twelve hours.[45] "Just think," Wheeler would remind listeners. "I used to make the trip from Canyon City to The Dalles in my stage loaded with passengers in jig time, we thought — 200 miles in two days." He would pause. "Of course, we whipped the horses under and over and changed 'em ever' so often, too." He would stroke his bushy white beard

Fossil, 1901. Courtesy of the Fossil museum

45 Ibid.

Fossil School, 1906
Courtesy of the Fossil museum

in the areas of his old wounds, reminiscing, and there was no doubt among his audience what he was remembering.

1901 saw the establishment of the fire department T. B. Hoover had wanted for Fossil, and there were initially thirty-four members. The organization was soon fitted with the necessary equipment and was putting out small fires before they could spread. The building of the new gravity flow water system, built at a cost of $15,000, aided the group immensely.[46]

A substantial six-room brick building for a school with plans for the construction of two additional rooms to be added when need be, was erected in 1902. In 1904, an election was held in the county and, by a large majority, the decision was made to maintain a high school for the entire county, thereby establishing the Wheeler County High School. Up to this time, many families had maintained a second home in The Dalles where they would live while their children attended school. The luxury of remaining in their homes in the Fossil area appealed to the parents of school-age children, so the results of the voting for the county school were not surprising.

---

46 McLaren and Janet Stinchfield, "Fossil," in *History of Wheeler County*, p. 6

The high school was to be held in two rooms of the brick building and there would be a tax on the citizens of the entire county to maintain the high school, no matter that it would be mostly the children of the Fossil area who would benefit from the school. Professor A. J. Garland was the first principal and Miss Sophia Townsend the assistant teacher in the high school. At that time, there were four teachers in the elementary school.[47]

There was a fairly noticeable Scottish presence in the area, and the same year the fire department was formed, a Caledonian Club was organized as a means of helping the Scottish folks gather socially and to promote and enjoy their culture. The club had 100 members in 1905 and they held their meetings in different places, though their headquarters were in Fossil. The organization was known for providing good Scottish entertainment for the area, and talent was brought in from as far away as Portland. Some of the officers in 1905 included J. D. McFarland, John and George Steward, and James S. Moore.[48]

By 1905, the estimated population of the county seat of Wheeler County was 800 and all necessary businesses for a small and independent community were present and thriving. The news that wasn't published in the weekly paper, the *Journal*, could be spread by the use of the established telephone system supplied by the Wheeler County Telephone Company with headquarters in Fossil. Locals could boast of long distance connections.[49]

The first movie theater was built in 1913 and the first Wheeler County Fair was held that year. The Fossil Public Library Association opened the city's library in '17, with an inventory of 600 books available to the public, and four years later the city took over the operation of the facility.[50] Culture had come to the new county.

---

47 Kathleen T. Buhl, "The Professions; Schools," *Glimpses of Wheeler County's Past*, p. 73
48 Shaver et al., p. 651
49 McLaren & Janet Stinchfield. "Fossil", *History of Wheeler County*, p. 6
50 Ibid.

In 1913, yet another push was made to have a railroad built to connect Fossil with Condon. It was in July of 1905 that the first train had traveled from Arlington to Condon, and a twenty-mile extension into Fossil seemed logical and probable; however, many of the stockmen in the area initially felt that their range would be reduced, and their increase materially decreased. That belief slowly changed to a general feeling of progression, as the farmer would benefit from the railroad to market his produce. The possibility of the connection had continued to be exciting to the locals, surveys were made, and there was much speculation about the endeavor

Addison Bennett, a reporter for The Morning Oregonian, who visited Fossil and its surrounding area to gather information for an article, "Wheeler County Land of Plenty Without Railroad to Interior," heard that the land was capable of producing much more than it was currently, but that the farmers lacked transportation to get their goods to market in an economical manner. A railway connection would alleviate that problem, as cheaper and available transport would encourage higher production which, in turn, would lead to more farms being established.[51] Bennett was wined and dined and given royal treatment and the ensuing article showed he was duly impressed.

> Now comes the question as to what is most needed to bring the country into the best state of development. Some people claim that Wheeler county is now over-populated, while others, with equal good judgment, say that the county will support double its present population. The above statements are made by two classes of people; the former comprising a class who enjoy monopoly and, if they could carry out their personal desires, would own the earth. The latter statement is made by a class of public-

51 Addison Bennett in *Morning Oregonian.* July 10, 1913

spirited people who are desirous of seeing the resources of
the country fully developed, who can see the benefits to be
derived from intensified and diversified farming. That the
country is rich in agricultural resources is demonstrated
by the fact that many of the large ranchers own beautiful
homes in large cities, cottages at the seashore and, in many
instances, make trips abroad and educate their children in
large universities of the East. Where it is possible for one
man to do this without coming in personal contact with
the work, it is possible for several men who are satisfied
with a more moderate home and surroundings to succeed
in their occupation likewise.[52]

For whatever reason, and some folks speculate it was politics that
interfered, the railway was never built to Fossil.

With the closing of local lumber mills, trade and population
dropped in the county seat. Improved vehicles and highways had made
travel easier and what had been a twelve-hour trip from Fossil to The
Dalles in 1900 was now a two-hour drive. Unfortunately for local businesses, residents of Fossil often opted to shop where there was a larger
selection than they could find in their town.

Though there had been concern when the population and businesses declined in the small town, the community has maintained its
status as county seat, which, along with the public schools, brings a certain amount of stability to the area. The roads must be maintained and
road departments for state and county highways provide employment
for some of the locals. Residents of the county's ranches and farms provide a smattering of customers, and during the tourist and hunting and
fishing seasons, the businesses benefit from travelers to the area.

---

52 Ibid.

Several of the larger ranches in the area take advantage of the increase in the size of the elk herds after the closing of Kinzua by offering "hunt for fee" on their lands. The charges help land owners pay the taxes on their grasslands that sustain the large animals. There seems to be no shortage of folks from more populated areas eager to spend whatever is necessary to bag a hat rack to hang on their wall.

The area around Fossil with its rich geological history brings many geologists and scientists to the area to study what has become an everlasting source of interest. The John Day Fossil Beds National Monument on the banks of Pine Creek ensures a steady flow of traffic through the northern part of the county during the warmer months of the year.

It is the same fossils T. B. Hoover first noticed, those remains from ancient creatures from millions of years ago, that attract many of the folks who contribute largely to the city's economy today, as well as to that of the county. Perhaps that founding father knew what he was doing when he chose to settle near those ancient reminders that life is ever-changing. Sometimes there is an advantage to being surrounded by the old.

"The recent advance in prices of agricultural and grazing lands has not as yet reached this far south and there is an excellent show now for the newcomers with the ready money to invest in farms and stock ranches at prices that are right and safe. There is no government land in this vicinity worth living on. It is not a community which offers inducement for poor people, except they want to rent or work for wages, but people with means will scarcely find a healthier climate or a better stock country for raising for market either horses, sheep or cattle, than the vicinity of Fossil and Wheeler county in general. The recent low prices of range cattle have discouraged some who would now sell their ranches and ranges at very reasonable figures, and in every community there are some people who cannot even stand prosperity long in one place,"[53] wrote H. H. Hendricks of Fossil a little more than one hundred years ago.

---

53 H. H. Hendricks, "Fossil, the County Seat," *Pacific Northwest Homestead*, p. 38

Chapter 9
1867 —Mitchell, Mostly Forgotten Communities & Well-Remembered Disasters

While T. B. Hoover's city was starting to build to the north, Meyer and Hewot took a rare trip together in the summer of '67, spending the morning riding to peruse the narrow canyon where the "crazy man" had built a home smack dab in the middle of a flood plain. They studied the rocky, almost vertical basalt bluffs bordering the valley on the north and the steep and rocky grass-covered hills to the south, and shook their heads. There was need of a stage stop in the area, that was true, but locating it in the constricted valley? Not a mile west of the proposed town site, the valley opened up onto a wide, grassy area high above the occasionally flooding Bridge Creek, an area that appeared to be a more logical location.

For a few days after their excursion, there was much speculation between the two farmers as to why I. N. Sargent would chose to locate a settlement in such a narrow, stone-walled canyon with obvious signs of previous severe flooding. Too, although the locale presented a certain rugged beauty that was appreciated by many, it was scorned by some. It is said that "Polk Butler climbed to the top of one (of the surrounding hills) and replied to a question as to how he liked the country, 'This is hell with the fire put out.'"[1]

---

1 Shaver et al., "Mitchell," <u>History of Central Oregon, p. 652</u>

Sargent built his homestead cabin in '67, the same year Al Sutton opened his post office, although Sargent didn't plat the town of Mitchell until '85. He envisioned a new settlement being built in the narrow basalt canyon and that a portion of the town would be within the boundaries of his holdings. A new arrival, William Chranston, soon settled near Sargent. Said to have been the earliest settler to establish squatter's rights on the site of Mitchell,[2] he joined Sargent in his planning.

Chranston and Sargent proved to be an effective combination, their ideas meshing in such a productive way that the determined men soon had the beginnings of a small town well under way. They were often seen together, Sargent's thin body moving nervously as he removed his dilapidated top-hat and scratched his balding grey hair when considering a proposal made by Chranston. His co-founder's shorter, heavier body didn't have an ounce of fat on it. When he knitted his bushy dark eyebrows together in concentration, his piercing dark eyes focusing on a problem, his audience took notice.

The two men assumed that businesses in the new settlement would be established strategically on either side of the military road leading through the narrow canyon. "There's a wider area just up there," Sargent reminded his friend, gesturing to the west of where the two men stood planning. "More room to spread out. 'Course, it's further from water, I guess."

"This'll work like a crowdin' alley," Chranston had explained. "Can't control folks like cows, but get them headin' through a narrow valley, get the wagons running through here, be pretty darned close to businesses. They'll be more apt to stop." He grinned, running his long fingers through the dark bush of hair on his head, and the location of the town was firmed up.

Homes could be built on the higher level of hills above the dust and

---

2 Ibid.

the noise from the thoroughfare running through the town, the men decided. The first business established on the flood plain of the creek was a blacksmith shop in '73, owned and operated by William W. Johnson.[3]

Johnson arrived in the vicinity of Mitchell heading east on the military road, herding his road-weary cattle before him. The angry bawling of separated cows and calves late in the afternoon brought Chranston and Sargent from their homes to see what was causing all the noise.

Silhouetted against the setting sun in the narrow canyon, Johnson's broad shoulders grew even wider in the men's eyes as the newcomer and his men turned the tired and foot-tender animals from the road and drove them back towards the west to avoid the town and to bed them down for the night.

"That's one broad man, I'll say," declared Chranston as Johnson worked his stock away from the small settlement.

"Broadest shoulders I ever seen," agreed Sargent, minimizing his thin shoulders as he rolled them forward in mockery of his slight build. Johnson was nicknamed "Broady"[4] even before he introduced himself to the two men.

"Born in a covered wagon on the way west," Broady told the two men over his plate of beans and venison a few hours later as he and his crew shared supper with their hosts. "Near Ft. Hall in '47." He ventured he had learned the blacksmith trade near Jefferson.[5]

"Heard about this country from a fella named Waterman," explained Johnson, trying to get comfortable as he shifted his stocky and muscular body on the pine chair that seemed dwarfed by the man. "He and his son have the farm up here," and the blacksmith gestured to the east. "And they got a mercantile business in Jefferson. Said this was gonna

---

3 McLaren & Janet Stinchfield, "Mitchell," History of Wheeler County, p. 8
4 Also spelled "Brawdie" by some historians.
5 Betty Jean Goodman Brown, "William Warren Johnson," in History of Wheeler County, p. 128

be a boomin' place. Come here to build myself a blacksmith shop." His audience openly welcomed him. Surely a blacksmith shop would be needed in the town they planned and Broady would fit the bill, if the man's ability could be judged by his physique.

Soon after he moved his cattle to an unclaimed region near the small settlement, one of the first orders of business for Broady was to ask that a post office be established. When requesting the sanction for that requisite for a town, Broady was asked by the Postmaster General what the population of the village was. A man of few words, Johnson reportedly replied: "No village. Just a blacksmith shop."[6]

He would be the postmaster, and he asked that the new settlement be named after Senator John Hipple Mitchell, who was currently serving his second term as senator of the state of Oregon.[7] Looking him up and down, taking in his broad shoulders and muscular build, there were no dissenting votes from the assembled town fathers.

One of the most delightful story tellers of all times, Ned Norton, penned a second version of the origin of the name Mitchell and, though his account has been repeatedly copied and revised and retold, no one has been able to tell the story quite like Ned. He attributed the original story to Anthony "Pike" Helms, Jerome Parsons's nemesis, who had told the story to his nephew, A. W. Helms. Upon hearing Pike Helms' story, a listener could conclude that Parsons definitely had competition.

To sum up Ned's account, an enterprising soul, on his way to Canyon City with a load of liquor in his Mitchell wagon[8], broke down near the site of I. N. Sargent's homestead, located on the well-traveled mili-

---

6 Ned Norton, "Communities Past and Present" in *Glimpses of Wheeler County's Past*, p. 39. A contradictory claim was made in Shaver et al, p. 652, that R. E. Edmonson "...succeeded in getting a post office located, with himself as postmaster" in 1877.
7 McLaren & Janet Stinchfield, "Mitchell," in History of Wheeler County, p. 8
8 This large, open wagon was built by the Mitchell Wagon Company in Racine, Wisconsin, from the 1850 through the early 1920s, the name "Mitchell" plainly stamped on its side.

tary road. He unharnessed his mules and, using his wagon, improvised a "store" for his wares, safe in the knowledge that customers would come. And, come they did. They sampled his wares and relieved the freighter of his load, ensuring a handsome profit for that proprietor of the Mitchell wagon liquor store and saving him the inconvenience of traveling the additional eighty miles to Canyon City. Those travelers who had chanced upon the source of refreshment decided there had been no finer wagon than the Mitchell wagon, and they declared that the location would from that time on be called by the same name.[9]

There were few buildings at the site of Mitchell when Broady set up his blacksmith shop, though there was a large trade area to draw from. Johnson was to find that too many of the locals were self-sufficient to the extent they did much of their blacksmithing themselves. His busi-

Advertisement for the Mitchell Wagon, conveyer of fine whiskey
www.wheelsthatwonthewest.com

---

9 Ned Norton, "Communities, Mitchell," in *Glimpses of Wheeler County's Past*, p. 40

ness wasn't becoming as lucrative as Waterman had led him to believe it would be, as it seemed settlers were slow to move in.

"Give 'er time," Chranston implored, his dark brows overshadowing his intensely focused eyes as he encouraged his friend. "Folks'll come. It just takes time for word to get out that we have a blacksmith in town."

The first school held in the county had been established in '72, the year before Johnson's arrival, and was located one-half mile from Mitchell. Two years later, the log cabin was abandoned and school was then held in a home in the developing city.[10] School did bring a few families to town, just as Chranston and Sargent had assured Johnson, but the small population offered only limited business to any merchant in the area.

"Can't make a living out of little kids' horses throwing a shoe on the way to school," Johnson grumbled. Even though this seldom happened, Johnson was just as apt as not to do the work at no charge; he could tell from the youngsters' well-worn clothing and hungry looks that there wasn't much at home and he couldn't bear to take money that might be spent on groceries for the little tykes.

"Heard Edmondson might set up a store soon," Chranston encouraged Johnson. "That'll bring a few more folks to town. They'll probably stop by, get some work done on a plow or somethin'. More and more farmers startin' to settle in 'round here. Maybe Waterman might need some repairs done."

"Does his own work," Broady said shortly. "Told me so himself. 'Course, he told me there'd be lots of work here for me, too. Folks 're just too damned independent. Don't have the money to get their work done, I'm findin'. I do a lotta 'put 'er on my account' work."

Sargent chimed in, adding his two-bits' worth of wisdom. "Town's gonna be growin' some soon. Just hold tight." He gestured at a loaded

---

10 Janet & McLaren Stinchfield, "Mitchell," History of Wheeler County, p. 8

freight wagon pulling up to the blacksmith shop. "Here comes someone needin' you right now," and he nodded and smiled in encouragement at his disgruntled friend.

The driver of the dray pulled his team to a stop and, leaning over from his seat, asked the gathering of men by the blacksmith shop, "How far to Canyon City?"

"'Nother eighty miles or so," Johnson offered, and the freighter nodded his head in thanks, flipped his reins, and clucked at his team to start. The men watching him drive slowly out of sight knew he'd get over the top of the grade leading out of Mitchell to the east and would pitch camp for the night alongside the road to the gold field. Like many travelers passing through Mitchell, he left nothing behind in the small town except a few wisps of dust. Hard for a man to make a living on that.

Despite reassurances from his friends, Johnson figured business wasn't going to build up for him in his small town. He worked his blacksmith shop and cared for his cattle for just two years in the area before he sold out his holdings in and near the small town he'd named and moved back to Marion County.[11]

"I just hate to see him go," Sargent told Chranston as the two men watched their friend drive away, his wagon piled high with the tools of his blacksmith shop.

"If he'd just wait a bit longer, I know business is going to pick up," was his friend's reply, as the two men stood in the dust of the narrow street leading through the small town. His words would prove to be true, to a certain extent, but they would be repeated fruitlessly again and again throughout the years of Mitchell's existence. Broady may have been the first merchant in the tiny town to grow weary of waiting for cash-carrying customers who never materialized, but he wouldn't be the last.

---

11 Betty Jean Goodman Brown, "William Warren Johnson, in History of Wheeler County, p. 128

Still known as the Winebarger Hotel after the long-time owners, this picture was taken before 1910 in downtown Mitchell. From the Dan Cannon archives

Meyer and Hewot made trips to Mitchell often for one pretense or another, interested in watching the development of the small town. Located as it was on the main freight road to the gold field, the settlement was a natural outfitting point for the developing Spanish Gulch mining district. A year after the school was built, in '75, R. E. Edmondson built the first store in the new city and for the next twenty years the little village nestled on the banks of Bridge Creek in the rocky canyon grew steadily, if not slowly.

Meyer and Hewot seldom left the fort-house at the same time, but occasionally they took a drive on Sunday and visited with nearby neighbors. One such day, when no one was at the stage stop, one of Samuel Carroll's hired hands stopped by on his way home from the growing settlement in the narrow rocky canyon some ten miles distant where he had spent more time in a saloon than was prudent. "On his way back to the ranch, he stopped at Meyers place not finding any one at home, and knew they kept hard cider he proceeded to drink 5 or 6 bottles, so by the time he made it to the Carroll place (walking) he was pretty drunk and thirsty, only thing he could find was a bottle of iodine, after drinking that he didn't last long."[12]

Chranston and Sargent watched the development of their town with interest, and by '81, Mitchell had two stores, a second blacksmith shop to replace the one Broady had vacated, and one hotel, and the residents were taking steps to build a grist mill.

"That grain's good for something besides fine whiskey," Chranston chuckled, "Though this is mighty good liquid barley," and he tipped a blue-enameled tin cup to his lips and took a sip. He and Sargent were among those citizens who encouraged the building of the structure that would house the mill for grinding local grain crops into flour. The residents of the town subscribed one thousand dollars towards the building of a grist mill; flour was ten dollars per barrel,[13] which was pretty spendy for that time, but venison was plentiful and the soil fertile for vegetable gardens, so the settlers survived.

Sargent woke to screams one dark night in September of '81. Scrambling from his bed and hurriedly pulling on his canvas jeans, he grabbed his hat hanging on a peg by the front door and, buttoning his pants as he ran, hurried out to see what the commotion was. He could smell smoke even before he left his front porch.

Sargent could see flames leaping out the windows of Richards's store, smoke billowing over the small structure. A frantic crowd soon assembled, some darting into the burning building to save what they could. Half a dozen men grabbed buckets and ran to the creek to fill them, and then ineffectively dump the meager contents onto the roaring flames before the intense heat drove them back.

I. C. Richards and his wife stood by with the crowd and watched helplessly as their store burned, the acrid smell of blazing wood and

---

12 George Cecil Carroll
13 Shaver et al, p. 652

merchandise filling the small valley, a light breeze blowing up Bridge Creek and moving the smoke to the east.

"Darned smoke's gettin' to my eyes," Richards explained as he wiped his large handkerchief across his face. "Just glad I got my wife and the little gal out of the house," and he motioned to the area where the house had stood, butted up against the store. Seeing his friend, Sargent was likewise overcome by the smoke and, pulling his handkerchief out of his pocket, dabbed at his own eyes.

Richards and his friends had saved only a small part of his inventory before the entire structure was destroyed. The early morning light fell upon a large pile of smoldering debris, a smaller pile of smoke-damaged goods lying some distance away. A gathering of onlookers was scattered near the burned store, on the lookout for wayward sparks that might travel to nearby structures.

"Might be I could use that shovel there," Sargent informed Richards, as he reached into his pocket and selected some coins. He placed the amount of his purchase in Richards's hand, beginning a parade of customers who had suddenly realized they were in need of an item in the pile of salvaged merchandise.

Chranston walked to the fire-damaged goods, selected a smoke-grayed sack of flour, and handed the price of his purchase to the merchant. A few of the other bystanders wandered over to the stack of merchandise lying on the ground, selected an item or two, and paid for their purchases with whatever money they happened to be carrying in their pockets. The smoke bothered Richards's eyes again.

"Reckon I'll just start over," Richards declared, squaring his shoulders. "Folks 'r' goin' ta need supplies." With the help of the townspeople, he scraped up the debris when it had cooled, tossed it into wagons, and hauled the remains of his first store half a mile to the top of the grade leading into Mitchell from the north. There the debris was tossed into the deep canyon where the locals had been dumping their garbage, the steep slope carrying the waste away from the dumping place.

The loss from the fire damage was assessed at $7,500 by Richards. He also had notes, accounts, and cash amounting to $3,800. Richards was insured for only $4,800.[14] He rebuilt his store and his business soon started again.

As had been planned by Sargent, Chranston, and Johnson, the location of the saloons and the places of business were along the creek and most of the residences and a church were built on a second level, up on a hill. This gave rise to the two nicknames for the areas of the town. Downtown would be known as "Tiger Town" as this was the center of activity made even more active by the number of saloons. Uptown would be called "Piety Hill" as that was the location of the church.[15]

Later, when the logging industry necessitated the addition of residences for the loggers, a second hill above the town would be populated with folks who had moved to the area from Oklahoma. Though the area was named Huddleston Heights after the family who had instigated much of the building, many of the locals jokingly called that part of town "Okie Flats," a name that even the residents from Oklahoma used with mixed pride.

Election Day on June 2, 1884,[16] dawned hot and muggy, though the sky seemed unnaturally bright cerulean blue. Sargent and Chranston, as was their custom, each left his own front porch early in the day and ambled down the street to sit on the bench in front of Richards's new store and discuss small town politics, religion, and anything else they could find to talk about. Once they got the town lined out, they would return to their homes, eat breakfast, and be ready for their day.

14 Ibid.
15 Ned Norton, "Mitchell," in Glimpses of Wheeler County's Past, p. 39
16 Stinchfield, "Mitchell," in History of Wheeler County, p. 9

"It's gonna be a hot one, for sure," Sargent complained, tugging at the neck of the one-piece woolen long-johns he wore twelve months a year.

"I'd get rid of those long-johns, if it was me," Chranston advised. "Feels good to not wear 'em," and he rubbed the front of his woolen shirt smugly. Then, using a red handkerchief, he wiped sweat from his broad forehead.

"Yeh, but you got a' extra layer of warm there," Sargent retorted, eyeing the mat of Chranston's chest hair showing above the top shirt button. "Little guy like me'd freeze to death 'thout no long-johns," and the two friends laughed.

"Be a big crowd today," Chranston commented needlessly. "Be good to see some a the folks that don't come in often. Still miss Broady, though. Wish he'd a hung on longer." Sargent nodded in agreement, wiping away a streak of sweat tracing down his grey-stubbled jaw. The men visited for a short time longer, and then each returned to his home.

The day moved sluggishly on, heat building in the narrow canyon with no breezes to move the warmness building along the creek. Close to noon, the tops of dark thunder clouds appeared to the south, building up rapidly, and an eerie greenish overcast began to overshadow the town. Birds seemed to have disappeared and not a sound, other than manmade, was heard as the residents of the little town moved to the streets, a pervading sense of doom building, the gathering talking quietly with each other. The first distant clap of thunder was almost a relief, breaking the strange silence that had hung over the town.

As the thunderheads quickly grew higher and darker and drew nearer, the thunder became louder and closer and echoed off the rocky cliffs to the north of Bridge Creek. A forceful wind blasted unexpectedly through the canyon, terrifying those who had assembled to wonder at the phenomenon.

"Wind's gotta be at least 80 miles an hour," Chranston guessed, and he ran for cover under Richards's store porch to join the crowd assembling there as large hailstones pelted down. The citizens of the town watched in horror as the small creek quickly became a raging torrent and they ran for higher ground, abandoning the heart of their community nestled along the flooding Bridge Creek. An acrid, heavy cordite-like smell permeated the air as lightning struck nearby again and again, drilling into the basalt outcroppings with an intense fury. The small creek became a raging torrent, and was estimated to become thirty feet deep and 300 feet wide in places,[17] spreading out over almost the whole width of the town. The deafening roar of the incessant thunder, the noisy rushing of the flood waters, and the grinding of the rocks tumbling along the path of the destructive waters permeated the souls of those who watched, rendering them numb and helpless.

Many residents of the town, as well as those settlers from the outlying area who had come to vote, watched powerlessly as the torrent ripped a deep gulch through the livery barn, carried three wagons away, deposited mud on the floor of Chamberlain & Todd's saloon a foot deep, carried away Fred Sargent's house, and damaged property all along the creek.[18] Huge boulders, the size of small homes, were washed from the banks and left standing in fields and along the raging stream.

The storm abated after less than half an hour, moving away from Mitchell almost as quickly as it had arrived, leaving behind its swath of destruction and an eerie silence, broken only by the rush of the still-swollen stream. A dazed population assembled to assess the damage. Fortunately, no lives were lost in the small town but it would take weeks to repair the damage. The fear of the potential destruction of a thunderstorm and flashflood would never leave the souls who had witnessed the devastation that day. It would be the next day before word of the tragic fate of the Wilson family reached the sobered community.

---

17 Ibid.
18 Shaver et al., p. 652

In 1913, a parade would follow the path of the
flood of '84 down the main street of Mitchell.
From the Dan Cannon archives

"See? What did we say?" Meyer asked Hewot, shaking his head
sadly, when they heard the news of Mitchell's disaster. They could com-
miserate with all the Mitchell folks, but the ones who had chosen to
locate on the flood plain? Well, there wasn't much to say, they didn't
figure, but they also figured the folks would rebuild in the same place.
After all, the traffic passing through wouldn't detour up to the second
level of town for a dish of venison stew or a shot of liquid courage. The
men were right; the city fathers in Mitchell were unfailing in their deter-
mination to build where they could take advantage of the crowd-chute
along The Dalles-Canyon City Military Road.

The Honorable Robert E. Misener, who had served in the Oregon
legislature and thus earned his title, arrived in Mitchell in '85 and "...
soon took up the saloon business."[19] Sargent and Chranston were among
those folks in Mitchell who were pleased to see him come, appreciating
the skills he brought with him. "He has been identified with the growth
and development of this county and town for a number of years and has

19 Ibid., p.685

Mitchell, December 7, 1887
Courtesy of the Fossil museum

always manifested a liberal spirit and an enterprise in building up that have done much good."[20]

By 1906, the grade school was built at the present site of the school gymnasium, but there were no facilities for high school students at that time.[21] Part of the good done by Misener in later years was the donation of the saloon he owned with the Honorable W. L. "Al" Campbell, who had served in the California legislature, to be used as a high school for the town. The school for which they donated their saloon sometime in the early 1920s had one room and one teacher for all four grades in high school.[22] The saloon was not in business at the time, needless to say. As the donation was made during the years prohibition was warming up, Chranston and Sargent chuckled and thought perhaps the federal government had a hand in inspiring the gentlemen's civic gesture.

By '93, with a population of 50 residents, the *Antelope Herald,* April 14, wrote, the town of Mitchell could boast of the following businesses:

20 Shaver et al, p. 685
21 Marbel Blann interview, 1996
22 Ibid.

"Oakes & Wilson, general merchants (these gentlemen are just completing a fine thirty by seventy store building), W. H. Sasser's large cash general merchandise store, Max Putz's flouring mill, J. T. Chamberlain's blacksmith shop, George Collins' carpenter and cabinet shop, Dr. Huck's office, the large Central hotel and feed stable owned and conducted by O. S. Boardman, Al Campbell's blacksmith shop, Miss Stella Boardman's millinery and dressmaking establishment, W. H. Sasser's hotel and livery stable, R. E. Misner's (sic) saloon, Dr. Hunlock's office and drug store, S. A. Chipman's boot and shoe shop, and the calaboose."[23]

The second destructive fire the small town would suffer began in March of '96 when the flames broke out in the rooms of W. T. Palmer on the lower story of the new hall in the lower part of the town. Within two and a half hours, nine buildings in the town were in ashes. These included the saloon building owned by R. E. Misener and Al Campbell, two residences of Mr. Misener, and also his new hall building. Al Campbell's residence and blacksmith shop were destroyed, as well as Sam Bennan's residence and some other buildings. An energetic fire brigade prevented any more of the town from catching fire.[24]

Three years later, in August of '99, a third major fire started in Mitchell. Children playing with matches were said to be the cause of the conflagration and parents in the town could finally look at their children and with some credibility ask them, "What did I say would happen if you played with matches?" By the time the flames were extinguished, some sixteen thousand dollars' worth of property was lost. Among the ten buildings destroyed were a store, a hotel, a livery stable, and a saloon. For the third time after fire had destroyed a good part of the businesses of Mitchell, the citizens dug in and rebuilt their town.[25]

23 Shaver et al, p. 652
24 Ibid., p.653
25 Ibid.

Dr. White, Dentist from Echo, Oregon, and John J. Pack, Optician. For a time, traveling practitioners would set up in Mitchell and then move on when they had completed their work. Notice their assistant resting near Dr. White.
Courtesy of the Fossil museum

The second recorded flood struck in July of 1904 and two lives were lost in this cloudburst that had begun at the head of Bridge Creek. The town of Heppner had been hit by a devastating flood just a year before, and many of the residents of Mitchell were undoubtedly thinking of that catastrophe and the flood of '84 ripping through their town as they fled to escape to the sides of the canyon.

By the time the roaring waters had subsided, the citizens could count twenty-eight buildings with all their contents that had been swept away. One of the two folks who were killed was eighty-year-old Mrs. Agnes Bethune, who was swept away with her hotel building. The second person was ninety-year-old Martin Smith. His daughter, Mrs. M. E. Parrish, had succeeded in getting her mother out of the house in time, but was unable to save her father.[26]

---

26 Shaver et al, p. 654

Thanks to a rider mounted on a fast horse out-distancing the flood waters, the residents in the nearby area were warned in time to escape the torrential creek. Many of the inhabitants of Mitchell, however, were left penniless and with only the drenched clothing they wore on their backs. Neighbors took in the homeless and, as soon as the debris could be cleared, the citizens began rebuilding their homes — again in the bottom of the rock-walled, narrow canyon. A second flood in September of that year struck in the evening, but as it was not as high as the one in July, and, due partly to the channel formed by the first flood, it did not do much damage.[27]

By 1905, there were two large stores in town, the largest "owned and conducted by H. A. (Hanley, grandson of Ezekiel) Waterman & Co., the members of the firm being W. A. Waterman and Jos. G. Fontaine. The business was established at Caleb in 1890, and in 1900 they moved to Mitchell, where they are doing a large and constantly increasing business."[28] The building was twenty five by ninety seven feet and the business was conducted on the first story with the second story being used for a public hall. Three clerks were employed to take care of the booming business that had an inventory of $15,000 and an annual sales amounting to $22,000. All merchandise was shipped in by way of Shaniko and the cost for that was an average of one cent per pound.[29] Waterman also had a branch store in Richmond.

By now, the town of Mitchell had two hundred residents supplied with a gravity-flow water system carrying water from a reservoir high above the town, giving assurance to the citizens that their town would have some protection from fire. Besides the two large mercantile stores, there were also several small stores, two liquor stores, two hotels, a flour

---

27 Ibid.
28 L. E. McDaniel in Pacific Northwest Homestead, p. 46
29 Ibid.

Members of a visiting car club line up outside the Oregon Hotel in early 1900.
From the Dan Cannon archives

mill, drug store, blacksmith shop, and livery stable. Mitchell could boast of two local papers, *The News and The Sentinel*.

The school had three large rooms and a capacity for 125 pupils, which required the services of three teachers. And, the Baptist church, built in '85, had wisely been located on a hill some 100 feet above the flood plain of downtown.[30] The congregation apparently felt they needed to rely on a bit of common sense along with their dependence on the Lord.

Through the years after Broadie Johnson's dust had settled on the road to Marion County, Sargent and Chranston visited often and visited long, reminiscing about the development of the little city located on the flood plain bordering Bridge Creek and nestled in a basalt cliff-lined valley. They had experienced the birthing pangs of the small country town and had memories of the disasters and of the successes, and were willing to share with those who would listen. With each telling, the disasters became worse and the good times better, as is often the case when old-timers reminisce.

---

30 Ibid.

Chapter 10
Mitchell Memories

The third recorded flood that struck Mitchell was Friday, July 13, 1956. A major portion of the downtown was washed away by a raging Bridge Creek, and the best accounts of this disaster can be given best by those who witnessed the event.

"I was right in the middle of the flood," Bob Cannon recalled. "Roy Smith had a convertible Ford sitting on one side and Clarence Jones had a pickup just above him, which shouldn't have washed away. But, Roy's convertible set right there and Clarence's pickup just kinda moved out and got in the stream and away it went.

"And Junior Jones, he had an Oldsmobile settin' on the hoist inside the garage. And that flood just sheared that hoist off right at the bottom. And I found the front end of that car over on my property, years later. And it wrapped one of those pickups of Clarence's around the bridge right here, too. Broadside. Just wrapped it around it. Didn't think the flood had that much power.

"And they was a young fellow from Portland here gettin' gas there at Clarence's and he picked up and run into the house. So he run and jumped up on the bed and it had a rubber mattress on the old bed. And he stayed in that house that was against these poplar trees over here. Threw him out on the bank. All he had on was his shorts. Tore his clothes off."[1]

"The flood was Friday the 13th, July 1956. I had a barn back of my place, and it went out about 4:00 p.m." George Schnee said. "There

---

1 Bob Cannon, long-time Mitchell resident, interview, 1996

were thirteen buildings went out. A 45 foot trailer house went over the bridge down here by the highway like a cork; it just went right over. The water gutted out the post office and took the safe down to the Painted Hills."[2] Several of the witnesses to the flood could remember for years the money that had been in the vault. When the safe was recovered, the money was pinned on a fence by the post office bordering the town's main street. There was no thought about the money disappearing as it dried within easy reach of anyone passing by.

The Mitchell flood was well publicized due largely to Jack Collins. "My father had an airplane and because the roads were blocked and no cars could get through, he landed his plane on the highway to see if he could help anyone. A reporter from Portland wanted to get his story back to Portland before anyone else did, and he walked up to my father and asked him if he would fly him to Portland. My father said, "Sure," and he flew the reporter to Portland," Bobby Collins Ferenstein recalled.[3]

"We lived here when the flood came, in '56," recounted Ethel Mc-Fadden. "We just got moved here. Anyway, I had water running out back and here it was, raining like everything, you know, and I was kinda laughing at myself, the sprinkler going on and here it's raining.

"And finally, when Carolyn [Ethel's daughter] and I went out to look out over the bank, that creek was a river. It was just a suckin' under the bridge down there. So we stayed on the hill. We didn't go downtown! Carolyn was seven at the time, and the next morning, it got cloudy again and she come in and she said, 'Momma, it's cloudy.' And I just passed it off, you know.

"And she said, 'Yes, but, Mom, they're all balled up!' She was thinkin' we was goin' to have another waterspout."[4]

---

2 George Schnee, long-time Mitchell resident, interview, 1996
3 Bobby Ferenstein, long-time Mitchell area resident, interview, 1996
4 Ethel McFadden, Mitchell resident, interview, 1996

Carolyn's fears are shared by many of the old-timers who remember the flood of '56, and the threat of a destructive thunderstorm is very real. Some feel Mitchell is long past due for a major flood, and often the old-timers eye heavy thunderclouds with trepidation.

When the post office was moved from its location in the old bank building near the center of town, some folks doubted the U.S. government's judgment of locating the new structure so close to Bridge Creek. Remembering the many first-hand accounts of the flood of '56 he'd heard, as well as those of the first two floods that had devastated the town and taken lives, Robert Cannon, a local young man who had been employed to help with work on the new building, commented on the location: "It's okay. It's job security."

The fourth fire in Mitchell that affected residents deeply was the one in 1983 that burned the two-story rock building that was the 60-year-old Mitchell School. The fire was determined to have been started by a faulty oil furnace and by the time it was discovered, the flames were too intense to be extinguished. Onlookers could only stand by helplessly and watch the building burn.

Many memories remained, however, of the "good old school days" in the substantially built gray-rock building. "My first look at Mitchell School liked to scare me to death! There was a principal, Elders, and when I went to register my freshman year, his first remark to me as I walked up to the desk to sign up was, 'Next victim!' Well, I already knew the school was called 'The Rock' and he was called the warden!" remembers Evelyn Fitzgerald,[5] though she was to learn her fears were groundless.

John McCulloch recalled the pranks the high school students used to play on Halloween. "They'd generally take all the boys out of school the next day and we'd go and fix our pranks. Outhouses moved from

---

5 Evelyn Fitzgerald, Mitchell area resident, interview, 1996

their holes and woodpiles would end up in the street. So, the next day we'd get to go put the outhouse back where it belonged and stack the wood where it belonged. But, see, it was a day out of school. Maybe there was a method in the madness besides the meanness!

"I remember one time we was moving Lupe McPhetridge's outhouse and he come out the back door and caught us, and we all about got hung on Lucille Cherry's clothesline. We was running through her backyard and everybody got their chin up on the clothesline and it about killed them!

"When I was little, in school, I used to get tied in my chair. I liked to go talk to my neighbors! But, I was not very popular with the girls because every time recess came, we was always tied in our chairs with their jump ropes!"[6] This method of behavior modification would surely be frowned upon in modern schools.

During the booming years of the timber industry, when nearby forests were prime for harvesting, the small town in the rocky canyon enjoyed prosperity. Sawmills sprung up in the midst of large stands of timber and the logging camps soon followed. The general stores enjoyed their years of success, the school and the churches increased their members and their assets, and the thirsty loggers contributed to the coffers of the local taverns. Unfortunately, like the over-grazing of the grass that had been belly high to a saddle horse before the large influx of settlers, the timber harvests took a toll on the old-growth trees and the logging industry dwindled, then ended.

Mitchell was to suffer the same fate as many frontier towns: periods of growth, periods of prosperity, and an ongoing period of economic decline and of reminiscing about "the good old days." For those who enjoy the way of life in the small town, the memories of the old days can be bittersweet.

6 John McCulloch, Mitchell area resident, interview, 1996

Many of the old-timers who lived in Mitchell have shared story after story about their life and the history of the small town. Their lives are very similar to those of some of the citizens in both Fossil and Spray, and the accounts give a sense of what the development of Wheeler County was like. Each story adds to the rich history of the small town of Broadie Johnson's that has been baptized with fire four times (1881, 1896, 1899, and 1983) and water three times (1884, 1904, and 1956), and many of them are well worth sharing, using the storytellers' own words.

"My great-grandfather, R. K. Nelson, came here in the 1870s," Dale Cole related. "William Tell Maxwell married his daughter; that was my grandmother, Sarah Nelson. The creek and street in Mitchell are named after her family.

"Dad was part owner in the Wheeler County Trading Company, and then they went broke during the Depression, in the '30s. He sold the buildings — the store, warehouse, and the dwelling house — to Clarence Hudspeth. Hudspeth rented them out to a guy named Phil Brady, and I went to work for Brady in the fall of '40. Come spring, '41, Brady sold out to Joe Norton.

"The first I remember, Albert King was the manager of the store. Paul Lynch was the bookkeeper and Herbert Smith was the clerk. They used to stock up a bigger supply of things than they do now. When the supplies came in, they came in wagon loads and the things were stocked in the warehouse. I guess there weren't many freight rigs come through too often. I'd say they came from Prineville or The Dalles those days.

"The store was robbed way back. I don't know what year it was. Anyway, when my father owned the store, the floor and underpinning rotted out and there was an old safe there that had been busted into. When we started working on it and rolled the safe back, it started to break the underpinning and we let it fall on the ground, Lyle and I, and we buried it.

"The back part of the store, years ago, was warehouse. Back there under the mezzanine. When I worked for Brady, he'd get truckloads of flour and beans and stuff like that. I'd just fill it up with stuff back there — bulk food. It wasn't in little packages like you buy nowadays.

"We had bins to put the stuff in. I remember a pair of Levis was $1.85. We used to sell farm equipment. Rakes and mowing machines. I remember Father went to town to get a rake one time. A ten foot rake was, I believe, $50.00. Horse drawn. And, he got a mowing machine."[7]

Dale's brother, Lyle, contributed more information about the Wheeler County Trading Company. "The building used to be higher so the wagons could unload on the dock in front of the store." The building was lowered after wagons were no longer used. "The business used to be an awful lot of credit. Back in the Depression, all the ranchers would come in to get maybe a whole wagon load of groceries in the winter, but they didn't have enough money to pay for it. So, Dad let out a lot of credit to the ranchers. They wouldn't come in but maybe once or twice a year. They didn't pay for it, and pretty soon the store couldn't give them credit any more. They went broke."

Lyle remembered his schooling in Mitchell and that the Cole family lived as many of the local families did. "We had a house in town, where the parking lot is for the Baptist church. That's where I was born. We lived on a ranch and in the winter we would move to town so we could go to school. We had a barn, and we would haul hay down in the summertime. We'd trail our milk cow to town when we came on Sunday night and would drive her home Friday after school. Didn't have anything to haul her in!"

Lyle and his brothers Dale and Loy and their sister Erma lived with their parents, Charles Anderson and Ella Maxwell Cole on a ranch four miles south of Mitchell. "The first year there were four of us and we

7 Dale Cole, life-long Mitchell area resident, interview, 1996

drove to school in a buggy, a one-horse shay. Then, it got down to three of us and we had a cart. When there were two of us, we started riding horse-back. Sometimes it was a cold four miles!"[8]

"My first year out of high school," Dale Cole remembered, "I worked for my board (at the Wheeler County Trading Company store) and then the next year, I got a dollar a day. From there, I went to $50.00 a month. When I quit, Norton offered me a $10.00 a month raise, but I had all of that I wanted, I guess.

"Dad had the first Dodge in Mitchell. 1914. We still have it. We (Dale and his wife, Claudia) got our first car, probably in '42. Model T. Cost $25.00. Oh, it'd go, I tell you! No top on it!"

Dale's wife, Claudia, added: "I got all dressed up to go to church. And we went in that and the first thing he did was drive it through a mud hole. I about lost my cool!"

"I was going to tell you about the time she went out to help me," Dale said. "Was going to rake hay. And, I was explaining to her and one thing and another. I, uh, guess I didn't explain something just right and she crawled off the rake and all the time we was on the ranch, she never did come back to help! This was a horse-drawn rake."[9]

Mary Christy Beldon reminisced about her early years as a child on the family ranch about seven miles north of Mitchell: "My mother's family, T. J. and Maryann Monroe, crossed the Oregon Trail in 1865. In 1869 they moved from Coburg, Oregon, to the ranch. In 1872, the family took up government land here and they were possessors of 960 acres while their children owned half as much more.

"I grew up on the Monroe cattle ranch. My great-aunt, Dorcas Monroe, married H. H. Wheeler. He was quite an old gentleman, I heard.

"I milked cows, made butter, drove derrick for neighbors and our

8 Lyle Cole, life-long Mitchell resident, interview, 1996
9 Dale Cole interview

own grain. I loved to ride horseback to salt the range cattle as salt blocks were unknown. My mother and I would take a bag of salt horseback and put out salt licks."

"I didn't start school until I was seven. Pike Helms used to pick apples and put the buckets of them on the school grounds so the kids wouldn't climb on his fence for them. He lived in the house right by the school yard.

"I remember the first car I seen. Mother and I were coming to Mitchell with a team. About at the Mitchell city dump, here comes a nice model T Ford Coupe. The horses reared and the fellow driving the car helped with the horses. We made it home in good time!"[10] That was Mary's first encounter with a car, but she soon learned the advantages of such a contraption over the horses her family owned: cars didn't need to be fed when they weren't working and they didn't leave piles of manure behind.

Jack Collins chuckled as he related an experience that had soon became local legend. His story was a bit more credible than those of Jerome Parsons and it has been verified by several of the old-timers. "I used to have the garage in downtown Mitchell, right after the war, in '45 or '46. One Fourth of July I was on the city council. That's the first thing you get on when you come to Mitchell. And, they had eight sawmills in the county then, and four or five of them were around Mitchell.

"One time on the third of July, a guy named Pat Buckley come through there and he had guns sticking out all the windows of his car. And he went down the street and turned around and come back. Well, he was going to shoot all the fellers that were from Oklahoma that were in the Pastime (the local bar). And I didn't know about it. He circled through town and came back and stopped by my place.

"And a feller named Monk Bailey was in my garage; he was the mar-

10 Mary Christy Beldon interview, 1996

shal. Well, anyway, when Buckley stopped at my place there, he had his pistol shoved in his belt here and it was cocked, ready to shoot. And he stopped and wanted a match to light a cigarette.

"And I was standing there pretty close to him and the door was open and I said, 'Well, Pat, let the hammer down on that damn thing. Don't shoot yourself right here in the garage. You might make a mess on the floor!'

"And, he let the hammer down. Then, we were standing there and he was trying to get his cigarette lighted and old Monk Bailey come in right at the door about 15 feet away from us and said, "Drop that gun!" And he had a pistol aimed right at Buckley. And, of course, that was not a good thing to say, because if Buckley reached for the gun and dropped it, he could shoot Monk.

"So, that come to Monk's head, I guess, because he started shooting at Pat Buckley and I was getting powder burns on me, so I moved over a ways. And he shot Pat three or four times. And Buckley thought he was going to die and I kinda thought he was right. He was bleeding a little around here and there.

"Anyway, Clarence Hudspeth was the mayor, so we got ahold of Clarence and we loaded Buckley in the station wagon and they started over the mountain on the old road, and the station wagon slid in the ditch. They got it out and went on to the hospital. In about two weeks, Pat was back!"[11]

"I come over here from Fossil in 1947 and bought that old station uptown. (The building was next to the house that Henry Wheeler had built and that Bob Cannon and his family lived in.) Run it for twenty-one years. Then, when the flood come, why Clarence Jones built out on the road and our business just quit, so we bought this property (just west of town) and built this station over here in 1969 and been over there ever since," Bob Cannon related.

---

11 Jack Collins, life-long Mitchell area resident, interview, 1996

"The people in Mitchell are altogether different than they used to be. The biggest change is when the mills went out. It was just a flourishing town, you know, and then everything just dropped to nothing. In fact, I looked around to find the best place to go and never did find one. Just as well I stayed here."[12]

"What do I like most about Mitchell? I like Mitchell because it's in the country. Any window you look out, you see beauty. And, it's the people you get to know. That's what makes Mitchell very special. It's kinda like two treats — frosting on the cake. The scenery and the people," summed up Carl Naas.[13] It seems he and Polk Butler had a difference of opinion concerning the scenery, but for the many people with fond memories of the little town located in a flood-prone canyon, the people are the treasure that lures them back again and again.

The connection with the land that had enticed first Biffle, then Meyer, then T. B. and Sergent, to settle in the middle of nowhere was the same connection that lured Ralph Fisk and John Spray to settle in the area where the town of Spray would be built.

12 Bob Cannon interview, 1996
13 Carl Naas, Mitchell resident, interview, 1996

Chapter 11
1869 – Spray

Meyer had first begun visiting with Ralph Fisk in the late 1860s as Fisk passed by the Meyer's Gulch stage stop, pausing for a break from his travels and a quick dish of stew. With the development of the road to the north of the county that would link T. B. Hoover's town with the Haystack area, Fisk usually took advantage of that shorter route from his holdings near the future settlement of Spray to The Dalles. The small town was the last of the three main settlements in Wheeler County, and the community would be slow to become incorporated.

Fisk began raising stock in the Haystack Valley along the John Day River in '69, a few years after Parsons had arrived in Twickenham. The newcomer's holdings were located about 30 miles north of Camp Watson and his valley had been named by a group of soldiers from the fort. They were on a scouting patrol when they noticed a small knoll, about 50 feet tall, that appeared to look like a round haystack with a greenish hue, and the name of Haystack was added to the military map. The mound was never called anything but Haystack — no "hill" or "mountain" or "butte" seemed to be appropriate — just "Haystack."[1] The first permanent settler in the valley was Isaac C. Holmes[2], who settled there the same year as Fisk.[3]

At first glance, Haystack Valley didn't look like it could amount to much, but, as Fisk commented to Holmes when he arrived, "Any land

---

1 Candy Humphreys interview, 2011
2 Shaver et al, p. 640
3 William Masiker in History of Wheeler County, p. 14

The "haystack" hill that gave the area its name.

that's free starts to look more desirable when the price is considered. It'll either be profitable or we'll get back what we paid for it." The men looked at the 'dobe-streaked soil, the sparse vegetation, and the lack of trees nearby and speculated on the potential for crops.

"Well," Holmes commented, wiping the early-morning sweat from his forehead with a work-roughened hand, "Free's a good price." He hitched up his canvas pants to his thin waist, knowing the effort was futile as they'd slip back down as soon as he started walking. "Seems I lost a bit of weight since I headed this way," he grinned at Fisk. "Bound to lose a bit more afore I get a field or two tilled up."

The lowland the men were surveying was surrounded by rounded hills streaked with white and green clay banks and scattered with basalt outcroppings. The sagebrush and bunch-grass were scrubbier than that found closer to Camp Watson, they would hear, showing the results of hotter summers and less rainfall than the soldiers were experiencing at their base of operations closer to the Ochoco Mountains.

Water would be the key to successful homesteads in the area, both men knew, and Fisk had sought out a waterway when looking for a place to settle. There was a creek running through the Haystack basin, giving hope to Fisk and other settlers who followed him that crops could be raised there, and that there would be water for the stock grazing on the hills before the summer heat shriveled the spring grasses. Timber, found not five miles north of the valley, and could be harvested for building homes, the men knew.

The following year, Fisk and Holmes welcomed Joe and Rodney Tompkins and Charles Masiker[4], all of whom settled in the Haystack country which included land from Kimberly to Service Creek. Settlements for miles around Haystack were originally known by that name, though specific individual locations soon began to be known by other titles.

One of the place designations that became familiar to local homesteaders was Kahler Basin, named for George and Andrew Kahler. Like Fisk, those early settlers found a stream running through their land and Kahler Creek would provide the much-needed water for their farm. Other nearby locations were Corn Cob Valley, Alder Creek, Mule Shoe, Service Prairie, High Spring Valley, and Lake and Parrish Creeks. Hogan's Bottom was named for the settlers there. Additional place names that soon became familiar to the locals were Balogna Creek, Balm Creek, Sore Foot, Honesty Flat, and Villainy Gulch.[5]

The terrain appeared to be ideal for raising sheep, and many of those animals were brought to the area, though the earlier settlers also raised cattle. Within a decade, nonetheless, it became apparent that the increase in the number of animals grazing on the well-known natural grasslands was obviously going to make short work of the pastures. This led to the necessity of establishing fields for growing hay to sustain the livestock during the winter, and the settlers were kept busy planting and tending their crops in addition to tending their livestock.

Early settlers in Haystack Valley lived some 110 miles from The Dalles

4 Shaver et al, p. 640
5 William Masiker in History of Wheeler County, p. 14

and it was usually in the fall that most of the families would make their annual trip to that city to buy supplies for the winter. What the area lacked was a driving force to develop a settlement to accommodate the early settlers. The answer to that problem arrived in a buckboard jouncing and clattering down from the north on the rough road leading into the area by the John Day River.

John C. Spray, a United Brethren minister for over thirty years, and his wife apparently had grand aspirations for their new son. Perhaps they had hoped for an adventuresome lad when they named their baby boy John Charles Fremont after the explorer of that name who had helped to open up the Oregon country prior to '42. That adventurer, explorer, and scientist who would become a surveyor and an expert frontiersman, turned into a politician, and in '64 he had run against Lincoln for president. He was forced to withdraw from the race due to money problems, and by '73 had declared bankruptcy. It was surely those accomplishments by Fremont prior to his failed campaign for the presidency that his parents hoped their son would acquire.

John Charles Fremont Spray arrived in the area of his future town in '84[6] and settled first in Kahler Basin.[7] "This will be home," he proudly informed his bride of a year, Mary Ellen. The young lady was not impressed with the high desert climate, the clay banks and sparse vegetation of the little valley; she was accustomed to the more lush flora of Lane County where she had been born.

Spray and his wife built and operated a little store in Kahler Basin. There they sold groceries, dry goods, and whatever else they felt their neighbors might need. The Wagner post office had been established by Carl Wagner[8] near the head of Kahler Creek in March of '82, and with

---

6 Shaver et al, p. 674
7 Rose Spray Warfield in *History of Wheeler County*, p. 214, writes that the Sprays first moved to Heppner where they operated a butcher shop for a few years before moving to Kahler Basin.
8 Stinchfield, *History of Wheeler County*, p 13

the addition of Spray's store, the new settlers in the area felt the country was becoming civilized. While John worked at building up their land holdings, Mary remained at home and operated the small store and went about her business of rearing the couple's five children and running the household.

Spray wisely acquired holdings scattered around the area. The energetic landowner followed the practices of many of the first settlers establishing holdings; he filed on scattered acreages and was able to utilize the land between his claims for grazing. Spray first filed claims to two parcels, 160 acres each, in '91 on Kahler Creek: one claim about two miles north of the future town of Spray and the second claim about six miles northeast of the future city. Not until 1915 did he file on 160 acres south of Spray on Hide and Seek Creek. Next, in '24, he claimed 320 acres between Lefthand and Chinahat creeks and about four miles south of Spray. John Spray also laid claim to an additional 240 acres close to his first holdings on Hide and Seek Creek.[9]

According to the adventuresome Spray, he joined W. O. Minor of Heppner and the men "…went gunning for a suitable location for a road to tap the country south of the John Day, and open up for the stockmen a nearer and better road to Heppner. After getting the road in place and a ferry established in '96, the history of Spray begins to open up."[10]

"I'm going to build myself a town," Spray had proudly announced to his wife, Mary, upon returning to his Kahler Basin home after a day of riding around surveying the nearby land to the south. He unsaddled his mount, harnessed him to a small buggy, and took his wife for a ride to show her the site of their future home.

John Charles Fremont Spray, city founder
With permission of McLaren Stinchfield

Located in a long, flat valley on the banks of the John Day River, the area of the proposed city was bordered to the southeast by a fairly level-topped mountain punctuated with ribbons of rock outcroppings and light tan or green or brown-red banks. Continuous ribbons of colors and layers of varying strata of soils surrounding the valley in the different formations showed the land had been formed by eons of settlement of soils under ancient seas. The ensuing pressure of layer upon layer of sediments falling to the sea floor had formed the marine-life filled rocks that would give credibility to those who talked of the ancient presence of oceans. The north hill of the valley was crowned with more basalt cliffs footed with sloping hills running to the river-level land. Here, again, as elsewhere surrounding Spray's site, scattered clay banks of various colors broke the bunch-grass-covered hillsides.

From a high vantage point above the flowing John Day, Spray pointed out to his wife how he planned to establish the new city above the lower floodplain. The town would be close to the river but located so high flood waters wouldn't encroach upon the inhabitants. Although J. M. Connelly lost his entire crop, estimated at a value of $7,000, on his farm at Cherry Creek some thirty miles downriver from the future town of Spray in '94, the high waters did no appreciable damage to the town site.[11] The gentleman had chosen the location well.

Spray and his family had spent fourteen years on their Kahler Basin holdings before relocating to the site of the developing town in 1900.[12] Spray was typically dressed in his three-piece suit complete with a narrow-brimmed dress hat when he was about his official business. He removed his suit jacket, rolled up his sleeves, and began planning the locations of a public hall, hotel, saloon, livery barn, and several dwellings. With help from like-minded individuals, and in due time, the buildings were erected. There was not much being done in his town that escaped the watchful eyes of the clean-shaven Spray.

"In 1899 the present town site was purchased by the writer,[13] and the next year found Spray fully established, with a large general merchandise store, public hall, good hotel, saloon, livery barn, and several dwellings and last, but not least, a good school house. The next year a blacksmith shop, drug store, printing office, gravity system of water works, and several more dwelling houses appeared."[14]

Mary Spray platted the new city on March 5, 1900. Located in the east central part of Wheeler County, the settlement would be named Spray after her husband, the founding father of the small country municipality.

In 1900, the newly-platted city received 82 votes for the position

---

11 Ibid.
12 Shaver et al, p. 674
13 John F. Spray in *Pacific Northwest Homestead*, , p. 49. There is no record of a land patent in the name of John F. Spray for the area of the town of Spray in the Government Land Office records
14 Ibid.

of county seat of Wheeler County; however, Fossil received 436, so it won the title. At that time, the county boasted a population of 2,243 residents, though not many of those were located in the city by the John Day River, which undoubtedly helped to account for the small number of votes for Spray.

John Spray operated the horse-drawn ferry that ran across the John Day River. Plans were soon underway to build a steel bridge for an estimated cost of $7,500. The passage over the waterway would be located close to where the ferry was operating, and the convenience of a bridge would benefit all travelers as well as the local folks. Spray donned his predictable three-piece business suit, harnessed his horse to a buggy, and drove around the newly formed county to collect funds to use for building the bridge.

In 1904, Spray wrote in *The Pacific Northwest Homestead, Inland Empire Edition,* that "Situated on the John Day river in Wheeler county… the picturesque town of Spray, which sprang suddenly into existence about five years ago, and which, situated as it is in the center of a fertile farming and stock raising country, seems to have a bright future in store."[15] The area of the town was settled about thirty years previous to Spray's article, though the town itself would not be incorporated until 1958.[16] Perhaps, much like a good wine, a slow aging was the essence of the quality of the small city of Spray.

By 1905, the mercantile store in Spray owned by Minor, Gilliam & Company, could boast of annual sales somewhere in the neighborhood of $30,000. Minor had accompanied Spray on the quest for a suitable road linking the towns of Heppner and Spray, and both men were equally proud of the profitable business that resulted from the highway being successfully built.

---

15 Ibid.
16 Stinchfield in *History of Wheeler County*, p. 9

Spray — early 1900s
Courtesy of the Spray museum

This store sells everything, within the bounds of reason, which might be expected to be found in an interior store, including dry goods, clothing, boots and
shoes, groceries, canned goods, books and stationery,
crockery, stoves and ranges, shelf and heavy hardware,
plumbers' goods, harness, saddles and whips, furniture,
carpets and matting, paints and oil, drugs and patent
medicines, guns and ammunition, flour and feed, coal,
agricultural implements and machinery.[17]

The men who owned the store were based in Heppner, more than
forty miles north of Spray on a rough, winding road. W. O. Minor, the
senior partner, owned a large stock ranch there and also had sizable
interests in land, cattle, and sheep in the Penland Land and Livestock
Company. Mr. Gilliam was the mayor of Heppner and also had a hard-

ware and crockery business there. The two other partners, W. R. Irwin and M. D. Clark, were in partnership with Minor in a large general merchandise business in Heppner.[18] Establishing the general store in Spray was a natural and profitable extension of their business in Heppner.

One of the first settlers close to John Spray's town in 1905 was Wm. H. Templeton who owned 160 acres of desert land with twelve of those acres in rye and five in alfalfa. Three other 160-acre ranches were owned by A. N. Foster, P. C. Martin, and I. F. Reed, and these men grew wheat, barley, and alfalfa as well as fruit trees. All three men raised cattle,[19] and all three men profited from Spray's advice and from his newly established town.

The land continued to be put into crops, and the Wagner post office was moved into town and renamed the Spray Post Office. Spray visited with the landowners coming to town to gather their mail and to do their shopping. Among those he advised in their new endeavors were Samuel Hughes, W. H. Gates, T. R. Smith, G. N. Robison, Albert Carsner, Archie Hunt, John V. Martin, the Dennison brothers, Charles Boyse, F. A. Hale, William Coates, and Richard and James Paul. Those men all owned holdings which they developed[20] and Spray kept the property-owners abreast of the progress of the area.

Of these early ranchers, the Dennison brothers were best known for their bands of sheep. Owning 2,200 acres of property eleven miles from Spray, half of which was tillable land, their principal business was 3,300 sheep that made up their three bands. In 1904, John F. Spray noted that the previous year Wheeler County had sold 1,500,000 pounds of wool. The Dennisons also ran fifty head of cattle and fourteen horses on their holdings, in addition to the sheep.[21]

---

18 Ibid.
19 Ibid.
20 Ibid., p. 49 and 50
21 Ibid., p. 50

William Coates, located about five miles from Spray, chose to raise fruits and vegetables on his property. All crops were irrigated, and he harvested apples, plums, prunes, cherries, peaches, and pears in his orchard. His large garden was filled with watermelons, muskmelons, and strawberries, as well as tomatoes and other vegetables. He marketed his produce in Fossil, Hardman, and Spray, and was able to get "large prices." [22]

The *Spray Courier* was published by David E. Baxter. This enterprising soul was also engaged in the insurance business and was studying law in '05, expecting to be admitted into the bar soon. Spray kept close communication with Baxter; surely that individual would be helpful in the event the new city needed municipal advice.

Another individual who did much to establish the growing town was S. L. Cross, who built the Hotel Cross, the main hotel in town. He also owned a store building, a barn, and eight building lots which he had for sale. Cross had arrived in Oregon in 1882 and settled in Spray in 1900. [23]

John Spray, using the title of Business Man and Ranch Owner, modestly (?) wrote in his article in the *Pacific Northwest Homestead that:*

> The town of Spray is springing up as if by magic in the midst of what was a short time ago nothing but a wilderness, and the credit for this transformation is wholly due to the efforts of John F. Spray, who laid out the townsite. He is probably the largest landowner, both of town property and farming land, of anyone in that section of the country, his ranch consisting of 2,440 acres of land, lying on both sides of the John Day river, and including much bottom land, which is very rich and productive.

22 Ibid.
23 Ibid.

"There are 200 acres of upland, and 200 acres of river bottom land which are tillable, and he is cultivating 200 acres on which he raises 20 acres of wheat, 40 acres of barley, 60 acres of oats and has an alfalfa field containing 80 acres, which is irrigated with water from Parrish creek. He is a sheepman, and at the present time has 7,000 head of sheep in his flocks running on the ranges, which are growing wool for market.

Mr. Spray's town property consists of his residence, a livery barn, store building, and 50 building lots which are now for sale. He owns the city water works — a gravity system, with a covered reservoir having a capacity of 15,000 gallons of water, and furnishing good fire protection.

Mr. Spray owns the ferry which crosses the John Day river at that point, but this will soon be abandoned, as the county is erecting a steel bridge cross the river, Mr. Spray, with true public spirit, being the principal donator to the enterprise. He also donated the site for the school house.

Besides his large mercantile business, Mr. Spray also conducts a real estate business, and will be found reliable in all matters pertaining to town property, alfalfa land, stock ranches, or timber land in Wheeler county, especially in the neighborhood of Spray. Anyone desiring to receive information regarding such property would do well to correspond with him at Spray.[24]

---

24 John Spray in *Pacific Northwest Homestead*, p. 51

Spray also encouraged settlement in the county, saying that "If you are not satisfied with your present condition, go to Wheeler County and invest in land at rock-bottom prices, such as is now offered for sale by some of the great stock companies which are retiring from business to give room for more diversified agriculture and more people in the county."[25]

After about twelve or fourteen years in his little town by the John Day, Spray sold his land and buildings and moved to Cottage Grove. He stayed there for some years, and then moved to Fossil, where he started a creamery and ran a feed store. Always a promoter, always interested in development, Spray lived out his life in Wheeler County, dying in 1929. He was buried at Cottage Grove, doubtlessly clad in his dependable three-piece business suit.

Typical of the inhabitants of the small towns that were established in Wheeler County, there were many independent characters that developed along with the new cities. One of the well-known families of

Early Spray Auto Campground, R. E. Wright, Prop.
From Dave and Candy Humphreys archives

25 Ibid.

the Spray area is the Snabel family, and there are many stories of that clan. Ezra Snabel and Sarah Hope Kirby eloped in '05, riding horse-back from Richmond. Ezra's father had drowned when his son was thirteen years old; to help support the family, Ezra ran moonshine to the Indians near Puget Sound, Washington. He fed the mash left from the liquor-making process to wild geese, which he would knock in the head with a stick when they became dazed from eating the fermented grain. The fowl meat would be used as food for his family.[26] His wife Sarah, who was called Hope by her family, lost her father, Louis Kirby, when he was trampled by a runaway team and wagon and killed at Richmond in 1911.

In 1909, Ezra and Hope moved to their homestead three miles from Spray and up what would be called Snabel Creek. Ezra helped to build the rock structure in Spray where the Snabel's eight children attended school: Bill, Effie, Ellen, Velma, John, Della, Roy, and Pansie.[27]

Effie married Jim Stirewalt, whose brother, Dave, chased wild horses with him. The men would sometimes ride to the Red Hills below Twickenham, chase and trap wild horses, some of which had been turned loose by their owners to fend for themselves and were free for anyone wily enough to catch them. The brothers would drive them to their ranch at Spray where they would rough break and sell them.

Bob Huntington recalled one time when the Stirewalts came through Twickenham. "Stirewalts came through Rowe Creek when I was pretty small and they had a crazy old horse, a John Creiger horse. He had a hell of a scar across his nose. They said Sid Wattenburger had him and hit him with a monkey wrench. The horse was crazy.

"But, Jim and Dave come in with horses. They wanted to know if one of us kids could help them through the timber. They were going to Spray. I went — on that crazy horse. Something spooked him and

---

26 Effie Snabel Stirewalt in *History of Wheeler County*, p. 221
27 Ibid.

he went right through that bunch of horses they was driving. I couldn't stop him.

"Jim Stirewalt hollered, 'Get off him!' He said, 'Roll off him, you dumb little simpleton!' And, I did. The horse piled up in a thorn brush and they darn near had to pull him out of it. Jim saved me from getting hurt, anyway.

"Jim and Dave stayed with Bill and Neva Keyes one night when I was working at the Sutton Ranch. For a joke, they went upstairs and took the door off Neva and Bill's bedroom and they hid it out in the attic. It was a long time before they found it, I guess.

"One time, before the war would've been, Bob Taylor was in high school. Jim and Dave, they had hogs all over. I don't know how many hogs they had. There was an old granary that caved in over around Condon and they gave the Stirewalts that old moldy grain, and it sprouted. They got me and old Bob Taylor to go with them and help sack up the grain. They said they'd give each of us a pint of whiskey, so we worked to beat the band all day long. Finally, they give us each a pint of Sloe Gin. Probably did us a favor because that made me so sick I left it alone for quite a while after that."[28]

With the presence of a mill in the town, Spray prospered from 1940 to 1973. The mill, first owned by the Heppner Lumber Company, employed many of the locals and business was lively in the little town. Through the years, the mill changed ownership and others who would purchase the mill were Frank Crawford, Hudspeth, Walt Lindstom, Barney Malcolm, and the Kinzua Corporation.[29] With Kinzua closing the mill in '73, the population of the last of the small towns to be incorporated in Wheeler County dwindled.

Spray citizens, largely influenced by the outlying ranching population, established a rodeo in '43. The rodeo soon became one of the big-

28 Bob Huntington, old-time Wheeler County resident, interview, 2010
29 Bernadine Nelson et al. in History of Wheeler County, p. 9

gest events in the county and each year it drew scores of contestants and spectators from great distances to attend the annual action on Memorial Day weekend.

The parade before the rodeo on Saturday is one of the highlights of the weekend. The procession is unique in that the line-up of entrants parades in a loop along the route — twice — making the event truly one worthy of watching!

In '65 the Eastern Oregon Half Marathon was instigated with a wager between two good jogging buddies, Lyle Rilling and Tom Nash, both dedicated athletes. The men began bragging to each other about their good running times and a bet ensued: a breakfast for the winner of a race from Service Creek to Spray, and a race was arranged. The distance was thirteen and a half miles, the exact distance of half a marathon, and the competition became an annual event, held each Memorial Day weekend in conjunction with the Spray rodeo.

Spray continues to hold on to its school, even with its dropping enrollment, and activities there help to form a strong bond among the members of that community. River floating and fishing add to the local economy, and the never-changing fossils and the monuments to those ancient remains bring a certain number of tourists and geology students each year.

Christian Meyer never visited the settlement of Spray; the developing town was a good day's ride from his fort-house and he never had reason to venture that far from home. He figured that someday, perhaps, the roads would be improved along with transportation, and folks might head to the developing city to take care of business. Meanwhile, for him, a buggy ride into Mitchell would suffice for any of the supplies Spray might have to offer; Spray was just too darned far away for him.

Chapter 12
1876 and later —Small Communities

For forty years, Meyer had sat at his large table at night after his day's work was done, sipping his whiskey and smoking his pipe and visiting with Hewot and any visitor who had stopped by. The country as he saw it that first day he and his partner had pulled up their wagon in Meyer's Gulch had changed dramatically. Amazingly, the big German farmer could give a full and detailed account of the history of the county and he did so with enthusiasm. He was proud of the new area he'd helped develop.

Meyer was quick to remind his visitors that he had earned the title of being the first permanent settler in Wheeler County. His good friend Biffle, the first settler to pound in stakes around a home section in the area, had died, and Waterman had obligingly, if not reluctantly, moved on and solidified Meyer's claim of being the premier pioneer. The farmer had seen the formation of settlements in the county and the ensuing incorporation of Mitchell and of Fossil and the building of the town of Spray. He had witnessed the results of Indian attacks and floods and fires. And, he had seen the birth of Wheeler County. The gentle German was content.

The land Meyer had settled on and the surrounding area would continue to be developed by folks who would move in with great expectations. Some of these families would prosper and would help build up the county; others, often for no apparent reason, would fail and move on, their time in Meyer's land becoming a memory to some and forgotten by many.

While Fossil and Mitchell were building up their municipalities and Spray was becoming established as a community, there were several small, almost forgotten post offices and communities created. Of these, Winlock and Richmond grew to the biggest sizes but the towns of Fossil and Mitchell, and later Spray, would draw citizens from the small settlements and the smaller post offices would be disbanded. From where he sat on the original The Dalles - Canyon City Military Road, Meyer kept a mental record of the communities and the post offices, no matter how short-lived, and of the characters that inhabited them.

Huntley was never much more than a post office established in February of 1876 near Clarno. Named for the Huntley family who homesteaded there, the name was changed to Pine Creek in June of that same year, the name taken from the creek that flowed through the area. The post office again changed names in December of '77 and became known as Crown Rock, so called because of a huge outcropping of basalt by that name that stood guard over the area.[1]

Another short-lived post office was established in Caleb, named for Caleb Thornburg, in 1876. Located on Badger Creek about fifteen miles east and slightly south of Mitchell, the town was begun by John Waterman and originally included the home of Jim Keeton, where the post office was located.[2] E. B. Allen and S. G. Coleman were among the first settlers in this area[3], and the town soon had the post office, a hotel, livery stable, blacksmith shop, and Biggerstaff's Saloon. E. O. Fling had been one of the first settlers in the area, arriving there in '70.[4]

The small community also had bragging rights to being the first of the early settlements in the area to operate a house of ill repute — the

1 Grace Younce et al., "Huntley Post Office," in *The History of Wheeler County*, p. 12
2 William Keeton et al., Ibid., p. 130
3 Jack Steiwer in *Glimpses of Wheeler County's Past*, p. 25
4 Shaver et al., *History of Central Oregon*, p. 640

husband being the owner and proprietor, and the employee his wife. "Don't 'spose I'll need to visit Caleb," Meyer had remarked with an ironic grin when he heard of the new business venture.

Caleb at one time had a population larger than Mitchell, though in 1905 when it had begun to decline as a settlement, it had a population of only 26. With no school, the settlers there gradually moved to Mitchell and only a small cemetery marks the former location.[5]

Meyer noted with interest that, among those folks laid to rest in the small cemetery, there was one argumentative fellow named Cal Chambers who, while he lived, could not get along with his neighbors. His reputation for being contrary and thoroughly unlikeable was manifested when he died and the locals didn't want him buried in the cemetery. Common decency prevailed, however, and the poor soul was given his final resting place off to one side of the cemetery, far removed from the early settlers who were laid to rest in the graveyard, his isolation ensuring he could no longer torment his neighbors.[6]

A one-room school near Highway 207 between Service Creek and Mitchell marks the area that was at one time known as Waldron. Word reached Meyer's Gulch that a post office was established there in 1879 on Shoofly Creek; it would be closed in 1902. At one time, the few residents of the area platted a town with the intention of becoming an official community in the county, but this effort never came into fruition. All that remains of Waldron is the school and a sign marking the area as a century ranch owned by the Jackson family.

Grade was a short-lived post office located on The Dalles-Canyon City Military Road where a grade had been cut into the side of a hill near the John Day River, just south of the mouth of Cherry Creek. The first postmaster was George M. "Monty" Wasson, who had set up a toll house at the cut in 1880. Though the post office was renamed and moved to Burnt Ranch in '96, it was closed permanently in 1901.[7]

Mr. and Mrs. VanBibber were two of the few settlers in the area of the Grade post office and home of Monty Wasson. Mr. VanBibber set up a blacksmith shop and his wife served meals to travelers. The charge for each horse, regardless of the number of wagons, was twenty-five cents. "We could not charge Indians and preachers, and naturally there was no charge to the neighbors," Mrs. Van Bibber's daughter, Mrs. Charles Putnam, explained.[8]

Carl N. Wagner's name was given to the small post office that was established March 21, 1882, near Kahler Creek. Established in Grant County, as Wheeler County did not become a county until '99, the post office closed in April of 1901 and the locals were served by the new Spray post office. George Hayden established a saw mill at Wagner and there was also a store operated by Hayden and Bob Carsner, as well as a dance hall. The justice of the peace for the Wagner precinct was W. A. Fisher.[9]

Another small settlement that was short-term was Winlock, with a post office being established there in 1888. The name of the small community came from Winlock Steiwer, the pioneer settler who became T. B. Hoover's son-in-law. The post office's locale was transitory, being housed in Al Howden's grocery story, then into a building built by Mr. Burton. It was then moved into the confectionary, card room and grocery store operated by Eddie Matthews. The post office was closed permanently in 1934 when ill health forced the postmistress, Cora Wallace, to leave Winlock.[10]

Although the population of the Winlock area exploded in 1906 when the Nelson Mill was established south of the community, the set-

7 Steiwer, "Communities Past and Present: Grade," in *Glimpses of Wheeler County's Past*, p. 37
8 Mrs. Charles Putnam, "Grade," in *Glimpses of Wheeler County's Past*, p. 37
9 Younce et al, "Wagner," in *History of Wheeler County*, p. 13
10 Stinchfield in *History of Wheeler County* , p 13

tlement would lose much of its population when the mill was moved in '27 to Dutch Flat. While Winlock thrived, it boasted of a United Artisans Lodge that was established in '04. In '08 a building was built for the lodge, and it was there that dances and socials were held, as well as meetings of the local Grange No. 497. Church services were also held there.[11]

A grist mill was built on the Howden property by Ben Glenn and O.P. Bunker on the small creek that ran through the area, and there different grades of flour were made. A blacksmith shop was built by Archie Boyce in 1914 near the Howden hotel. John C. Myers built a store west of the blacksmith shop, and he carried all kinds of merchandise.[12]

The store was looted and burned in '31 by robbers, and the three men responsible would eventually serve time in the state penitentiary. The woman who was their accomplice lost her appointment as postmistress of Winlock. A Nazarene church and a school completed the necessary buildings of any small settlement, but when Nelson's mill moved, the population of the town dwindled and the small community died.[13]

Located almost in the geographical center of Wheeler County, Richmond got its name from a dispute between two strong-willed settlers of the area. Feelings were still fairly tender from the recently ended Civil War, and settlers from both the Union and the Confederate states arrived in the area. It was in 1889 that folks in the Shoofly country saw a need to establish a town for the large number of settlers there. Among those early inhabitants in the region were the Gilliam, Donnelly, Helms, Keys, and Walters families.

R. N. Donnelly donated the land for the settlement, and one of the first items of business was to establish a school. The location of the school was disputed heatedly by William Walters, and Donnelly dubbed

---

11 Ibid.
12 Ibid.
13 Steiwer in *Glimpses of Wheeler County's Past*, p. 64

R. N. and Rebecca Keyes Donnelly
Courtesy of the Fossil museum

Walters "Jeff Davis" because of his stubborn approach. At Donnelly's suggestion, the new town was called Richmond, thereby linking Walters's personality with the capital of the Confederacy.[14]

Donnelly, who had married Rebecca Keys, came to the area from Tennessee. He had sent for several young men to come to the area to work, and the region soon became known as "Little Tennessee." The men would work for a few years for wages and then venture out on their own to obtain their own land. Because of his "leading his people home," R. N. soon became nicknamed "Moses." After entering into politics, he served a term in the state legislature and introduced the bill to cre-

14 Younce et al, "Richmond," in History of Wheeler County, p. 12

ate Wheeler County. Upon completion of his term, he preferred to be called "The Honorable R. N. Donnelly" and the gentleman got his wish.

When the legislation passed to create Wheeler County, Donnelly, who had worked to form the county, sent his constituents this message: "The child is born — its name is Wheeler!"[15]

Although the small town boasted a store, a hotel, a livery stable, and a good public school, it was not long-standing. Like many of the early settlements, the business gave way to larger towns that were more centrally located to more heavily populated areas of the county.

Fred Dunn remembered attending a dance in the dance hall that was built about a mile from the town of Richmond. The owners of the hall had thought that would be the location of the town, but, true to form, the strong-minded founding fathers had other ideas and the town itself was located a distance away from the structure. The hall served through the years as a social center for the community, and a party was held there when Fred was in the second grade.

Richmond, 1901
Courtesy of the Spray museum

---

15 Fussner "Fossil," in *Glimpses of Wheeler County's Past*, p. 31

"I saw someone get shot; I don't know who he was. Nobody knew who he was. Us kids all liked Frog Wilson 'cause he was full of it, you know. It just run out of him. And, we was all around him inside that door at the dance hall door there at Richmond and that guy come through the door and that guy stood there and looked at Frog and his substantial stomach and he said, "I'm going to let some of that out," and he just cut him right across the belly. Cut his front open. Didn't get into the entrails. The knife blade must not have been long enough or his clothing stopped it, but it cut him open.

"But, being a Dunn, I went after the guy because out the door he went. Down the back stairs and he took off up that road going up towards the post office. Then a big old light come on and a voice yelled, "Freddy, lay down!" so I hit the ground.

"And that gun went, "Boom! Boom! Boom!" You know what I remember the most? The flashlight the sheriff was carrying was about fifteen to twenty inches long and the lens was huge.

"And they searched all over there, and "Get back in that dance hall!" you know. I went back in there and they'd taken the door off the closet and had Frog laying on it and up on the table. And, there was Grandma, sewing him up. Needle and thread. And they took him on that door, carried him down the stairs, out into a wagon, and hauled him over to the Wilson place and took him in the house on that door.

"Three, four days later they found that guy that Ed Kelsey had shot. He was under the bed in a bunkhouse. He'd been shot three places. Gangrene had set in and killed him. It all happened just like that.

"But, the flashlight, I'll never forget! It was probably one of the first I'd seen in my life; the biggest damned flashlight I ever seen in my life! We was living up at the Graham place and we'd walk back and forth to the dance hall and going to school in the dark, just by feel. We didn't have flashlights.

"One night there, at one of the dances they was having, some guy come in packing a banjo. And could he play that thing?!! Oh, man, he played! Never seen him again. Nobody knew who he was. He was somebody's sheepherder or something around the country.

"We'd have a dance and there might be one guy with a violin or a fiddle and maybe somebody with a guitar and maybe somebody with an old squeezebox. And, that was the music you had. There was a Davis from down in Twickenham always trying to sing, a red head.

"They had a dance over in Kinzua and she was playing the piano. And all of a sudden, she just reared up and she fell over backwards on the floor. Kerplunk!

"Hey, what's the matter?" we wondered.

"Mom said, "Oh, I think she's probably pregnant. Leave her alone." Somebody threw a cup of water in her face and she jumped up and she shook and went over and started playing the piano again."[16]

When Barney Thomas, a resident of Richmond, sent for a mail-order bride, he hired Fred's mother, Elsie Sarah Mabe, to clean his house for his new wife. While cleaning, Fred, his brother Robert Lee, and his mother stayed in Barney's house.

"Barney's wife came and we had a big party down at Richmond in the old dance hall. Shivareed them after they went to bed; banged on pots and pans and made a terrible racket. Then we moved down to what they called the Forest Graham place then. That's where Zach and Linda Keys lived. Grandpa Dedman built that place.

"Graham had six or eight kids and they went to school at Richmond. Bill Thomas had three or four kids in school. I think Bill Thomas had thirteen kids. There was 43 kids in school and there was two teachers at Richmond school house."[17]

---

16 Fred Dunn interview
17 Ibid.

J. W. Clarno, whose family name was given to the settlement which never had a town site, settled his farm in '65 about twenty miles southwest of Fossil. Of his 800 acres, he cultivated 160 acres and by 1905, he wanted $6,000 for the ranch, which by then supported 200 head of Hereford and Shorthorn cattle and 200 horses and boasted of an orchard with 200 fruit trees.

There was no post office there at the time; that would be established in 1894. The grade leading westward from Clarno towards the small town of Antelope in Wasco County was named the Chichester Grade after the family of Nannie Chichester, the first postmistress for Clarno.

Andrew Clarno's son, Charles had a fondness for the steamboats that traversed the Columbia River and he built a miniature, naming it the "John Day Queen." The small water vehicle served both as a ferry across the river and as a pleasure boat until the boiler blew up, ending Charles' venture. John Silvertooth, an old-timer from that area, related that the incident was due to the over-consumption of alcohol impairing the judgment of the involved parties.[18] The spark arrester from that famous Queen can be seen at the Fossil Museum.

Although there was some hope at one time that oil would be found in the Clarno area and residents were encouraged to invest in stock for the endeavor, nothing came of this plan. The biggest draw to the area was to be the rich geological finds. Oregon Museum of Science and Industry (OMSI) would eventually construct a camp there, naming it Camp Hancock after Lon Hancock, a prominent geologist who spent much time in the area. The fossils that were so plentiful near Clarno were abundant throughout the region of new settlement.[19]

Perhaps the shortest-lived post office in Wheeler County was Francisville. The building, located on upper Pine Creek, opened in January,

18 Steiwer in *Glimpses of Wheeler County's Past*, p. 28, 29
19 D. Frederic Carnes in *Pacific Northwest Homestead*, p. 51

1883, and closed in June. The small "community" by that name was located on what is known as the Charles Conlee ranch.[20] The post office was so short-lived that the only recollection of the facility is noted on the Bureau of Lang Management's General Land Office map made in 1899.

Another very small forgotten area of settlement was Barite, located near Antone in the southeastern corner of Wheeler County. The tiny community was never much more than a few homes and a post office established in 1901 and closed in 1906. The postmaster of the fleeting mail service was Reuben Fields, who also operated the small saw mill there. Barite's connection to the outside world was the semi-weekly stage that carried mail between Barite and Antone.[21]

Rock Creek Lake, in the mountains near Antone, was a resort for fishing and boating, picnics and dance, and was established in the early 1900s. An early entrepreneur, George Coleman "Buck" Glover, built the dance floor by the Rock Creek Lake. This gentleman was in charge of the dances and he capitalized on the social gatherings by selling candy, tobacco, hot dogs, fire crackers, and other necessities of celebrations. Two of the musicians were Bill and John Peterson.

Old-timers recalled the celebrations at Rock Creek Lake with many memories of the horse races held on the quarter-mile race track around the lake. Families often spent a night or two camping near the lake and fishing, taking a few days for a break from their work-filled lives. When the dances became a memory, the floor was torn apart and the lumber hauled to Dayville where it could be used again.[22]

In 1918 the Service Creek post office was established with May Tilley serving as the first postmistress. Located on the John Day River in a narrow valley, the small settlement never boasted enough of a popula-

---

20 Fussner in *Glimpses of Wheeler County's Past*, p. 36
21 Ibid.
22 Irene Glover, "Rock Creek Lake" in *History of Wheeler County*, p. 16

tion to attain the status of a town though there was a small store and a school. The nearest settlement was Richmond, which could be reached after winding around on a very steep road known as Donnelly Grade.

There were twenty pupils from age five to twenty the first year Service Creek was listed on the county school census. The school first opened in '08 and closed in '44. The school, like most in the area, was used as a community center and for church services and Sunday school.

An interesting note is that Service Creek went through various spellings through the years. It was known as "Sarrice Creek" in 1918 and marked "Sarvis Creek" on early maps, and the name was changed to "Sarricecreek" to "Servicecreek" and finally to Service Creek. [23]

As the settled areas developed, some were naturally geographically more suitable for larger populations. Too, residents gravitated towards the areas with more businesses, bigger schools, and more potential for immediate employment and growth. Not a small part of the movement was brought about by the rhetorical skills of some enterprising souls who, though definitely civic-minded, also could see potential for personal gain. Many of the smaller settlements were abandoned as the residents moved to more populated regions to pursue their visions for their families. Several of the early communities became lost to all but the memories of those who had struggled to build their own niche in the newly inhabited land.

There are few remains, if any, to mark the sites of several of the earlier settlements. Kinzua Corporation totally wiped out the area of its booming lumber town, replanting the area and returning it to the original natural state. Caleb can boast of a small cemetery with Cal Thompson's marker, among others, a silent reminder of past residents of the area. Antone's square stage-stop building with its small lookout tower

---

23 Fussner in *Glimpses of Wheeler County's Past*, p. 55, 56

Twickenham Grade School
Owned and renovated by Tom and Mary Fitzgerald

perched on top where residents kept watch for Indians and for the approaching stages still stands, but just barely. Richmond's status as an early community is evident in the buildings that endure, marking the area as a ghost town; the church is used occasionally as a place for community gatherings. The old dance hall toppled a few years ago and only memories remain of the events held there.

Grade has long been vacant with only a token grave remaining; nearby Burnt Ranch cemetery is used infrequently and is all that is evident of that historical area. No known local resident can remember any mention of Francisville. Waterman is merely marked by a road sign and the ruins of an old building becoming part of the soil.

The old livery stable still stands in Twickenham, though the picturesque but crumbling Riverside House was taken down a few years ago to prevent injuries to the curious. The Twickenham Grade School, built in 1905, was moved to a new location in time for its centennial to be celebrated. The small building is being renovated and the library-turned-bedroom was occupied by Bob Huntington when he was an overnight guest. The morning after he slept there, he reported hearing noises in the night.

"You suppose there is a ghost of an old student in there?" he asked with a grin on his face.

Perhaps. If there are spirits of the first settlers residing in the locations of the old settlements in the area, an old-timer would be the most likely to experience them with tongue in cheek, reliving the past and enjoying the memories. The reveries can be fun, and occasionally a story about the men involved in the beginning of Wheeler County's sheep industry will be recalled along with the reminiscing of the long-ago settlements.

Chapter 13
Wheeler County's Sheep Industry

Christian Meyer and the earliest of the adventurers who passed through Wheeler County found lush stands of bunch grass growing abundantly on the hillsides and in the meadows. However, they watched with concern as more and more stock cropped down the stands of grass as the stockmen entered the area. The initial settlers brought sheep and cattle with them, though sheep were the favored animal. Meyer preferred to tend his gardens for his livelihood, but he watched with interest as the sheep industry grew in the area.

"Sheep are better for this country than cattle for three reasons," Meyer contended, holding up a broad fist and raising a finger as he enumerated his points. "Number one, a good breeding ewe costs a whole lot less than a cow and most of the new settlers are living pretty close to their pocket books. Number two," he raised a second finger, "sheep produce two cash crops a year — both lamb and wool. Number three, the women need those fleeces to make the cloth to make the clothes," and the German raised his third finger.

The sheepmen were to learn that along with the benefits came the pitfalls which would eventually drive them to convert to raising cattle. Plagued by scab, severe weather, coyotes, and cattlemen, the sheep were to prove to be an important, albeit not long lasting, part of the economy for the young county.

"Can you smell 'em?" a traveler asked, wrinkling his nose as he pulled his horse up beside Meyer's fort-house one day late in '72.

"What?" Meyer asked, sniffing the air to the west, the direction from which the horseman had come, as he looked for the odorous culprit that was causing the undetected stench irritating the rider.

"Sheep. Hundreds of sheep. Stinkin' little bounders," replied the rider in disgust. "Eatin' every scrap of grass they come to, leaving stinkin' piles of secondhand grass in the dust behind 'em." He dismounted, leading his horse to the hollowed-out log full of water butted up against the pole corral where several sleepy-eyed horses stood switching their tails against the eye-flies that hummed busily around them.

"How far back?" Meyer asked, eyes on the road, expecting to see the wooly animals round the bend at any minute.

"Down at the creek," was the answer. "Afore you get to the Burnt Ranch, you know, back down there," and he gestured vaguely towards Cherry Creek fifteen or more miles to the west. "Couple a herders draggin' 'long behind, keepin' the wooly boogers movin'. Said cousins, Zachary Keyes and James Keys,[1] owned the sheep, movin' 'em to that area for the winter. Said there was 600 a them meadow maggots. They'll move 'em on up this way in the spring. Need to stop to rest 'em up fer now, let 'em lamb. Plan to settle east of Mitchell next spring on some land they got up there."

"I s'posed they was gonna come, sooner or later," Meyer shrugged. "Guess there'd been some brought up to Oregon as early as '43 from California.[2] S'posed to be a good investment. Can't fault a man fer tryin' ta make a livin'," and he eyed his fields proudly.

"Keyes's have 'bout 600 head," volunteered the traveler. "Cotswold ewes. Said they borrowed $600 from their Uncle James Keyes in Benton

1 Judith Keyes Kenny noted the difference in spelling the family name Keyes or Keys, depending on the family member's ancestor, Zachary Keyes or James Keys, each side claiming their spelling is correct. "Early Sheep Ranching in Eastern Oregon." Oregon Historical Quarterly. Volume LXIV, Number 2, 1963
2 Buhl in "Sheep Ranching in Wheeler County," in Glimpses of Wheeler County's Past, p. 83

County.[3] 'Bout 600 too many, you ask me," and he slapped his grimy hat against his dirty trouser leg, ridding the cap of any remnants of sheep dust.

Meyer rode to the sheep camp early the next spring, noting the young nutrient-rich grasses on the rounded hills east of Cherry Creek where the band of sheep had not yet grazed. With such an unusual abundance of native grasses, he figured the Keyes cousins had chosen a good year to begin their venture. As he drew near the sheep, he sniffed the odor the lone rider passing by his fort-house had commented about, but he didn't find it terribly offensive. The German kept hogs in a pen, horses in a corral, and cows in the barn; the varying scents of the livestock's droppings merely meant they were eating well.

He observed in awe as the herder's small brown and black shepherd dogs worked the sheep, watching the commanding gestures of the man with questioning looks, then springing into action to move in the direction indicated by the motioning hand. The dogs circled the wandering sheep and returned the straying animal slowly to the herd without causing as much as a ripple in the grazing flock. He marveled at the cleverness of the dogs; they would be worth their weight in Canyon Creek gold for the Keyes cousins.

The stories he'd heard about the sheepherder's hospitality proved to be true. Meyer ate lunch perched on a handy rock near the makeshift camp. There were beans, copious amounts of beans, paired with mutton steaks practically deep-fried in bacon grease in the large cast-iron skillet nestled among the coals. The herder had dumped a portion of his sourdough into a kettle, added flour, and patted the stiff dough into rounds, and then cooked the flattened circle in a frying pan placed on the campfire.

"Dough gods," he answered, noting Meyer's eyebrows raised in an unasked question. The men sopped up their bean juice with the fried

---

3 Kenny. "Zackary Taylor Keyes." <u>Oregon Historical Quarterly. Volume LXIV, Number 2,</u> <u>1963</u> (Author's note: Keyes's first name is misspelled; the correct spelling is Zachary

bread, then used the rounds to polish their plates clean before eating the last of the dough god. They licked their spoons clean, and then polished them on their pants' legs. Putting their inverted plates and tableware into the wooden box containing various cooking utensils signaled the end of the meal. Dishes were done.

Before he left camp, Meyer noted a few small lambs teetering on wobbly legs near the camp.

"Born this morning," the herder gestured towards the new babies. "Bit earlier 'n we 'spected. Make a slow trip to the ranch, but gotta start tomorrow, trail 'em there. Need to get more grass," and he motioned to the nearby hills where the herd had nearly depleted their grazing. The thirty or so mile trip to the Keyes's ranch would take several days with new lambs being born every day and slowing down progress. The herder would take advantage of the abundant fresh grass along the route.

The lambs grew rapidly from their mother's rich milk and from the plentiful spring grasses the herders found on the Keyes ranch just east of Mitchell. Nestled in a valley just under a rise about three and a half miles from town, the top of the pass soon became known as Keyes Summit, the creek as Keyes Creek. By the time the lambs were five months old, they were marching east on The Dalles — Canyon City Military Road to market. The cousins invested their earnings in yet more sheep, and their herds grew quickly to the typical size of 1,100 head in each band.

"Best get those letters sent," Zachary advised, and he and James wrote to young men they knew in Tennessee and Kentucky, asking them to come to the area to help during the lambing and shearing seasons, and to work as herders. The Keyeses appreciated the men "from home" and, as they all brought their traditions with them, the new area began to take on the feeling of their former state. Indeed, the area around Richmond was soon known as "Little Tennessee" by the locals.

Some of the workers would stay for a season and then return to their native state; others saved their wages until they had a nest egg and then branched out and began their own homestead and built up a small bunch of sheep.

Biffle's bottom land along the John Day, as well as that of his neighbors, was planted into crops that did well in the valley. As it was so resilient, alfalfa was often one of the first hay crops of choice. Three yields could be harvested from the fields and the sheep could be moved in to graze the stubble that was left. Providing grazing for a neighbor's band brought in a little much-needed cash for the farmers in the area.

"If we could get someone here," James explained to Zachary, pointing to a location on his map of the area, "and then here and here," and he established two more points with his pencil, and then drew a triangle connecting the dots.

"Get those homesteads proved up on, buy 'em back, and we can use all this unclaimed area in between for grazing," Zachary remarked, tracing the proposed land with his finger. This was a common practice for the earlier settlers, and it was to prove very beneficial for the sheepmen and, later, for the cattlemen.

As they contemplated the map, the cousins reached into their shirt pockets in unison, drawing out their pipes and their cotton bags of tobacco, filling the smoke-tarnished bowls and tamping the contents gently before lighting them and then leaning forward to study the map James had marked. They sat puffing their pipes contentedly, looking at the map thoughtfully, deciding where homesteads could be filed most strategically.

"Trail 'em to the mountains here after they're sheared in May," Zachary added, pointing to the general area of Badger Creek in the Ochoco Mountains south of Mitchell, "and summer 'em on the free grazing. Then, trail 'em back to the low country for winter and for lambing in March," and he settled back in his chair, running his fingers through his thinning hair which was receding from his forehead, satisfied that he and his cousin had chosen a profitable operation for their new venture.

"Need to watch the grass," James cautioned. "Some of the neighbors seem to think the grass'll bounce back soon's the sheep're off the pasture. Some of 'em have might near eaten the grass down to bare ground." Zachary nodded in agreement. The cousins were well aware the native grasses would serve the sheepmen well if they would, in turn, care for the pastures. Judging from the numbers of sheep moving through the area, the balance could easily be tipped and the range overgrazed, the animals left with too little feed.

"Market's good in Idaho for mutton in the gold field there," Zachary had reported after trailing a small bunch of mutton to hungry miners in the Canyon City gold field. "And, there's a good price to be had in The Dalles for the wool.[4] And, I'm thinking of Prineville for a market; might be the best route to go. Looks like we've got a winner, no matter how you look at it." Initially, he was proven to be right.

The cousins dissolved their partnership sometime in '80 or '81; James kept the horses and mules and the first home ranch, and Zachary moved the sheep to his permanent home on Keyes Flats, five miles north of Mitchell.[5] There, a son, Walter, was born to Zachary and Amanda Viola Booth. A second son, Henry Dick, was born in '85, and later Custer joined his brothers. Henry developed his father's love of sheep and remained a sheepman until his retirement, his operation typical of those of the surrounding area.

In addition to the devastation from scab and severely cold winters, Zachary and other sheepmen also had to contend with the cattlemen, who despised the wooly creatures, and the mutton-loving coyotes. The cattle-sheep wars of the late 1800s and early 1900s provided great en-

---

4 Buhl, "Sheep Ranching in Wheeler County"
5 Kenny. "Early Sheep Ranching in Eastern Oregon."

Zachary Taylor and Amanda Viola Booth Keyes
Judith Keyes Kenny archives

tertainment to those far removed from the problem; for those whose welfare depended on the sheep, however, the problem was a matter of life or death and there were lives lost before the matter was resolved.

Whenever he could, Zachary talked wise range management with his neighbors, but he could see that the early stock owners, sheepmen and cattlemen alike, eager for a profit, overstocked and mismanaged the rangeland. Not many years after the large influx of sheep and cattle to the area, it became obvious that the legendary grass would only support so many animals for a limited amount of time.

Zachary watched helplessly as the cattlemen and sheepmen disputed over the open range. The cattle tended to crop the tops of the grasses and move on; sheep were more apt to eat the grass down to the ground before moving to a new grazing area. As everyone had the right to use the public domain as they saw fit, there was no way to exclude one stockman or the other.

Crook County cattlemen became notorious for their persecution of the sheepmen and news of their escapades brought a fearful watchfulness to the ranchers in Wheeler County. Vigilante committees were formed and night raids on sheep bedding grounds were not uncommon. The sheep-killing men remained "anonymous" though many knew who they were; threats were made to those who could identify them, and, in one instance, a store-keeper who might have been able to identify the night-riders was killed.[6]

> ... certain it is the conditions to raise stock successfully and with fine financial returns exist well in Wheeler county. Being thus favored so especially, it seems doubly sad that the baser passions of men, blessed with this magnificent country, should so dominate them that they must seek revenge in that dastardly method fit only for the savage. We refer to the outrages of killing stock on the range. What a sight, to see the fair ranges of Wheeler county, stinking with the carcases of fine animals slain in mere revenge, perhaps of a fancied wrong! But such is the case and this blotch we are forced to chronicle, would we be faithful in writing the history.[7]

In '04, Zachary got word that the Sigfrit brothers had lost some of their cattle after an unknown person or persons placed poison on their range. Hearing about this, he charged into his house, knocking his shin on the small steamer trunk he'd packed on his back in '66 as he made his way across the Isthmus of Panama to catch the ship that would take

6 Buhl, "Sheep Ranching in Wheeler County"
7 F. A. Shaver et al. p. 647

him to Portland and then to his uncle's house. He had placed the small chest by his front door to remind himself just how far he'd come, he had explained to his wife as he set it down, and he wanted it to stay in that place of honor, despite an occasional sore shin.

"Where in thunder did that come from?" he scowled, and Viola sat rocking her baby and smiled patiently. Zachary's sore shin added to his anger and he ranted on and on about the dismal news of the ongoing war between the cattlemen and the sheepman.

> The *Wheeler County News* of May 27, 1904, says: "Poison was deposited on the range eight miles east from town, a short distance from the Canyon City road and the result of this cowardly act is that twelve head of range cattle belonging to Sigfrit Bros. died last week. The motive for this deed is unknown.
>
> "Following the poisoning episode came the news to town early Monday morning that about three a.m. five men attacked a band of yearling sheep in the corral on the place belonging to Butler Bros. of Richmond. One hundred and six sheep were killed and a greater number were so wounded as to either die or have to be killed. These sheep were being grazed on leased land, and no motive can be found why this should occur. It was thought, possibly, it might be the breaking out of another war between the sheepmen and cattlemen, and that the latter were responsible for the deed.[8]

Later that same year, Zachary's hands were again shaking and his deeply set dark eyes flashing in anger as he thrust the Wheeler County

8 Ibid.

News of September 23, 1904, towards his wife, demanding: "Read this! Just read this!"

> ...about five men, about eleven p.m. Friday... attacked a band of sheep belonging to Thomas Fitzgerald, camped at the side near the head of Westbranch. Thirty-eight were killed outright and twelve more died later. Two bullets passed through the herder's tent, and he quit the scene at once. Every law abiding person of the county was stirred at this fresh outbreak, and while there are grievances between the cattlemen and the sheepmen, and many of the law abiding citizens are on one side and many are on the other side, still, the consensus of opinion of all good men of sober judgment was that the matters above referred to were outrages of the worst kind and reflected great discredit on the fair name of Wheeler county, and cast a cloud on all citizens as though the place was filled with people not law abiding. But, such is not the case. The people of Wheeler county are law-abiding, and some day they will ascertain the perpetrators of such uncalled for deeds and mete out through the courts just punishment.[9]

According to some accounts read later in local history books, the number of sheep that were killed in the attack was 1,000, though Thomas Fitzgerald's grandson, Tom Fitzgerald, remembers the account as told by his grandfather differently.

"I don't remember just exactly when it was — about 1904, 1905. A herder, I think his name was Dick Bradshaw, handled some of my

---

9 Ibid.

Tom Fitzgerald's band of sheep in the early 1900s.
Sheep Mt. in the background. Courtesy of Tom Fitzgerald

grandfather's sheep; a band out in the hills and he was grazing them. One night a bunch of guys came by and killed about 100 head of them. I guess they were cattlemen. I don't remember — I've probably heard at one time who it was, but I don't remember.

"The detective that finally caught them was named Jesse Selkirk. He was a pretty skookum investigator, I guess, for that day and age. But, a man and his son were eventually convicted of that."[10]

Given that Fitzgerald ran about 1,100 head in each of his bands and that he was not wiped out by the night raid, the lower number of 100 head of sheep killed is probably more accurate, though not so sensational in the telling of the incident. Whatever the number of sheep killed, the Sheepman's Association paid a $2,500 reward and the Wheeler County government paid a $1,000 reward for the conviction of the culprits.[11]

---

10 Tom Fitzgerald interview
11 Buhl, "Sheep Ranching in Wheeler County"

Tom and Amy Fitzgerald with children, Ruby and Mark
Courtesy of Elsie Fitzgerald Simmons

Satisfied that justice had been served for that offender, Zachary knew, however, the sheepman's woes were far from over. There was still the boundary problem that seemed never-ending, compounded by overgrazing by the over-stocked ranches in the area.

To reserve grass for their own herds, large ranchers sometimes fenced off range land that may or may not have been within the boundaries of their holdings, ensuring the grasses could not be grazed by their neighbors' stock. That problem was resolved in 1905 with the formation of the National Forests. From that time on, a grazing permit was required for the stock growers, and this new regulation greatly alleviated the over eating, though stories have been passed down through the years of sheepherders professing their ignorance of the boundaries when they were caught foraging their animals far inside a dedicated pasture.

Zachary had to explain boundaries over and over to his herder, who could not — or would not — become familiar with the limits placed on the band of sheep grazing on the government land in the Ochoco

Mountains. The large "triangle pasture" which had encompassed huge areas of unclaimed lands could no longer be used, regardless that the grass always seemed greener where the neighbor had the grazing rights.

During the height of the sheep industry, the herds provided a good profit for their owners. One eastern sheep buyer came to the county and purchased 18,500 head to ship to the Chicago market. Some bands were trailed to either Prineville or to Condon where they were put into stock cars and shipped to their destinations by rail. Others were trailed to Heppner, where they would begin their trip to Montana or feedlots in the Midwest. By 1905, the number of sheep that were raised in Wheeler County was recorded at 200,000. The same year, there were 15,000 cattle and 8,000 horses feeding in the county.[12] Considering those large numbers of stock, no matter how lush the native grasses were it is no wonder that the range soon became overgrazed.

The sheep industry in the area had begun to draw statewide interest by the turn of the century, and the Western Historical Publishing Company from Spokane, Washington, had sent reporters out to interview locals. For a sizeable donation, individuals could have their biography published in History of Central Oregon, an Illustrated History, to be printed in 1905, as well as receive a copy of the book which would include a detailed history of the area.

"If I'm not important enough to be included without paying the money, I don't belong in there anyway," was Zachary's terse reply when approached by a reporter.[13] The money was better spent for a new Merino buck, he decided, and he traveled to the Fossil area to purchase just such an animal from Winlock Steiwer.

Among the best known families involved in the early sheep industry in the Fossil area was the Steiwer family. Winlock Steiwer had mar-

---

12 Stinchfield, "The Sheep Industry," in *History of Wheeler County*, p. 27
13 Kenny, "Early Sheep Ranching in Eastern Oregon." p. 122

ried Annie J. Hoover, the daughter of T. B. and Mary Jane Chambers Hoover. Born in Washington County, Oregon, Annie had arrived in Wheeler County in a covered wagon in 1870 with her family. Among her children was William "Bill" Hoover Steiwer, born in '96. William married Dorothy Kerns and they had two sons, Jack and William "Bill" H., Jr., both of whom remained in the county all their lives.

Bill helped manage the family ranch where they raised sheep, cattle, and hay. He entered into politics and served in the Oregon Senate for ten years, where he was president during his last term, Zachary was proud of sharing the story that his friend, Bill, was active in the Wool Growers Association, serving as president in both the Oregon and national organizations. He also was a director of the American Sheep Producers Council, president of the Northwest Livestock Production Credit Association ..."[14]

For years the Steiwers' billboard erected beside Highway 97 east of Fossil on part of their holdings encouraged passersby to: "Eat lamb, wear wool, for health, for beauty, and for goodness sake!" Passing travelers, especially the sheepmen, always grinned at the reminder beside the highway.

---

14 Steiwer, William H. and Jane Steiwer Campbell. "William H. Steiwer, Sr. Dorothy Kerns Steiwer." The History of Wheeler County, Oregon . p. 215

Chapter 14
The Sheep Business Changes

I know of no one more qualified to speak of sheep raising than my old friend Henry Keyes," wrote William
H. "Bill" Steiwer of Zachary's second son. "As a boy
and man he lived with the sheep, herded them, owned
them, through the lush years of high prices and favor-
able weather and through the years of drought and depressions. As county judge he contributed greatly to
the development of this part of the state.[1]

"Glad shearing is over with," Henry remarked to his wife, Grace
Apple, as she sat rocking their baby girl, Viola. Married in 1909 by his
grandfather, Robert Booth, the circuit rider who had started the church
in Richmond, Henry had first homesteaded on Dry Hollow just northwest of Twickenham, but later moved to the old Dedman Fort- House,
which he would own until '46. There he headquartered his own sheep,
continuing his father Zachary's sheep business in Biffle's valley where
that first homesteader had pastured his own band.

The sheep in Wheeler County had been sheared by shearing crews
of half a dozen men or so, depending on the size of the herd, beginning in May after lambing season and before the flocks were taken to
their summer grazing. The shearers had used hand shears, sharpened
to a fine edge to make the shearing easier. By 1900, the price charged
by most sheep shearers was somewhere in the neighborhood of seven
cents a head, depending on the sheepman telling the story, and Henry's

---

1 Kenny. "Early Sheep Ranching in Eastern Oregon," p. 101

shearing bill had crept up higher each year. He hoped each spring that the price of wool would increase along with the shearing cost. Within twenty years, the Twickenham-based sheepman would see the charge for shearing increase to around twenty cents[2], and by the mid-1900s, to a dollar a head.

In the early 1890s, the going price for wool was in the neighborhood of seventeen cents a pound. This increased to twenty cents at the turn of the century,[3] after some serious declines in prices due to the market being depressed.

"Just read this article on scab again. You might like to take a look at it," Henry told his wife, handing her a well-worn newspaper article. "This was written before I was even born, but it's worth reading from time to time, worth holding onto. Glad we don't have to worry about it too much. But, it's time again," he grinned wryly, referring to the onerous process of dipping his band of sheep in a liquid solution as a prevention against the disease. He rubbed his little daughter's head, fuzzing up the short unruly hair, and, shrugging his shoulders at the inevitability of the unpleasant task ahead of him, he went out the front door of his home.

In 1868, sheep had contracted scab, the dreaded wool-destroying disease and a condition that threatened annihilation of the bands near Prineville; the infection spread to some of the herds in nearby areas. The crisis was described as follows:

> These sheep had the doubtful honor of having the first case of scab in the settlement…we thought it was the mange..and we lost all our wool and nearly all our sheep before we learned what ailed them. Greasing the measly things with bacon rind did not cure them and some of

---

2 Buhl. "Sheep Ranching in Wheeler County." p. 90
3 Ibid. p. 92

Shearing shed in Twickenham built by Gordon Shown
Judith Keyes Kenny archives

us retired from the business with disgust. Why, the scab
is a native of this section. I have seen the coyotes perfectly naked with it; the rim rocks had it; the sagebrush
had it; it was in the grass, in the rocks, in the air and our
sheep caught it and had it bad.[4]

Fount Watkins[5] joined Henry, and the two men walked to the sheep
dip, opening the small gate at the end of the crowd-alley that led to the
forty-foot-long trench the men had dug earlier that week. They'd been
helped by an extremely gaunt passerby who had stopped at the ranch
for a few days to work for his meals. Once the dip-ditch had been dug to
Henry's specifications, the traveler had been sent on to Shoofly to help dig
another conduit there, and then a third one at the Robert Keys's ranch.

---

4 Ibid.
5 Watkins's first name, spelled as both "Font" and "Fount," is noted as "Fount" in BLM
records of his filing for ownership of an entire section, 640 acres, just east of Kentucky
Butte in Wheeler County, in 1923.

The ditch was wide enough to accommodate sheep without allowing them to turn around and deep enough that, when filled with water mixed with a sulphur and lime solution[6], the sheep could be submerged in the odorous mixture. Once it had been completely immersed, the animal would be prodded to the end of the pit where it would awkwardly shake off the wet concoction and stomp indignantly away from the place of torture.

Henry and Fount pushed the reluctant sheep into the crowd-alley and through the dip one at a time, stopping infrequently to rub a mixture of sulphur and lard on the sore mouth of a ewe. An occasional limping sheep was tipped over to the ground and Henry held the struggling animal down, gripping the sore leg and holding it still. Fount would prod a swollen lump between her hooves with his sharp pocket knife, lancing the infected area and dodging the putrid liquid that sprayed out. After locating the piece of cheat that had caused the infection, he would flip it to the ground, satisfied the infection would now heal quickly. The herder then applied a dab of the sulphur and lard mix to the infected area before Henry released the struggling ewe. She was ready for the trip to summer grazing.

"Lambs are starting to put on some weight," Henry observed as he, his son, Bill, and Fount stood watching the flock grazing on the foothill under Sutton Mountain, "but the grass is getting short. We need to start to the mountains in a few days, keep them on the Howard place for a few weeks, and be ready to push them onto the allotment when it opens up on July 1." Fount nodded in agreement. This was the practice many of the sheepmen in the area observed.

"Hard to believe this area had up to 12,000[7] head of sheep at the turn of the century, isn't it?" Henry asked his herder. Fount's eyes widened.

6 Buhl, Ibid. p. 90
7 Buhl, Ibid. p. 86

"12,000? You don't say," he declared in amazement. "No wonder the grass is so short," and he shook his head sadly. The two men stood quietly for some time, looking towards the north side of the river where the grasses was already beginning to wilt in the warm days of late-spring.

"Thankful we had an easy winter," Fount remarked to Henry. "Those poor Butler brothers. Took quite a beating in '90, didn't they?" he commented. Henry agreed, a hand-rolled cigarette bobbing from his mouth in time to the nodding head as he put a foot on the bottom rail of the juniper-pole corral fence the men stood near and leaned his arms on the top rail. Bill copied his father's movements, content to be an observer; he figured he'd be given an active part in the family business soon enough and for now he'd listen and learn. The two sheepmen stood quietly, content with the day, and reminisced, their eyes constantly scanning the valley before them, assessing the terrain with its natural pasture.

"The brothers are doing okay for themselves, though," Henry remarked. "They bounced back."

Two of the Keyes's neighbors were the Butler brothers, George and John, who had homesteaded on what was called Butler Mountain on their Shoofly holdings, land that would eventually be sold to Bill Jackson in 1944, after four generations of the family had lived on the ranch. They had two bands of sheep, a total of 2,400 of the wooly animals. During the unusually severe winter of '90, they had lost all but about 600 head of their stock. Despite the severe financial blow, the brothers wanted to stay in business. They rented sheep from Henry's father, Zachary, who would have shares in the lamb and the wool crops, an arrangement which proved to be mutually beneficial. The Butlers would stay in the sheep business until John's death in 1917.[8]

The "double winter" in the 1890s was Mother Nature's contribution

---

8 Jessie Butler Sharp in The History of Wheeler County Oregon. p. 56

to the miseries that plagued the struggling sheepmen in the area. Hundreds of sheep froze to death in their bedding grounds, despite the best efforts of the herders and their dogs to keep them alive. Stories about the severe weather would be passed down through the generations.

Years later, Richard Mortimore would remember that his grandfather, Harry Mortimore, had a band of sheep in the '90s. "Granddad got to talking about a double winter. I didn't know what he was talking about. Said, "Yeh, we had winter." He was going out to tend camp and take out groceries and what-not. Got out there, and, damn, it was getting cold. Anyway, the herder, he was off to town, drunk. So, Granddad took care of the sheep and cooked himself some supper and took care of the dogs.

"And he said, "If it hadn't been for those dogs, I'd froze to death." He put them dogs in bed with him. Anyway, they lost the whole damn band of sheep. Got wet, sweating, stuck together. Couldn't get apart and smothered."[9]

Leaning on the top rail of his corral fence, Henry took a sideways glance at his herder, feeling he was as much a friend to him as he was a hired hand. He'd heard a lot of stories about one of his favorite characters, the man beside him with his wool shirt tucked haphazardly into the waistband of his well-worn canvas pants, his high-topped shoes covered with sheep manure and mud from the dipping trench. He grinned to himself as he observed Bill copying the herder's every move, straining to put his booted foot on the same high juniper pole Fount was using as a prop.

By Fount's own words, he was run out of Tennessee because he was just too good a shot. Henry had heard the story often.

"Fount Watkins was, by his own admission, the best shot in all of Tennessee, all of Oregon and, for that matter, probably all of the area in

---

9 Richard Mortimore interview

between. Why, it was in part this very skill that got him into trouble back in Tennessee and prompted him to head west to Richmond, Oregon, where his cousin worked on a ranch.

"He didn't really understand why all the local highbrows were upset with him, when all he did was shoot a fox — the last fox in Johnson County, or so they claimed. But hell, if they didn't want it dead, why on earth did they chase the silly thing around every Sunday with hounds, horses and guns. Any fool could watch the whole affair twice and see that the fox always made his escape through the same hole in the stone wall that bordered Fount's place.

"It was an easy matter for Fount's trained eye to pick the fox off that last Sunday before he left because the fox always paused and looked back just before he darted through. Fount reckoned he'd help those fellers out when he heard their hounds baying and saw the fox coming across his field. How was he to know they would get so upset? Oh well, it didn't matter much. He never needed much of an excuse to start out on a new adventure and those redcoats looking down their noses at him was all it took.

"After arriving in Oregon he worked for several outfits herding sheep. The folks out here sure didn't seem to mind him picking off a coyote or two. In fact, the more the better. His handiness with a firearm paid off many a time out there on the range. It didn't hurt any for the local "revenuers" to know what a good shot he was either as he also brought some other skills with him from Tennessee.

"One time he told me a story that I just couldn't believe, though. I was still just a little guy, 'bout nine or ten and he had told me so many stories I never knew what to believe. Every time I thought I had him, he'd go out and show me some fancy shooting or dig out a gallon jug just to prove he wasn't lying.

"Well, one evening we were sitting around my Uncle Bags' house

(George Donnelly) at Richmond. It was just my uncle, Bill Asher (Fount's cousin), Fount and I. Those three were having a great time filling my head with stories about sheep camp and coyotes and bears. So I asked Fount if he had ever shot a bear. He said no, he had never shot a bear, but he had killed one once with a water pipe. I couldn't believe that one so he proceeded to explain it all to me.

"It was like this. Fount was herding sheep out in the desert country by Fort Rock. He had to use water trucks and get water from wells and haul it out to the sheep every day. Well, a neighboring allotment of Lafe (Lafayette) Jones of Mitchell had a huge storage tank. It was about six feet high and eight feet across and had a two foot opening in the top, just a manhole, I could guess. And there was a ladder which you could climb to check the water level.

"One day a little bear came down out of the mountains and walking across that desert country must have made him pretty thirsty. He must have smelled water and climbed right up that ladder and jumped in the tank. Luckily, or maybe not, there was not enough water in the tank to drown the critter, and who knows how long he had been in there when Fount came along to look at the tank. When Fount climbed the ladder, I don't know who was more surprised, him or the bear.

"Fount did not know just what to do. He couldn't leave the bear in there to eventually die. He couldn't shoot it for fear of puncturing the tank, and how would he get the bear out? So he decided to put the ladder down the hole. The bear wouldn't climb up the ladder as long as Fount was sitting there, and Fount couldn't jump off for he'd never get back up there again to retrieve the ladder. So he sat there and pondered his dilemma for a while. Then who should ride up, but Bob Palmer, the government trapper. Bob had a rope on his horse, and he and Fount decided to lasso that bear and pull him out.

"It took some doing because the bear was not a willing party to these shenanigans. Eventually they got him out but they still didn't know what to do with him. Fount still did not want to shoot him for fear of puncturing the tank (regardless that he was the "best shot in all of Oregon"). He remembered seeing a piece of water pipe nearby so he got that and decided to see what he could do with it. He walloped him a good one over the head with it and it didn't seem to faze the bear at all. He hit him again and the bear started to sink a little. So he kept going at it until the bear was dead.

"I couldn't believe it. I figured Fount was lying to me this time. I was building up my nerve to call him on it when the dogs started putting up quite a ruckus. We all looked out to see who was coming, and who do you think it was? Bob Palmer, the government trapper. We had just finished supper and I was ordered to put the beans back on the stove and get out the fruit and biscuits, standard fare in those days. I kept my mouth shut just long enough for Bob to get his mouth full. Then I asked him, "Say, Bob, what do you think of someone saying he killed a bear with a water pipe?"

"He chewed his biscuit very slowly, swallowed and said, "Well, if I didn't know better, I'd call him a liar, but the fact is Fount here and I did just that once out in the desert country by Fort Rock. It was like this…"

"Fount had me again. The only person who could prove his tale had appeared like the Angel Gabriel, bearing the truth. I never doubted Fount again."[10]

A serious problem the sheepmen faced from the minute the first of the Keyes' band stepped into Wheeler County was that of the growing population of coyotes, a voracious predator. An article in the Fossil Journal in 1895 declared "…that each coyote destroyed 11 — 50 head of sheep worth $1.50 - $2.00 each year. In 1895, the Gilliam County

10 Linda Donnelly Miller and Roderick Donnelly, "Fount Watkins" in *History of Wheeler County*, p.234

court granted a temporary bounty on coyotes... They paid $1,300 in coyote bounties 'to the incalculable benefit of the county' in March 1896."[11] One of the best-known of the government trappers in the history of Wheeler County would be Bob Palmer.

Bob Palmer, the son of Charlie and Lizzie Palmer who set up their homestead on Rowe Creek in 1884, trapped predators most of his life, and it was said that in his career he trapped 5,000 of them.[12] Bob rode a horse while he ran his trap lines and wherever he ended up at night was his home; he timed his days to arrive at the home of a host where, sometimes, he had a clean change of clothing to change into if a trip to town were in the making.

Bob, a truly liberated and memorable individual, kept the tools of his trade stashed at strategic places on his trapping route. Traps, stretcher boards, and poisoned bait were part of the necessities for the "coyote trapper" as his friends called him, and the trapper was an independent-thinking soul.

"Bob would step up on Dad's workbench and reach high onto the top of a rafter and retrieve his jar of coyote bait. The mixture of strychnine, pieces of fish and deer that had been dead a year or more, bits and pieces of flesh scraped from the hides of the animals he'd trapped, and Bob-only-knew what else, had an odor of its own not easy to forget.

"...The stench was unforgettable and we kids looked forward to a whiff of the strong smelling potion, trying to outdo each other by seeing who could stick their noses closest to the jar and sniff the hardest.

"One day Bob opened the jar to add some fresh flesh and stirred the mixture with the blade of his knife. He fished out a piece of rotten flesh that was too big for his liking and, placing it on the greasy shop bench, he cut the meat into several pieces. Finishing with the bait, he recapped

---

11 Buhl. "Sheep Ranching" in *Wheeler County's Past*, p.91
12 Patsy Younce. "The Descendants of Charlie and Lizzie Palmer." in *History of Wheeler County*, p. 178

the jar and put it back in the place high above the reach of little hands. Then, he wiped his knife blade on his well-worn and little washed jeans, took the apple Pete offered him, and whittled off a few pieces to eat.

"I don't think Bob owned more than two pairs of jeans at once. One was for work, one for special occasions. One morning when I opened Bobby's bedroom door to wake Bob, I saw his jeans seeming to literally stand beside his bed.

"My brothers got to share their bedroom with Bob and related how he'd wear a tee shirt frontwards, then turn it around backwards when the front was dirty. Then the shirt would be turned inside out and worn both frontwards and backwards. He kept a few shirts scattered around at his hosts' homes, so he did get that apparel washed more often than his jeans. Bob got a lot of mileage out of his clothes."[13]

Bob was a favorite of adults and children alike and he spent time at night playing checkers or card games with the youngsters and card games with the men of the family, Henry Keyes among them. On occasion, he was known to "accidentally" tip the game board over if it were apparent he was going to lose.

After the children went sent to bed, Bob sat and visited long into the night with his hosts, sharing stories in a loud and clear voice that the eavesdropping children, supposedly tucked snugly into their beds, could hear just fine from their hideaway in the stairwell.

Henry heard Bob repeat a story that had been passed around for some time and by so many folks that no one can remember who first told the tale or when. The account was worth repeating over and over, though, to the delight of his hosts and to the amusement of the snickering, supposedly-sleeping hidden children sitting with their hands over their mouths to suppress their snorts of laughter.

---

13 Mary Fitzgerald. *My Twickenham.* .Xlibris Corporation. United States. 2007

Seems like some tender-hearted environmentalists were objecting to the trapping of coyotes, declaring it was inhumane. A meeting was called to discuss the problem and sheepmen, lawyers, politicians, and a few environmentalists attended, each intending to give their opinions to the assembly.

Statistics were given by the sheepmen for the number of sheep killed, the number of coyotes trapped, and the estimated number of kills per coyote per year. One of the fair ladies from the "Valley," a name given by locals to residents of Oregon west of the Cascades, stood to plea her case from the animal-lovers' point of view.

"Trapping," she declared, "seems so inhumane and unnecessary. Surely there can be a solution to the problem other than trapping; perhaps sterilization to prevent further propagation of the coyote? Possibly they could be fitted with prophylactics?" She nodded intelligently at a nearby sheepman, smug and sure of her solution.

The gentleman looked her up and down, noting her tailored suit, her neatly coifed hair, her beauty-salon fingernails, and her flawless make-up. The lady had come prepared to win the battle.

The sheepman rose to his feet, shoving his seat back gently with his well-muscled, jean clad legs, his threadbare plaid shirt neatly pressed, his worn and scuffed cowboy boots cleaned of sheep manure and polished to a shine in deference to the occasion.

"Ma'am," he said softly, looking her straight in the eye. "The coyotes are eating my sheep; they're not screwing them." There would be no condoms dispensed in Wheeler County that day.

Henry Keyes would continue his sheep ranching in Twickenham across the river from his first home on the Dedman place. Although his family had suffered during poor economic times in '05 and '06 and he had investigated the possibility of homesteading in Canada, Henry had returned to the family ranch and remained there with his sheep until he retired in the mid '50s, moving to Fossil, where he sold real estate for a number of years.

Henry recalled warmly how, as a youngster, he had enjoyed his days of riding for the cattle of Henry Wheeler, whose ranch had adjoined Zachary Keyes's ranch. As a young man when Henry ran for county judge, Wheeler had asked him to drive him to the polls. Henry Keyes would hold the office of county judge for twelve years, from 1913 to '25, and was remembered as "Judge Keyes" by many of the old-timers in the county.

His wife, Grace, became diabetic and died in 1914 at the Dedman Fort-House. Henry remarried in '17, to Bonnie Anna May Stransky, and the couple had three children, Dickse, Pete (Henry Dick, Jr.), and Judy.[14]

Henry's second daughter continued her family's sheep business, the third generation in the Keyes family to work with the wooly critters. Her years in the sheep business seemed to mark the transition from a time of Wheeler County's profitable sheep industry to one of a supplemental industry for local ranchers.

Dickse Keyes Williams, and her little sister Judy, along with their brothers Bill and Pete, had, as youngsters, helped trail the herd of sheep to their summer pasture, and then back home, where older sister Viola waited for them. Fount Watkins was one of their father's employees they remembered especially well.

Part of the thrill of the herding was the sharing of the meals with the sheepherder, the food made tastier because of the energy expended while helping with the sheep. Meals usually included beans, fried sour dough, bacon or mutton, and dried fruit — three times a day. Henry's children looked forward to the time spent with their father's sheep and the colorful herder, and Dickse became her father's right-hand man at an early age.

---

14 Judith Keyes Kenny, "Henry Dick Keyes," in History of Wheeler County, p. 136

Each March and early April, until she was sixteen years old and left for college, Henry's shadow worked beside him, her brothers, and the sheepherders, helping lamb out the bands in Twickenham. Extra help was hired for the season, and the lambing was done in sheep sheds. The use of the shed lowered the lambing losses considerably and, as a bonus, added to the sheepmen's comfort.

A band consisted of about 1,000 to 1,200 head of sheep, depending on which sheepman was telling the number, and as Henry kept three bands of 1,000 sheep, there always seemed to be more work than the herders could manage. Big brother Bill left the family ranch when he was old enough to work for wages, so Dickse's help was continually encouraged and welcomed.

Sitting on some scattered hay to avoid sitting in lamb scours, and then leaning her back against a wooden panel, Dickse would cuddle a weak lamb on her lap, a rubber nipple-topped bottle in her hand, coaxing the orphan to drink. She'd croon softly, rubbing the knobby wool on the newly born animal's side and stroking its throat, trying to save the life of the little creature that seemed to have been born with a will to die.

The lambs' tails were bobbed and the little males castrated after it appeared that they were going to survive, which was about a week after their birth. As a child, Dickse's first job was to squirt KRS, an odorous black disinfectant, on the wounds. When she grew strong enough to hold the wriggling, terrified lambs, she would grit her teeth and hold the lambs up while Henry cut their tails off; then, if she held a male, the lamb would be castrated. A squirt of KRS on the wounds and the lamb was released.

Although Dickse learned to use the knife expertly, she never did like that part of the marking process and usually left the bloody work to Pete and Bill. It was more fun to squirt an unsuspecting brother with a bit of the KRS, a prank that was sure to earn her a scolding from Bonnie, as the disinfectant left a black mark on clothing that no amount of scrubbing on the washboard would remove.

Dickse looked forward to the shearing, which was done early in May. The ten-man sheep-shearing crew would set up and Dickse's job was to keep the pens full, moving the unshorn sheep down the narrow crowd chutes. The noisy thump-thump of the gasoline engines used to run the shearing machines, the choking smell of the spent fuel, the bleating of frantic sheep panicked by the whole episode, the barking of the darting sheepdogs as they helped control the animals, all added to the confusion in the packed space.

Henry's daughter would force the reluctant sheep through a swinging section of burlap and into the holding pens made of wood panels on two sides, and covered on the side next to the shearer with a large wool sack. The large brown burlap bag allowed the shearer to reach in, grab a leg, and drag the bleating, wildly kicking sheep into position to shear.

Dickse's body was too slight for her to handle the odorous task of tromping wool; after the wool had been sheared from each sheep, a fleece-tier formed a bundle of the wool with his feet, tied it into a semi-secure package with twine made from heavy, twisted brown paper, and tossed it into a large sack hanging in a woolsack frame. The burlap bags were easily six feet deep and about three feet in diameter.

Dickse volunteered once to tromp wool. Once. She'd waited until the bag was about a third full, then dropped from the top of the sack into the soft pile of lanolin covered, tick infested wool and tromped for all she was worth, trying to pack the fleeces tightly. The fleeces smelled of the oil still warm from the sheep's body, freshly mashed manure, and splatters of the oil from the shearers' hand-pieces, but Dickse learned quickly she couldn't hold her nose and tromp wool at the same time.

Little brother Pete kept tossing the tied bundles into the large burlap bag with a mischievous grin on his face, hitting Dickse on the head until she was covered with traces of sheep droppings mixed with bits of sticky weeds, ticks, and the fat from the wool.

The noise of the smoke-belching gas engine, the barking of the dogs, the bleating of the sheep in the crowd alley, and the cursing of the shearers at the struggling sheep, drowned out Dickse's insistent demands that Pete quit pelting her with the filthy fleeces. When his smiling face appeared at the top of the wool bag, the little wool-tromper screamed at her brother to stop, whereupon he cupped his hand behind his ear, mocked a questioning look, and, grinning at her discomfort, threw another bundle of wool at her.

She saw an occasional tick attached to the fleeces as she worked the bundles into the bottom of her temporary burlap prison, and she squirmed away from the bloodsuckers. By the time she had packed the large wool bag as best she could and had stomped her way to the top where she could grab the circular sack frame and swing out, she could imagine a dozen of the bloated ticks feasting on her body.

"Don't think you've got enough weight to be a wool tromper, Dix," Henry observed with a wry grin, looking at the loosely packed fleeces in the wool sack and leaning close to her ear so she could hear him above the noise in the shearing shed. She agreed readily, shaking her head vigorously, made a face at Pete, and stomped back to the crowd chute gratefully.

When the last sheep had been sheared and the bleating, freshly shorn animals pushed out of the shed, the shearing plant was turned off. The silence was deafening in its suddenness, leaving a void in the round barn Gordon Shoun had built for his family and shared with his neighbors.

After the sheep shearers had packed up their tools and had headed up to Richmond to their next job, Henry would have the large bags of wool loaded onto a flat wagon bed and he and his children would make the trip to Shaniko, at one time the wool-shipping capital of the world. The eighty-mile trip would take a few days, the team of horses straining to pull the heavy load up the Rowe Creek grade leaving Twickenham.

There was another slow downhill pitch in the road out of Fossil to the south, leading down to Pine Creek, and an even longer and harder climb from the river at Clarno to the top of the hill near Antelope. Then, there was the final steep and winding grade from Antelope to Shaniko, and getting to the top of that last hard pull was always a good feeling. Dickse and her brothers rode their horses much of the way but often would walk for a break from the saddle. Even walking, they could easily keep up with the horses pulling their heavy load of wool up the steep pitch in the winding road.

Once in Shaniko, Henry left his youngsters to fend for themselves while he dealt with the wool buyers. With a few dollars in their pockets, Dickse and her brothers wandered the main street of Shaniko, looking into shops and occasionally purchasing some small item for little sister Judy or for their mother. They met Henry for dinner at the Shaniko Hotel, sharing their meal with wool buyers and sheepmen, then sought their own amusement again until they made their way to the camp for the night. Hauling the wool to market was an annual trip made easier when Henry purchased an old truck that could make the journey in one day.

When the snow had melted from the high peaks east of Mitchell and the tender young grass was high enough to provide feed for the sheep during their journey, Henry would announce, "It's almost time to move the sheep." The sheep-dip treated band of sheep would be trailed to the Ochoco Mountains above Mitchell to the old Howard place that Henry's father had bought. This was Henry's base of operation for the summer, and from there the sheep would be grazed on the Forest Reserve land where Henry had an allotment for twelve hundred head of sheep.[15]

"Can I go? Can I go?" Dickse would ask eagerly. "May I go?" she would amend, glancing at her mother to see if she was impressed with her proper use of English. Bonnie, amused at her little daughter, would glance at her husband and the Judge would smile and nod his head.

15 Kenny, "Early Sheep Ranching in Eastern Oregon," p. 108

The herders would drive the band pastured on the north side of the river to the wooden bridge crossing the John Day, cursing and thumping the lead sheep with a branch of sage until the scared animal pattered over the wooden planks. Once a few sheep crossed, the others followed quickly.

They wound their way out of the valley, past Sam Davis's ranch, following Girds Creek so the sheep would have water throughout the day as they grabbed quick bites of the fresh spring grass growing in the narrow valley worn through the ages by the creek.

The tiny hoofs of the sheep pattered on the packed soil until the dew-dampened dirt was churned up into a cloud of dust that filled nostrils and choked the herders at the back of the band. The pungent odor of fresh sheep droppings mingled with the dust, but even more strongly came the smell of juniper and sagebrush.

To break the tedium of trailing the band of plodding sheep, Bill or Pete would grab a handful of the fresh sheep droppings and bombard Dickse, who would immediately gather her own soft handful and return fire. The skirmish over, she would wipe her hands on her pants leg and reach into a pocket where she'd tucked a handful of the dried corn she'd taken from the sheep feed the night before. She would put half a dozen kernels in her mouth, and chew on the snack as she ambled after the part of the herd that was her responsibility.

When the little herder became thirsty, she'd stretch out on the rocky bed by Girds Creek and drink from a small inlet of water unclouded by the sheep's hooves, scooping the water into her hands and drinking from them.

"Will-ya, Wont-cha, Do-ya, Don't-cha, Repeat. Will-ya Two, Wontcha Two, Do-ya Two, Don't-cha Two, Repeat Two." Dickse chanted the names of her bummer lambs as the ragged white backs of the freshly sheared sheep bounced up and down hypnotically and Dickse, plodding along at the rear of the band. She'd sometimes name as many as two dozen lambs that had been separated from their mothers either by the ewe's death or by her inability to care for her offspring. The little bummers were tame to the point of being difficult to trail as they'd stay near Dickse, hoping for a bottle of milk.

"You've got to watch these sheepherders, Dix," Henry advised her as they sat near the campfire, enjoying a bit of warmth before they tumbled into their bedrolls spread on the ground for the night. "Learn the boundaries and where to drive the sheep. Those Irishmen are going to get the best grass for their band and they'll stretch the boundaries to the limit if you don't watch them. It's not the herders that catch what-for when they get on someone else's land.

"That Johnny Joyce! He knows the land better 'n I do. Got caught going for some good grass far inside the boundary of a rich pasture bordering my allotment last year. Pleaded innocence so pathetically with that Irish brogue of his that the poor landowner took pity on him and carefully drew a map on the ground, explaining just where the sheep belonged. Old Johnny, he just nodded and asked about the landmarks and convinced the old buzzard he was totally lost. Fellow offered his own herder to help Johnny get my sheep back where they belonged!"

"You gotta watch out for those cattlemen, too," he cautioned. It's not been all that long since they killed that hundred head of sheep that belonged to old Tom Fitzgerald. Biggest kill in Wheeler County."

"Who'd shoot a sheep?" demanded Dickse, squirming to get more comfortable on the large rock she was using for a seat, though she knew the story well; she'd heard it countless times through her early years.

"Five fellows raided the band at night. Herder hid and wasn't hurt. Man and his sons were the culprits. County had to take care of the wife and the kids while the fellows were in jail. Didn't like sheep."

"Why'd they take out their beef on sheep?" Dickse grinned at her choice of words. "Sheep're smart'n cows. That's what you always say."

"Sheep n' cattle war, Dix," Henry replied. "Sheep n' cattle war. Only so much open rangeland and the sheep eat the grass, move on, and the cows can't live on what a sheep leaves behind. Overstocking. Kills the grasss. That's why the herders have to keep moving the band."

"Tell me about the allotment," Dickse demanded. "If the land belongs to the government, won't they take care of our sheep?"

"National forests were created in '05. After that, the U. S. Forest Service required a federal permit. Limit of 16,000 sheep to any one of us sheepmen. Didn't affect me any. Never had more'n 16,000. It's working out. Still, have to watch those damned cattlemen," and Henry took a pull from his bottle. "Forest department won't watch them for us."

"Tell me about Walt Jordan's toes again," Dickse begged her dad, though she'd heard that story a dozen times, too.

"Walt was herding up in there somewhere," Henry gestured vaguely towards Sutton Mountain with his half-smoked cigarette. "He was supposed to be cutting me a load of poles while he was at it. Problem was, it turned out, he'd been sharing too much moonshine with some of his friends and didn't get the job done. Day or two before I was supposed to show up to get the load of poles, he went to cutting and hacking like a son-of-a-gun, trying to get the poles all cut before I showed up. Whacked off a few of his toes.

"His dog came down alone. Found him trotting down the road on the way to our place. Had a kerchief tied around his neck. I untied it and some toes fell out. Walt had sent his toes with the dog to let us know he'd chopped them off and needed help." Dickse wiggled her pudgy little body deeper into her bedroll, envisioning the severed toes and relishing the bedtime story she almost knew by heart.

Dickse graduated from Mitchell High School when she was sixteen; by the time she was eighteen, in '38, she had graduated from Oregon Normal School in Monmouth with her teaching certificate. The United States was recovering from the Great Depression in the late '30s, and

Henry had lost some of his land holdings simply because he could no longer pay the taxes on all his properties. The ranch the family was living on in Twickenham was purchased by Dickse for the back taxes amounting to about $1,400. Henry retained the old McAllister place, Biffle's original homestead area, as he felt the ranch had more potential than the land Dickse was purchasing.

Dickse borrowed $1,276 from Howard Mortimore to pay the back taxes and the ranch was hers. The eighteen-year-old taught school at Pine Creek for one year, then moved to Twickenham and began the work of clearing the land on her new ranch, planning to plant crops to feed the band of sheep she hoped to acquire. When she married Bob Williams the year she turned twenty-four, the couple began raising children — eight of them — and a little band of sheep on the property bordering the John Day River.

Dickse's oldest son, Pete, learned to shear sheep while he was in high school and did so for many years. He entered and won the state 4-H sheep shearing contest one year. While he was practicing on one of the bummer lambs belonging to his parents, a younger sister heard him utter the word "Damn!" That kind of language by their children was not acceptable to his parents, so the little sister dutifully tattled on her big brother.

When questioned about his slip of the tongue, Pete replied to his mother that he understood why sheep shearers used the language they did. He didn't get into trouble as his mother had a firm knowledge of the temperament of sheep in general and of bummer lambs in particular, a philosophy shared by many of those sheep owning folks who were exposed to the unpredictable animals.

One of Dickse's friends, Dale Cole, remembered the ranch started by his father, C. A. Cole, as having a band of sheep for many years on his ranch near Mitchell. "Lyle and I, when we took over in '47, we ran a band of sheep for practically ten years. Sold them out in '59. Then we went to cattle and had them until '86.

"We had the sheep sheared; that was part of our payday, was wool from the sheep. It got hard to get the sheepherders. There were coyotes, too, you know. We had foot rot in the sheep, which is a bad disease, and then we had parasites that set us back pretty good.

"What did I like best about sheep? Selling them. They're a lot of work. Lambing time, we were up night and day. And, you had to keep an eye on the sheepherders.

"We'd hire a sheepherder in the spring. When we started lambing, we had two or three guys helping the herder when they were lambing, which was about six weeks. And the herder was with them on the summer range.

"Then, when they'd come in the fall, I'd look after them until feeding time. While the herder was out there, we'd have to look after him about twice a week. Carry him the groceries and whatever it took to maintain the camp. Hunt the sheep when he lost them. We had an Irishman herder one time and he'd lose half of them and when I was looking for them, he'd lose the rest of them.

"We've had a lot of dry years, which makes the grass grow less. Overgrazing. I believe the sheepmen overgrazed. There was a powerful lot of sheep in this country in those days. I was on a county committee way back and there was 110,000 sheep in this county."[16]

Someone who did his share to eradicate the pesky coyotes in Dickse's valley was Carl Naas. He married Irene Misener, whose parents, Virgil and Mary, raised sheep in Twickenham, and Carl hunted the predator every chance he got. Before Carl and Irene were married, he visited the Misener ranch and he and his future brother-in-law, John, killed a coyote.

"John Misener and I had killed a coyote and we wanted to know

---

16 Dale Cole interview

how to skin one, and we knew Blaine Winebarger was an old trapper and he knew how to skin. Well, he happened to be at the Pink Spur (the saloon in Mitchell) and we went and got him and he was drunk. So, he opened up the back of his jeep.

"He says, 'I've got a coyote in here I'll show you how to skin,' and he opened up the back and there sat the coyote, growling at him. He thought he had hit the coyote hard enough in the head to kill it, but he hadn't. The coyote was in the back, alive, and Blaine was drunk.

"We knew he couldn't help us, the way he was, and we often wondered how he got home with that live coyote in the back. That was strange! That was a Mitchell experience.

"We were coming home to Twickenham for elk hunting, and Chris Perry was with us. We saw a coyote out in the field, so Chris shot it. He went running out there to get it. And, he picked it up and hung it over his shoulder and started walking back to the pickup and the coyote came alive and bit him in the rear end.

"He threw the coyote down and went to shoot it at point blank range, and I said, "Don't, Chris! You'll ruin the hide!"

"So then he grabbed the barrel of the gun and hit the coyote over the head with the butt of the gun and finally knocked the coyote out and brought it in and then John and I wanted to administer first aid to his wounds, because they were very deep.

"And, he wouldn't let us help him! He was a very uncomfortable young man for quite a while. But, he went back outside and the coyote was sitting up in the pickup, still alive!"[17]

One of the few female trappers to work in the county was Evelyn Fitzgerald, who caught her share of the coyotes in the Mitchell area. "I used to trap," she explained. "The prices went down on the pelts, so I

17 Carl Naas interview

haven't trapped for quite a while, but it's real interesting. When I first started in, I thought it should be real simple to get those coyotes to stick their foot in that trap. But, there's an awful long ways from setting the trap to getting them to stick their foot in it!

"It really was fun. I trapped coyotes and cats and beaver and mink. Mostly coyotes and cats was what I went for, but I did clean out a bunch of beavers that were cutting up a neighbor's corrals and using them in their dams. I proceeded to fall in the pond one time at about 20 below zero!"[17] Despite her chilly dip, the lady trapper continued to do her share to eradicate the pesky coyotes.

The offspring of sheepmen learned to help early, and were always glad to share their memories. One of those youngsters was Fred Dunn, who spent much of his childhood near the Bob Keys ranch in Richmond. Though his parents didn't have sheep, Fred Dunn recalled going with a sheep-shearing crew when he was thirteen. "It was Cliff Beeson's crew. He lived in Condon. I think there was eight men on that shearing crew. Maybe just six. Two guys from California, Uncle Clyde and his partner, and there was two more people. Boy, it was a lot of fleeces for me.

"I didn't like working with the sheep. They stink! We started at Bob Keys's place. He had that big shearing shed there. We started there and I think we did three bands there. I don't know who they belonged to. I think one of them was Grandpa Mabe's. And, I think Keys had two bands, maybe. Donnellys bought some sheep. We sheared all those and then we took off and we went to Silver Lake. Five bands of sheep to be sheared.

"My hands. Remember those paper strings we used to tie fleeces? Big old heavy leather gloves on, by noon they're cut all to pieces by that paper string. Oh, my hands got so sore!

"I got home and Uncle Clyde, he went in the bedroom and he was in

---

17 Evelyn Fitzgerald interview

there a long time. Pretty soon, he hollered, "Freddy, come here!" I went in there and he had all this money laid out. And he said, "There's what you earned this year." Six hundred dollars. He paid me with hundred dollar bills.

"He said, "What are you going to do with it?"

And I said, "Give it to Mom." That's where it went. Bought her first car with it."

Dickse taught school in Mitchell for several years, to help supplement the meager income from her sheep and her ranch in Twickenham, and one of her all-time favorite people was Virginia Humphreys. The two schoolmarms shared sheep ranching stories during their breaks from their respective classrooms. After Virginia had married Bob Humphreys in 1949, the couple returned to Wheeler County to Bob's family home on Waterman Flat where Bob's mother was engaged in the sheep business. It was here Ginny learned about sheep ranching, Wheeler County style,[18] and she and Dickse could always laugh about their experiences with the wooly animals.

"I don't know for sure how long the Humphreys were in business," Virginia told Dickse. "Mr. Humphreys (Rhys) came here before the 1900s. I'm not sure when, but it was after your granddad. He'd been educated at Oxford and then he came to America. He worked at the bank. He was very good at figures. He could add as fast as the early calculators. He'd count the sheep in groups of over ten; he wouldn't count 1-2-3-4. He started at Buckhorn (east of Mitchell near Waterman Flat), taking care of other people's sheep, and he gradually built it up.

"He had sheep from way back then. That was a big industry from where he came from; in Wales. They had usually one band, 1,250 head of sheep[19], on the ranch in Waterman. They developed them through the

---

18 Virginia Humphreys interview
19 The number of sheep in a band varies with the person telling the story, but 1,000 to 1,200 is a common count.

years. Everybody in this country had sheep back then. You could have a lamb ready for market in five months. And the wool was a second crop. And he got the allotment in the mountains when the Taylor Grazing Act came along. It was back of Dayville, high in the Ochocos.

"Our ranch is just this side of the Cant Ranch, the John Day Fossil Bed. They're a Century Ranch, a 100 year old ranch. Bob's family has been there all those years. And his mom said to Bob, "There's a band of sheep at Silvie's Valley that I've bought. If you want them, you can go trail them home. (Silvie's Valley is out by Burns.) I put the down payment on a ranch up at Waterman, and you can take them to Waterman." And that's how we got the ranch there.

"The sheep shearing business was quite a thing. Mrs. Humphreys, Loula, had three sons, the Potters, when she married Rhys Humphreys. She'd been married to Andy Potter and he was a brother to George Potter. When Andy died, Loula moved to Waterman Flat where she proved up on a widow's homestead. Then, she married Rhys in 1910 and they had six more children. One girl in all the nine children. The Potter children were Raleigh, Emery, and Ray. The Humphreys were Lloyd, Rhys, Trevor, Gladys, and Bill and Bob.

"So, Mrs. Humphreys, one time, had all those children to take care of and all the sheep shearers to take care of. They sheared sheep up at Buckhorn. It's eight miles off Highway 19. There were eight shearers and you had a wool tromper and a wool tier. Besides that, you had the ones that got the sheep penned up and the herders and whatnot.

"And my mother-in-law was a good cook and she cooked lots for them. She even had pie for breakfast for them sometimes. And, always, biscuits. And, then, you always had cake or fruit for them at noon, too. And, at night it was a big meal, too.

"One time Mrs. Humphreys had the shearing crew stay with her for a week and she didn't have refrigeration or electricity or anything like

Loula Humphreys and son, Bob
From Dave and Candy Humphreys archives

we have now. And she cooked for them for a week, and then a guy that sold moonshine came over and they got drunk. After they could go to work. Oh, I think I would have taken a frying pan to the whole bunch! There were about ten or so men. I often told my boys that she had such trials and tribulations in her life that nothing they could face would be that tough, because that was down-to-the-earth survival.

"We had all sorts of sheep shearers. We had a Basque, Gregario, for years. He was good. He'd come over when they got permits granted to them to come. He was very anti-Franco.

"The sheepmen shipped their wool in the early days to Shaniko. They took it in the big mule-drawn or horse-drawn wagons. Then, in our time, Rhys took it to Baker a lot. There was a fellow over there that bought it. And, then, the lambs used to be that way, too. Buyers would come and buy them, like they did a lot with cattle, right at the ranch. Of course, in the early days, when the farmers mortgaged their crops, they had people to pay when they got the money. But they made it.

"Then, the sheepherders were a different breed of people. Much of the time they were alone. When they did get to town, for some reason it seemed to be written into their resume or their script that they were supposed to get drunk because that's what most of them did. I think because they were alone so much they got so lonesome for people that when they got to town that's what they did. I shouldn't make them out to be all drinkers because they weren't. They were some really great ones that didn't. It was just a lonely life, that's what.

"The one we had for a long time, the herder, was Mike Corlie. He herded for twelve years and it was so enjoyable. He was such a gentleman and he did such a great job. He didn't drink. He had a wife, Mabel, and she was a cute little lady. She'd go to sheep camp and on those little sheep camp stoves she could make cakes or biscuits.

"And, then, on the other hand, we had Albert Hancock for several years. His brother was where Camp Hancock got its name. So, Albert was just full of all kinds of stories about early days, Indians. He was a great person; the boys really enjoyed growing up with Albert. But he, on the other hand — his camp — he did dishes by turning the plate over so the flies couldn't get on it. Then, he'd turn the plate over and eat off it. And he survived to a nice age."[20]

Dickse would chime in with her Fount Watkins and Johnny Joyce stories, and the two schoolmarms would chuckle companionably.

---

20 Virginia Humphreys interview

"We'd mark the lambs and brand them and all that kind of stuff," Virginia continued. "Then, they'd get ready to go to the mountains about three days before July 1. They used a pack-string for years because tere weren't roads up there, and it's pretty tricky how they did the packing.

"The packsaddles have two handles coming up on both sides and you could hook a box over those horns and you could pack your little camp stove, your bedding — everything you had to get on that. But, you had to balance them out really evenly or it would make it really hard for the horse to go. I think it's a lost art now. They call them 'diamond hitches' that they would throw on them, you know.

"They'd go up in the Spanish Peak area up back of Antone. That was our allotment from there to Dayville. 35,000 acres. It was a government allotment. And no fences, except going around the outside of it, if you could imagine that. So, you had to have a herder with them, and the government required that you have a camp tender with them. The camp tender cooked the food and looked for lost sheep, and the herder moved the sheep from camp to camp.

"Bob's job was to help the herder and my job was to cook. It was a fairly relaxing life. It really was. We got our water out of a spring, if it were handy, or out of a creek. And we survived all the stuff people don't know about if they get water out of the creek, because a lot of the places we drank aren't fit for human consumption now. Just don't look up the creek!

"About once a week, the trappers would come through up there and Stan Thomas was the trapper then. He used to take his wife with him. She made really delicious pies. I told him I didn't know what was wrong with him; she made such good pies, why did he get rid of her? And he said, 'There's more to marriage than pies!'

"Our sheep allotment ran from right above Dayville to the west slope of Spanish Peak. A couple of days were needed to trail the sheep up there from the ranch. The drovers camped along the way. They had a camp where the flock and crew crossed Rock Creek, then on to High-way 26 just before you get into the gorge. So, we'd always have a big picnic down there in the meadow. Usually there were a couple of good rows, you know, with the tempers frayed and all that kind of stuff. Trail-ing sheep wasn't all peace and pancakes and sourdough. There were a few little thistles and thorns involved.

"We brought the lambs out Labor Day and they really grew big up there. That was after three months up there. And we trailed them down to the highway, which was a dusty, hot trail. Then, we had to take them down the highway seven miles or so, and it was really hard to do that because it was really crooked where you have to go through the gorge there, and we always worried about somebody running into them or stuff. And, just as you'd get the sheep to going really well, somebody would drive through and jump out in front of the sheep with a camera and turn to take pictures because it was something a lot of people hadn't seen. And, then they'd stop the sheep and it was so irritating. They were just honestly interested in them.

"The ewes would stay up in the mountains and the herders would bring the lambs out and they would ship them. Two or three big double-decker semis would come in and they would take them out to the mar-ket. Then, the herder would come back and they would work the ewes down towards the river and they would spend the winter there, then.

"Like this fellow, Shuler, says, "It takes tough minds to survive tough times." And those people (the sheepmen and especially Mrs. Loula Humphreys) had it. They weren't a bunch of whiners like we have now. And people that want to give it away. People want to give it away, and it's noble, but it sure does tear down the country, doesn't it? Gov-ernment subsidies. Stand in the line for their pittance — their dole.

"People quit running sheep so much because of too many pred-ators. The eagles would pick up the lambs. We'd start at the river with them and there'd be a big crop of lambs. And by the time they got to Buckhorn to be marked, it was just amazing how many of them had died in the process. It's very frustrating, because the eagles are endangered, you know!

"And, then regulations. They played a big part. I think NAFTA (North American Free Trade Agreement), where we opened up the market for other countries to come in. That probably did a lot. Australian wool. And, there weren't herders anymore, really. You tried to get by with having people come from the Pyranees or Mexico or wherever. It just wasn't profitable any more. And then we got all the nylon fabrics and this kind of thing, so the wool market fell."[21]

Dickse and Virginia lamented that sheep were almost a thing of the past and agreed they were glad they had enjoyed their years with the aggravating animals. It took a special breed of person to appreciate sheep, the two sheep-women decided.

Sandy McKay, a well-known retired wheat rancher in the Antelope/Ashwood area of Wasco County, Wheeler County's neighbor, remembered working for the Muddy Company when he was a young man, leading the typical life of an all-around ranch hand at that time. The spread was located near Burnt Ranch and gained notoriety when it was owned and operated by the Rahjneesh, and McKay's life typified that of many young men in Wheeler County at that time.

"I was born in Antelope," Sandy recalled. "Dad ran sheep. In them days, they was Merinos. Them are those little sheep with the good wool. They kept their lambs until they were two years old. Sold them for mutton. I don't know if they sell it for mutton any more. I know I don't like it in restaurants. My dad took his wool to Shaniko. There or to The Dalles. So, I learned about sheep when I was a young man.

---

21 Virginia Humphreys interview

"I left home when I was thirteen-years-old," Sandy recalled. "My mother got sick; she had a brain cancer, and that was during the Depression. All the money my parents had was in their pockets. I went to work to help buy the medicine for my mother so I never went to high school.

"I went to work at the Muddy. I worked there for five and a half years. At that time, people by the name of Hahn and Free owned the Big Muddy. They were the only outfit in the whole country that could give you any money. You got your pay every month. (This was during the Depression years.) I worked for thirty dollars a month. That's what everybody got. I got my room and board. I got tired of working cattle all the time and I worked with the sheep, too.

"The Muddy had summer range up at Summit Prairie. They owned two thirds of it. It's good pasture and they took care of it. And, every year, when the snow would go off and it'd start drying up a little bit, they'd have irrigators there to keep the meadows wet.

Sandy rode to the ranch's summer pasture near the old Carroll Camp in Wheeler County often, following the route taken by Sam Wilson when he had made the desperate ride to save his family from the flashflood.

"It was a long trip, as far as a good horse could carry you in a day from the Big Muddy. They would keep a couple of bands of sheep up there and all those heifers and steers. They'd take them to Prineville and put them on the train and send them to wherever the buyer was.

"What I did mostly when we were shearing was separate the sheep. Done that for a couple years. Yeah, I got in on the shearing. Lots of times I'd have to go to the lambing camp for a few days. They had six places where they lambed. They all lambed at the same time. A band was 1200. They'd get about half done and then they'd mix with another band. Some of them herders, working with the sheep, would take off and get to drinking, but most of them were good hands.

"It was a good place to work, the Muddy Company. They furnished everything that you could think of, but butter. No refrigerators. But they'd buy all kinds of jelly, in gallon cans. You could get all of that you'd want. They'd take it to the herders. I seen at the ranch there one time in shearing time, the shearers were there and they had fourteen shearers. They'd feed them all. And all the ranch hands, and anyone that came. There were 42 men there and one old lady took care of them. They had a man there to cut meat and help her build the fires early in the morning. Get everything warm. It took a long time to set the table!"[22]

Many of the earlier ranchers in Wheeler County ran a band of sheep and their children counted the herders as part of their family. Elsie Fitzgerald recalled: "I remember when Grandpa (Tom Fitzgerald) still had sheep. He had two bands, about 2,200. There were 1,100 head per band. They were crossbred Columbia and Ramboulet.

"I don't remember how old Leona [her younger sister] and I were, but we weren't very big. We followed the sheepherder with the sheep one day when he left our place and he was herding them on the foothills of Sheep Mountain. And, the folks missed us and they looked all over the place and couldn't find us.

"Finally, they wondered maybe if that's what happened to us and they got the field glasses and looked and, sure enough, they could see us running around with the sheepherder and the dogs. And the sheepherder shared his lunch with us. We stayed out all day! We had fun. I don't know how much fun it was for the herder."[23]

Mary Misener remembered her years of raising sheep in Twickenham. "We had mostly Rambolet sheep. Finn and Suffolk and Hamps, Columbia and Polypay, Merino. We didn't have cows at first. I liked the sheep best on the ranch."[24]

---

22 Sandy McKay interview
23 Elsie Fitzgerald interview
24 Mary Misener. interview.

Her son John remembers his mother's sheep. "Meadow maggots! I think the most sheep we ever had was about 500. We ran them all on irrigated pasture and it was a real mess because they got all kinds of parasites. And then you'd go out and have to catch a sheep that had fly-blows on it, and you'd shear the wool off and it'd be crawling with maggots all over it. It wasn't one of those things you'd want to do right before you ate or right after you ate! It wasn't one of those things you look forward to doing any time.

"Yeh, we used to raise sheep, but they were a lot of work and then the coyotes would get into them and kill them two or three a night. And you'd have to corral them.

"We had a guard dog, finally, that really stopped the coyotes from getting into the sheep. The only time he'd have problems would be if we moved them to a different pasture and he didn't know where they were and he wouldn't go hunt them up if he didn't know where they were.

"Sheep require so much more labor than cattle. I think probably the most interesting part of raising sheep is when they were having their babies because you'd go out and put them in the pens and they were cute. Half-way gentle and weren't causing a lot of problems yet. But, then, as they got bigger, uglier, and older, well — they got to be a lot more work.

"We got rid of the sheep because they just take too much work. You have to have someone there with them to watch out for them all the time. Take care of them. Keep the coyotes from getting them. They just seem to be more susceptible to disease, too, than cattle."[25]

Lee and Patsy Hoover ran sheep for a short time. "The sheep came from Pat Arrabara in Mesa, Washington," Lee said. "There wasn't anything wrong with the sheep except they all had foot rot. They were old sheep when we got them.

---

25 John Misener. interview.

"Patsy started driving school bus after we went into the sheep business. I'll tell you the story about that. I was working for the Forestry. Full time. And, so the sheep got left on the pasture. We had a couple hundred head. Anyway, the sheep had a tendency to get in the alfalfa field and bloat. Or, they'd take off on a rainy day and go to the top of Ball Mountain. Anyway, one day come along in the fall and it was foggy and Patsy couldn't find the sheep and she tracked them down and followed them around and she found them up on top of Ball Mountain. And the fog was thicker than her hand in front of her face. I think the sheep found her. Anyway, by the time she got them back in the barn, the sheep was over."

Patsy's version differed somewhat: "There was an ad in the Times Journal for a job in the extension office and I was 40 years old and I applied for it and because of who I knew, not what I knew, that I got the job!

"So, I went to work at the Extension office and you couldn't run the ranch and work at the Forestry, too. Lee came home and herded the sheep. Maybe two, three weeks. I got home one day and they were all going in the truck, one at a time. And, we went out of the sheep business!"[26]

The Hoovers weren't the only ones to go out of the sheep business. The growing popularity of beef over lamb and the decrease in the need for wool because of the development of synthetic fabrics made the sheep industry unprofitable. Ranchers who had depended on sheep gradually turned to beef as their main crop. For the old-timers, it would be a bittersweet economic necessity.

It was to be 100 years after the Keyes cousins brought the first herd of sheep to Wheeler County in 1873, that the last direct descendant of Zachary Keyes put her final load of wool into a pickup truck to have it hauled to the Portland Woolen Mills for sale. Facing the last few months of her fight with terminal cancer, Dickse Keyes Williams, possessing the

---

26 Patsy and Lee Hoover interview

strength of the pioneer spirit that had carried her grandfather and her father through the formative years of the sheep industry in Wheeler County, had sold her small band in the spring.

Standing beside her last load of wool, Dickse wasn't really seeing the large burlap wool bags stuffed as full as a tick on a spring lamb. Like so many other children of sheepmen, she was recalling long dusty days spent as a child trailing her father's band of sheep to his allotment in the Ochocos. She was reliving the excitement of helping pull a lamb reluctant to be born and celebrating with the unkempt sheepherder as the little creature struggled to its feet and took that first drink of milk from its exhausted mother.

She was remembering long days spent with contrary sheep being squeezed into the narrow chutes and into the holding pens for the sweating shearers sore from bending over, hanging in their pliable slings, as they sheared another sheep, then another, through the long spring day. She was remembering the drive to Shaniko with her father's loads of wool and the meetings with the wool buyers and the sheepmen. She was reliving those long days when she had escaped housework and walked to the sheepherder's noon camp, sharing his doughgods and his brown beans with him as together they watched her father's sheep graze on the hills in the valley she called home.

Knowing the sale of the bags of wool would be the end of a century of the Keyes's sheep ranching, she had remarked that she knew it was also the end of the sheep industry as it had been in Wheeler County. "The only sure thing we can depend on is change," she had quoted, her voice quavering slightly.

After her death, one of Dickse's daughters would find the following poem written in her mother's handwriting, presumably composed by the little sheepherder turned wife, mother, and satisfied sheepman:

Heaven won't be so lonely
If what I hope is true,
If a little lamb of God is there,
Or some old friendly ewe.

In those fields of heaven
Beside still waters deep,
May the years to come find me
With a little band of sheep.

Wheeler County was changing. Sheep had been the first major business in the fledgling county; cattle ranching complemented and then took over that industry. There would be good years and lean years, but always there would be those incidents that helped to develop the independent character of the folks who were involved in the enterprise. Always, stories of those old-timers serve as affordable entertainment for many a Wheeler County family on those occasions that bring them together. At times, there may even be a hint of the old animosity of the sheepmen versus the cattlemen, often fueled by those who, with a twinkle in their eye, see a heated argument as enjoyable and affordable entertainment.

Chapter 15
Cattle Ranching

"Someone has said: 'Wheeler County — the synonym for the greatest stock country in the world.' This may be rating it high, but, certain it is the conditions to raise stock successfully and with fine financial returns exist well in Wheeler county."[1]

There was sufficient and nourishing grass for grazing when settlers began to arrive in the area in the 1860s, and Christian Meyer watched many families drive their cattle past his stage stop. Most of the earlier families brought a milk cow with them and the more affluent also boasted of a few beef animals, many of which were Shorthorns and Herefords. Soon more and more beef animals were brought into the area and that industry would slowly replace the sheep.

"I'm getting myself some cattle," Henry Wheeler informed his friend Meyer on one of the rare occasions he traveled past the fort, stopping for a visit with his old friend. "Figure they'll be more profitable than running passengers, and they won't talk back as much," and both men chuckled. The former stagecoach owner absently stroked the thick white beard covering his scarred cheek as he shifted his weight in the straight-backed chair, settling in for a good session of discussing his venture and encouraging advice from the German. He had sold his outfit to the Holliday stage people and then worked with them for two years. In '70, he decided to enter the ranching business.

---

1 Shaver et al, p. 646 and 647

"You might find that cattle could be even more obstreperous than uncomfortable stagecoach passengers," Meyer badgered Wheeler, "but you'll have to work that one out yourself."

"Wood Gilman and I are working with the French brothers[2], stocking the ranch with good cattle. Figure I'll be there for a while, help get things going." Wheeler rolled his shoulders, limbering them up, feeling his forty-four years of activity. He knew he could only work another ten years or so before his body would start rebelling at the hard physical labor required of ranching. Though he'd be working in a supervisory position, a man had to be healthy to keep on top of the men handling the cattle that would be run on the holdings.

"Little land, good partnership, few cows. Now, all you need is a good woman!" Meyer teased his friend. The right woman, Dorcas Monroe, didn't come along until '73. Wheeler would abandon his bachelor status when he was forty-seven, and the couple would have one child, Clara, though the marriage was only a vague thought in the mind of the two friends as they sat recalling past adventures and planning future events from their seats in Meyer's Gulch.

Gilman had located the main headquarters of the Gilman-French Ranch at Sarvis Prairie, fifteen miles east of Fossil, and there was much work to be done. With eyes focused on the plat map of the area, the partners began "blocking" the ranch by choosing small homesteads to add to their initial acreage. The ranch holdings slowly grew to 35,000 acres.[3]

Wheeler oversaw the stock raising on the large ranch, riding to each of the six divisions of the property and working with each foreman as the herds grew. "Nealy, you need to fence off this valley and that hill there," Wheeler pointed out to Perry Cornelius Helms. "Keep the cattle here for the summer and then push them to the lower country for the

---

2 Ibid., p. 689
3 "Gilman-French Cattle Ranch" in Pacific Homestead, p. 37

winter. Make better use of the range that way." His foreman sat astride a tall saddle horse, the animal shifting impatiently, anxious to be moving.

The son of Anthony "Pike" Helms, who had established both the Waldron and the Twickenham post offices, nodded in agreement, his admiration of Wheeler evident in the deference he showed his boss. He knew from experience that the bearded ranch partner didn't give frequent or unnecessary directions to his hired hands; when he asked that something be done, there was good reason for the directive. Wheeler had become an honored and highly respected resident of the county after surviving the Indian attack on his stage, and his partners knew they could rely on him to make decisions that would benefit not only the Gilman-French Cattle Company but also their employees.

Nealy was proud of the care he gave his assigned portion of the large ranch, the holdings that were known as the Prairie Ranch, and he enjoyed overseeing the hired hands while riding his stock-savvy mounts. The long hours spent horseback, usually seven days a week, were enjoyable to a large extent because of his love of a good saddle horse. Nealy had also formed a lasting friendship with Wheeler, admiring the retired stage driver's dedication in developing the area, and Helms was proud of being treated as an equal by his boss.

Wheeler's faith in his foreman was well-founded. Helms's reputation as a knowledgeable stockman was surpassed only by his reputation for being a good horseman. One year, he and Fred Ball bought horses and planned to take them to Idaho for the winter. The thermometer dipped to minus thirty-six degrees and, coupled with deep snow, the severely cold weather caused the men to lose the entire herd. That was a bitter pill to swallow for a man who loved horses so much.[4]

Nealy's love for fine horseflesh would be echoed by later stockmen

---

4 Jesse Faye Morris, "Perry C. and Lucy E. Helms," in Wheeler County History, p. 110 and 111

in the county, and he would smile in understanding when he heard of the whopping big amount of $3,600 being spent for a good stallion. In 1910, six men purchased a German Coach stallion named Heros, pooling their money to pay the amount asked for the horse they bought through the A. C. Ruby Company of Portland. Mike Fitzgerald, Henry D. Keyes, S. B. Davis, R. A. Thomas, R. R. Keys, and G. O. Butler all signed their names on the contract. A third of the cost of the stud was due each year, and each of the six ranchers scraped together their two hundred dollars by January of 1911, '12, and '13 to honor the contract.[5] Investing in good horseflesh to improve the quality of their herds of horses was an action that Nealy certainly understood and approved of.

Reining his tall bay horse away from Wheeler, Nealy gave him a parting smile and wave and then turned toward the far end of the long valley, heading in the general direction of the fencing crew. There were cross-fences to be built for separating the pastures and maximizing the grazing, and he wanted to be sure the men were following the crudely drawn directions he'd given them a few days previously.

Watching Nealy ride across the pasture, Wheeler felt he and his partners had chosen a good man. Satisfied, he started towards what was being called the Sutton place to check on the progress of the barn being built. It was said to be the biggest on the Gilman-French Cattle Ranch, being 212 feet by 72 feet, and the half-built building was already an impressive structure nestled in a small and shallow canyon across from one of Sutton's fields. Wheeler had heard there was room in the barn for 300 tons of hay, and sheds would be built full-length on two sides with racks for feeding cattle.

Thinking of feeding, his stomach rumbled slightly and he hoped to arrive at the ranch just before noon so he could enjoy some of the cook's efforts. He'd eaten there before and knew there would undoubtedly be

5 Linda Keys archives

dried-apple pie to top off the meal. The foreman's wife, like all ranch cooks, would have cooked plenty of extra food as local residents had the habit of timing their trips so they could stop by the house of a good cook close to mealtime. Wheeler had noticed the best of cooks were honored by folks stopping by close to mealtime, considering it an attestment to their culinary skills. He had yet to stop by a ranch kitchen without being offered a meal or, at the very least, a handful of cookies or piece of pie along with copious cups from the ever-hot pot of coffee that had been set to one side of the stove top to keep warm.

The Gilman-French Cattle Ranch would soon be known as one of the very best breeding ranches west of the Rocky Mountains.[6] This was attributed largely not only to the wise management by Wheeler, his partners Gilman and French, and their ranch foremen, but also to the abundance of outside range and the large fenced pastures, besides the plentiful hay crops which could be raised on the holdings. With the many springs and creeks, the cattle would never have to go too far for water. Though there was snow in the winter, it was never very deep nor did it last long, and man and beast alike benefited from the climate.

The ranch ran from 4,000 to 6,000 head of cattle and 75 to 100 head of horses. There was a large amount of standing pine and fir for timber. By 1905, an estimated 200,000 feet of lumber had been cut on one of the farms.[7] In all, the ranch soon claimed to have 1,000 to 2,000 acres of cultivated land, and there were at least 2,700 acres that could easily be tillable. The fertile soil produced abundant crops of alfalfa, and wheat and other grains. Orchards of apple, peach, pear, and plum trees were soon producing large crops, as were vegetable gardens and berry patches.

Wheeler was proud of his work on the large ranch. The efforts of the partners were paying off with an efficient, smoothly running operation.

6 Pacific Northwest Homestead, p. 37
7 Ibid.

Henry Wheeler's Corn Cob Ranch in 1917
Courtesy of the Fossil museum

The eight years he'd spent on the development of the land were satisfying, but he had an urge to branch out on his own, and Dorcas was willing to help her husband.

"We call it the Corn Cob Ranch," Wheeler boasted on one of his visits to Meyer's Gulch.

"Now, that's a fine name for a ranch," Meyer commented wryly. "How on earth did someone come up with that name?"

"Figure some soldiers probably named it that in the '60s after seeing a pile of burnt corn cobs left behind by the Indians or somebody. Don't know. Lots of Celilo and other folks from the Columbia River area come through there, leave behind odds and ends. Trade with local folks. Fish, moccasins. Things like that. They coulda left the corn cobs." Wheeler shrugged. The name of the ranch didn't much matter to him, he figured.

Wheeler had established a post office in the area in '77, of which he was the postmaster, and then he settled on what would be known as Corn Cob Creek in '78, and filed for his homestead in '79. "Almost straight north of Spray's town," Wheeler told the German. "'Bout 160

Henry Wheeler's home on Girds Creek
Courtesy of the Fossil museum

acres. Township 8 South, Range 24 East, Sections one and two, if you want to look it up,"[8] the new land owner added with a proprietary grin. With his staking claim to more land two years later, the former stage-coach operator would own 240 acres, though he made liberal use of the unclaimed land bordering his holdings.

The gentleman later sold his Corn Cob Ranch to Gilman and French and he and Dorcas built a home near the head of Girds Creek, about eight miles northwest of Mitchell, settling on land patented to Dorcas's mother, Maryann Monroe,[9] who had crossed the plains in '65.[10] Later, Wheeler and his family left that home and built a residence in the heart

---

8 BLM Government Land Office Records
9 BLM General Land Office records
10 Mary Beldon interview, 1995

of Mitchell, near the Wheeler County Trading Company. Wheeler retired there, often conversing with visitors about ranching and politics
in Wheeler County. He was one of the first men in Wheeler County to
engage in cattle ranching, but there were many who followed who have
their own stories to relate.

"There's history at the Prairie Ranch," Lee Hoover said of the ranch
that is synonymous with cattle ranching in the county. "The ranch was
bought by Gilman-French who also owned the Corn Cob Ranch and
the Sutton Ranch. There were three homesteads incorporated into
the Prairie Ranch. The Hoyt, the Lester Hawk place, and the Beeson
homestead.

"The Hoyt is on Lake Creek. To get there, you'd go up Alder Creek
four or five miles and turn off. There are 90 acres of irrigated land up
there. They used it for raising produce — corn, watermelons, etc. Frank
and Melva Cecil were the last people who lived there. Frank worked for
Alec Johnson who had the Fossil Merc, the Smitty Place, and so on.

"The house Peggy and Bryce Logan live in now was built around
1895. I have an idea it was built by Gilman-French. We have a picture
taken in 1896 and Sid Gilman was sitting in the front in a rocking chair.
That's when Gilman-French had the Sutton Ranch on Rowe Creek and
the Prairie Ranch and Corn Cob in Kahler Basin.

"Helen Myers helped cook over at the Prairie Ranch during haying
season. Crew run as high as 40 men. The kitchen still has got the little
hand-out window. You served it up on a plate and you handed it out. Big
dining hall there."[11]

One of the larger ranches incorporated into the Gilman-French
land holdings was the Sutton Ranch. With Al Sutton establishing the
county's first post office there in 1867, folks who were looking for

---

11 Lee Hoover interview

homesteads began to feel a sense of permanence in the area. Many of the pieces of land that were settled on were established before the government had surveyed the area, so boundaries were somewhat tentative at times. Some of the earlier ranches are still known by the first landholders' names, including those holdings mentioned by Hoover.

Some of the first settlers in the area that would form the Sutton Ranch tried other enterprises before they turned to beef. Harry Mortimore raised turkeys for a time. The turkeys were herded on the range during the days and driven to their pen and house at the ranch at night. His neighbors, Jack Palmer and Tom Huntington, were partners in a neighboring turkey venture, and Bob Huntington, Tom's son, remembers well his turkey-herding days: "That was a terrible job. You know, I had to get up at daylight. I got to shoot a lot of hawks, eagles. I hung one of them on the fence. A cop came along and wanted to know about the eagle. "I said, 'I shot him! He was after my turkeys.' And then he said I had a perfect right to shoot him if he was after my property, but don't hang him up on the fence."

The turkey industry in Wheeler County didn't thrive for long due to the predators and the cost of shipping the finished product to market. Most of the land owners turned to beef animals for their main source of income, and the Mortimores, the Huntingtons, and the Palmers were among the turkey farmers who turned into cattle ranchers.

Bob Huntington was just one of the many young men who would work for the Sutton Ranch for a time. "I came into Fossil and I was broke and I didn't want anybody to know it," Bob began his story, echoing the plight of the many young men in the county after WWI and WWII who became hired hands on the cattle ranches.. "I was sleeping in an old car and I got down to a quarter. I went into the bar and that is when your luck turned! I went in there and I played the slot machine. They had a quarter slot machine. So, I put my quarter in there and I got five back.

Howard Mortimore was standing there waiting to play that and he said, 'Feed it up for me,' and so I put them back in and I hit the jackpot. Worth $25 then.

"And, you wouldn't believe this, but I went up to the other bar — they had two bars in Fossil until after WWII — and I hit the 10-cent jackpot for ten dollars." Bob's luck would continue; he landed a job on a cattle ranch that same night.

"Lee Carey came up town and hired me to go to work for the Sutton Ranch." Bob worked for Lee and the Gilman-French company for a time before he went on down the road, only to return to the ranch to work for Bill Keyes two different times in later years. Bob commented that Bill was the epitome of a good cattle ranch foreman, overseeing both the care of the cattle and the haying that was essential for feeding the livestock.

"During the first season I worked for Bill, I rough-broke a few saddle horses and was paid $10 per head whenever he sold one. This wasn't too bad as mostly they weren't finished breaking. It gave me a chance to make a little money, which came in handy as that was a rainy summer, which made haying for $1.50 a day not so good since you can't hay while the hay is wet.

"Bill and Neva were good to me. He had a haying outfit, a Jenkins' stacker. It was made out of spruce and it seemed like every time you turned around, something broke on that thing. Bill went up on Corral Mountain and he got poles. Hauled those poles down. It seemed like we used almost all of them, fixing that stacker. It needed good teeth for a derrick team.

"I guess it was the same time I worked for him, Bill got Clarence Hovey and his wife, Alda, and she was definitely a good cook. And, Bill gave Clarence the best team to run a hay rake and here I am with a mowing machine and I got a balky team. So, I got up way early one morning and I got Clarence's team and I'm out there mowing hay and I didn't even eat breakfast. Bill came out and he gave me a little talk and explained it was not proper etiquette to steal another person's team, especially if it was the cook's husband's. About all I accomplished was make Bill mad, mow a little hay, and miss my breakfast.

"Somehow, the hay got mowed. Also, somehow, Bill kept the hay crew going. Bill was a man of patience, a man who trusted people, and I believe you find that this sort is completely honest. He was a straight shooter and a loyal friend. He remained a kind man, though that kindness was not always returned.

"Bill kept a sharp eye on the haying progress, and was always present when the derrick pole needed to be moved and did his best to prevent an accident. There was only one accident. Bert Green was stacking and we were hauling a very damp first crop off the field so the irrigation could start on the second crop. Bert had me swing a load with the trip rope. He was to stand clear. The load tripped and buried Bert. We got him out before he suffocated but he claimed a leg injury and had to go to town for doctoring. The doctor was the liquor store. Bill went in a few days later and brought Bert back. After a few days, he was fit to work.

"In the meantime, I was chore boy, because I had crippled the chore boy; also because I could milk a cow or two. I believe there was a garden to hoe, also. I was glad when I got spelled off of that job. About now you can see Bill's philosophy of replacement. I guarantee you I treaded carefully around the cook and her husband.

"I played my last joke on the Sutton Ranch. There was an older man working there who was also a carpenter. After haying he was going to shingle that huge shed. I put a dead snake by his shirt that he had taken off while shocking hay. The snake didn't scare him too much, but he said no kid could make a fool out of him and he quit. The truth was he wanted to go on a hunting trip.

Bob Huntington could give Jerome Parsons a run for his money! His story telling provides a good insight on Wheeler County folks.

"Bill, as always in his wisdom, delegated the job to the culprit that ran the barn shingler off. If I wanted to stay on the Sutton, I could shingle the barn. I got up there and worked all day long nailing shingles. In the evening I climbed down and backed away and looked at that roof. I could hardly see where I had made a show. Since this job was gypo, I quit, never to work for Bill again."[12]

The barn Bob pounded some shingles onto was a large round barn, said to be the largest such structure in the state of Oregon at that time. Unfortunately, the barn burned as a result of an out-of-control range fire caused by lightning in the 1950s.

Raising hay was an essential part of the cattle industry in Wheeler County, and during the '30s when many of the men traveled to Portland to work in the shipyards, women and children took over the job of haying. Fred Dunn, born in '30, remembered his early days in the hay fields.

"When I was six years old, Bill Jackson called Grandma. "Can that kid drive a team of horses?"

---

12 Bob Huntington interview, 2010

"She said, "He sure can.""

"Bill said, "Well, send him over here. We need a derrick driver." It was two miles over there. So Grandma put a handful of clothes and lunch in a gunny sack and told me where I was supposed to eat. It was on the road that comes from north of the Jackson place through the saddle there on the side of Toney Butte. There used to be a granary that stood there in the saddle. I was to walk until I got to that. Before I got to it, I was supposed to get down and look all under it to see if there was any rattlesnakes. There was a big timber that stuck out to the side of it. And, I could sit on that and eat my sandwich that Grandma sent with me, and then go on down to the Jackson's.

"I got down there and Effie fed me some more. Put me to hoeing in the garden and I didn't have a hat, and, by God, I got sunburned! It wasn't hurting me but I'd look in the mirror and I was just burnt to a crisp.

"The next morning out to the barn we went to harness teams. Must have been eight teams in there. They had a lot of hired men. I couldn't lift a collar up to get it on their horses. I wasn't big enough.

"I went and fed the chickens and the hogs and Elmer Jackson had to harness all them horses. Damn mules. They had a team of mules. Once you got them harnessed, they were gentle as they could be. But, you went through the barn door and they went to kicking. They brought those mules from Bill Biggerstaff. Fine looking animals.

"Bill always rode a mule. He'd always come over there and have Uncle Hickey's wife to make his orders out, for clothes and stuff. She'd fill it out and mail it for him. And, he always come walking in. Hickey wouldn't allow the mule on the ranch. So, he'd just ride down until he could just barely see the ranch and tie the mule to a juniper and walk on in.

"Uncle Clyde [Mabe] come in a horseback one day. Bill Biggerstaff and a bunch of us kids and Aunt Ruby was in the kitchen at the table. Uncle Clyde came through the door and he said, 'I knew Bill Biggerstaff was here.'

"How'd you know I was here?"

"He said, 'A damn mule tied to a juniper up there!' Uncle Clyde, he didn't care what he rode. Mules are good animals. Man, they can go twice as fast as a horse can. They cover a lot of ground when you're working them.

"I could drive a team of horses when I was eight years old, all day. Men all went down to work in the ship yards. Every weekend, somebody would come home and they'd tell me what I was supposed to do the next week," recalled Fred.

"Uncle Clyde took me out there and he showed me all about that mowing machine. Sharpened the cycle bar for me. Boy, on Monday morning, away I went. That team stepped right out; they'd just go right along. Man, I'm a cutting hay like mad. Harold Dean [Fred's younger brother] he wants to start raking and Grandma told him no, it's got to cure a little while.

"So, I had the big field in front of the house all mowed and I'd started over on the other one and Grandma let him start raking. The ten-foot rake would catch up with a five-foot mowing machine in just a little bit. And, Harold Dean was caught up, but he wanted to get more. So, at noon I just unhooked my team, took their bridles off and tied them to the fence there by the yard. Took them to the watering trough and back up to the yard, tied them to the fence, fed them a handful of hay and let them eat. Not unharnessed or anything.

"Harold Dean's team was on the other side of the gate. We went in and ate, and he just wolfed his food down like it was going out of style and out the door he went. And Grandma said, 'Where's he going?'

"I said, 'I don't know.' I'm still eating. And, all hell broke loose! There was picket fence coming down, tin a rattling, and Harold Dean's a screaming bloody murder. Grandma and I was out there right now. There's that team going down across the field and Harold Dean standing there. One horse went under the granary porch, and it was two days before Grandma would let us use it; it banged up its shoulder pretty bad. But we got our haying done."[13]

Henry "Harry" Mortimore, grandson of Sir Joshua Reynolds, was born in England in 1867. He was trained to be a banker and for a time worked in Lloyd's bank in Barnstable, England. He came to Fossil in 1890 and set up a bowling alley. For a time, Harry packed for the Oglevie sheep outfit on Butte Creek and later he and Nat and Ed Shoun ran sheep near Camp Watson during the summer. The Oglevie sheep concern was purchased later by the Steiwer family.

In the late '90s, Harry filed on a homestead on Sugar Loaf west of the Rowe Creek road, and he bought up adjoining homesteads from those who were moving on. His home was on the old Fort Fitzmaurice place and, after several years of raising horses, he began to raise cattle on his ranch which bordered the Sutton Ranch. Harry married Elizabeth Welch and the couple had two children, Mary and Howard.[14]

"Grandad, he'd finance a lot of people to homestead," recounted Harry's grandson, Richard Mortimore. "Then, when they'd prove up on it, he'd give them "X" amount of dollars for the land. That's 'cause they got the land for nothing. Of course, they had to prove up, live there two years." Some of the earlier homesteaders Richard recalled hearing of or of knowing when he was a youngster were Rosenbaum, Nelson, Dedman, Heightman, Baird, Huntington, Palmer, Stevens, Jackson, Riddle, John Creiger, George Griffin, O.P. Bunker, Caldwell, Jack Castle, 'Club Foot' Clark, Jim Brown, Vera Prindle, Fitzmaurice, Neilson, Custer Keyes, Carpenter, and Thompson.

Richard remembered many stories of the earlier settlement of the portion of the Sutton Ranch that was located on and near Rowe Creek.

---

13 Fred Dunn interview, 2011
14 Howard Mortimore in *History of Wheeler County*, p. 167

"Granddad and old man Charlie Palmer had a feud. Charlie was a pretty good drinker and it didn't take much to get him a going. Grandpa would have to thump him. The story goes that they were fighting up on Sugar Loaf and went rolling down the hill. He (Grandpa) broke a rib. Charlie got a little obnoxious at times.

"There were some people by the name of Stevens. They were my first wife's family. Anyway, they didn't have nothing. They were living over on the Stanford place at the head of Robinson, the canyon that comes out down on Pine Creek. There was a little house up there. Stanford by that time had vacated or whatever, but they was living in it. I don't know how many kids there was. There were seven or eight kids. They didn't have nothing to eat.

"And, Granddad had Mac Huntington working for him. So he said, "Mac, gather up some eggs and hams." And Mac didn't want to do that, so, he gathered up all the rotten eggs he could find and hauled over there to those people. And Granddad damned near killed him. Yeah, Granddad was a tough old feller but he was fair."[15]

A ranch name well-known in the Waterman Flat-Richmond area is that of the Six Shooter. The origin of the name for the ranch seems to be elusive. The most prevalent thought, when talking with old-timers of the area, is that someone happened upon a six-shooter that had been lost by some early settler or cowboy passing through the timbered land, and the traveler named the area for that firearm. Although the old ranch has prime meadows and timberland, the name of Six Shooter has probably caused the area to be well known more for is name than for its history.

George W. Potter was born near Boone, North Carolina, and he traveled by train to Oregon when he was 17 years old. Gordy Shown, a rancher on Shoofly Creek, hired the young Potter, who worked for him

---

15 Richard Mortimore interview, 2009

for several years. When the young man had saved enough of his wages, he purchased the Six Shooter ranch from Dave Gilliland, who may have been the first owner of the ranch. Potter also purchased a ranch on Parrish Creek from Gordy Shown to round out his holdings.

Susan Rebecca "Callie" Thomas married George in 1906 and they lived on his ranch with their five children, Georgia, Pearl, Earl, John, and Virgil. Life must have been hard for the family, as it was for all early settlers, and, given George's reputation, Callie's life was surely a double-challenge. Their house was small and it had to have been crowded with the brood of five children. The house was known as "Callie's House" for years, until it burned down.

One story about Callie's husband that has been repeated several times was related by Betty Humphrey Potter, wife of Glen Potter, whose father, Ed, a cousin of George's, worked on the Six Shooter ranch and recalled that George raised about 50 pigs at a time. George had a reputation among the locals for being more than frugal. The story was that George would take a can holding about a gallon of grain to the pig pen, toss the grain over the fence, and tell the pigs to have a feast.

Around 1913, Callie ran the post office and store, which were in the Oddfellows Hall in Richmond. The children at first attended school in Richmond; later, Callie would take her children to The Dalles to finish high school and the family would return to the ranch in the summer.

George became well known for the fine whiskey he brewed and distributed in the surrounding area. There are several stories that floated around for a while involving stills set up near George's holdings. The stills may or may not have belonged to Mr. Potter, but the stories are worth relating.

According to one story, a still was set up in a thicket of little jack pines. It was so well hidden that, except for the smoke, it couldn't be seen from high points in the area. One windy, cold day the operator of the still went down and got it all fired up and sat there waiting for the liquid to start running. The wind was bad and he had a hard time getting the moonshine hot enough, even with the propane burners under it. So, he used a wool blanket or two that he had with him and wrapped it around the still, trying to keep the wind off it. His blanket caught fire and caused quite a smoke, but the neighbors never noticed it.

Another time, another story, and this may or may not have been George, but the incident occurred suspiciously close to his ranch. A still was set up and the owner would take his pigs down to the still to feed them the mash left over from the whiskey making. The pigs would get drunk and they'd just lie around there, and they would get up and stagger around and they'd fall down and they would just lay there and grunt. The pigs got "fatter than a son-of-a-gun" according to the storyteller.

A third story recounts how a still was set up in a cellar and the operator was in the habit of wearing loose bib overalls. The moon-shiner (George?) used propane heaters and when the still had a blow-out near the top, he took a wad of bread dough and tried to patch the hole where the steam was getting away. He was bellied up close to the still and he got too close and the overalls caught fire and the whole front was burned out of them. The wearer of the baggy bibs didn't notice the heat for a while, but when the heat reached his chin, he looked down to discover the overalls were on fire![16]

Although these stories may not be about George Potter, and there is no way of proving or disproving them, they reflect part of the society in the early 1900s in the Six Shooter area, an excellent ranch for cattle grazing by all accounts. Regardless of the stories, George Potter was known for his fine whiskey and the income added to his coffers and helped to support his ranch.

---

16 Roy Critchlow, long-time resident of the Mitchell area, interview, 1995

An old-timer near Mt. Creek east of Mitchell, Bob Collins, remembers his family driving their cows to Shaniko where the railroad provided transportation to various locations. Sometimes the family would pick up cows from nearby ranchers and sometimes George Potter would join in the cattle drive or send several head for delivery to what was the cow-shipping capital of the area.

"Grandpa Mabe was a riding for cattle some place and he was going up from Richmond up through George's place. He got to George Potter's, and George invited him to "Come on in and eat. I put a pot of beans on with a hog's head this morning." Grandpa went in and that old cook stove was a steaming away and that big old cast iron kettle was setting on the stove. George walked over there and pulled the lid off and Grandpa said them two eyeballs popped out on the stove top. George hadn't cleaned the head.

"George put the lid back on and said, "I think they're done!" There wasn't anybody to talk to; Grandpa was going up the road! Grandpa said, "I didn't eat!" George's pigs went and ate what they could find. George wasn't too ambitious but he had a hell of a nice ranch."[17]

George died in 1940 and there are two popular accounts of his demise. Betty Potter relates that he died in the Mitchell city jail where he was spending some time due to his brewing of the fine whiskey for which he was famous. He died from an infection when his caretakers failed to supply him with the antibiotics he requested.

According to Fred Dunn, "George Potter cut his own throat in Mitchell. I was working at the Fopiano Ranch when George died. The hired man was driving and hit that bridge abutment right above the park in Mitchell. They were going up to Waterman Flat. Hit that, and George's head went through the windshield and his throat was cut.

17 Fred Dunn interview, 2011

"George said, "I guess I might as well end it now." Went to sawing until he cut his own throat all the way through. His head was sticking out of the windshield. He was a character. I never drank any of it, but they say he made the best moonshine in the country."[18]

In the early 1940s, Callie Potter offered the ranch to Glen and Betty Potter for $40,000.[19] The young couple turned down the offer as they didn't have the money and didn't want to go into that kind of debt. The ranch sold to the Californians Fran and Lorriane Cherry in '47 and Fran ran the ranch until the '90s when he sold it.

The Six Shooter has gone the way of many of the old holdings of the early settlers in the area. The current deed to the well-known ranch carries the name of an absentee landowner. The once profitable ranch, with its lush natural meadows, sources of abundant water for cattle, its stand of timber and fertile soil, is no longer a cattle ranch. Instead, it is being treated as a wildlife preserve and as a hunting retreat and the huge red and white "No Trespassing, Private Property" signs contradict the old-timers' inclinations to invite passersby to stop for a meal of beans and hog's head and a bed for the night — and, just perhaps, a sip of fine moonshine whiskey.

The backbone of the successful cattle ranches was often the "cow sense" that was an integral part of those who worked with the cows, regardless of their proprietary interest in the stock. An old-timer, Joe Fitzgerald, was interviewed and gave an account of his work with cattle on the Jackson ranch north of Mitchell. He began working for the Jackson family in 1953 and after 58 years with the same family, he's still going strong, the epitome of loyalty to an employer.

"I'm 63 years old," Joe said in '95, "and I've done farming all my life. I really started to working steady when I was about nine. My parents,

18 Ibid.
19 Betty Potter interview

Mark and Vada Fitzgerald, had their own ranch. It had belonged to my grandparents, Thomas and Amy Fitzgerald, who had settled the ranch down on Bear Creek in 1870 something. And my dad was there until 1960. I left the ranch in 1953. Went to work here and have been here ever since.

"We just raise cattle here and then we raise all of the hay for them. We have about 600 acres of hay land on the place here. The Jackson family heirs own the ranch.

"I enjoy watching crops come up and grow. That's what I enjoy most about farming and ranching. And watching the baby calves grow and get big. If you've got good, healthy animals and they're doing good, I don't know — it's hard to explain, it's just a way of life. You've got to love it. It's all I've ever done, so I don't know any better. If you've never moved out of Wheeler County, you don't know what people are supposed to do, you know!

"Farming has changed quite a bit since I first started farming. I first started cutting hay with a horse-drawn mower with a five-foot cutter bar. Then it was several years before they finally got a power mower, a tractor-pulled power mower where it went behind and it had a seven-foot bar and we thought that was great, you know. That's what we used for years and years and years. Finally, we got into the self-propelled windrower. Now we run a 12-foot self-propelled windrower and we can cut more hay in three hours than you could cut in three weeks with teams, you know, and it's all ready to bale when it cures a little bit.

"We used to stack hay with wagons. Rake the hay after you cut it with a horse drawn mower, rake it with the team with a dump rake and then you had to go shock the hay in windrows with a pitchfork and then you come by with a team and wagon and you pitch the hay on the wagon.

"Before my time they pitched it off onto the stack, but we had a Jackson Fork to start with, a four-tined pitchfork that used a derrick pole to pull it up. And then we got farmhands that went on tractors, which was just a big buckrake type deal that was hydraulic controlled and you could go 20 feet high with that. I stacked that loose hay for years that way. Sometimes when I was home, we used to feed with a farmhand, too. Take it back out of the stack with a farmhand and scatter it out for the cattle.

"But, then, when I went to work here, we still stacked hay with a farmhand all the time and we had power mowers. We did some team mowing here, too, when I first started. But most of it was done with machinery. We still fed with a team for several years after I went to work here. Now, we do everything in bales and we stack it up with an automatic bale wagon. Then we have to feed it back out in the winter time.

"We used to have about six to eight men to put up the hay. But now two of us can do as much farming as six of us used to be able to, with our new equipment and stuff.

"I hate coyotes. I shoot at every one I see. We've had a lot of coyote problems with our calves. We had a heifer and a calf and the calf was too big for her to have and the next morning she was down and the calf was half out and half eat up. A coyote was eating it up while it was still in her. I assume the calf was dead before the coyote started eating, but it doesn't necessarily have to be. They will eat them while they're alive if the cow can't fight them off. But I got the coyote so he won't do that anymore.

"A time or two eagles were trying to kill calves. I saw them a few times run the cows away from the calves and then dive-bomb them. Try to get the calves, but the cows were smart to get the calves under the trees or something. This was in two weeks' time that I saw it happen; witnessed it happen two different times, but the eagles didn't get the calves. But they used to get sheep. My family used to raise sheep when I was a little bitty kid and eagles got a lot of lambs then.

"Wheeler County Stockgrowers decided that I needed the award for Cattleman of the Year, and there's two or three criteria: How well you manage your cow herd, how well you've taken care of the range, and what you've done for wildlife and different things like that. I got that award in November of 1993."[20]

Audrey Jackson, widow of Bill Jackson, was one of Joe's employers. She spent all of her life either on the family ranch or in Mitchell. Her parents had been married in the 1890s and spent their lives in this area, and the ranching operation eight miles north of Mitchell had been in the family since the 1930s.

"Although the ranch used to run sheep, it now runs cattle and the family raises hay for their animals.

"I can remember several droughts. During one particularly dry year, I can remember the rye hay sliding right off the wagon when the men tried to haul it. The coldest weather I can remember was during the '30s when the thermometer reached -30 degrees. The worse disaster I can remember was the flood of 1957."[21]

Audrey's nephew, Ronnie Quant, grew up working on the family ranch and for twenty-six years he would leave the ranch to teach in Madras during the school term and return to his home to work the ranch during the summers.

"My folks came to Mitchell in the 1890s and my father's folks about 1908. My ancestors came across on the Oregon Trail. The town of Sutherlin was named after my ancestors. Their last name was Sutherlin. They came across in the wagon train of 1847. They had a plantation and they had some money, so they built a false bottom in their covered wagon and filled it full of money. They built a mansion in Sutherlin; it's pretty good size. Then they came up to Mitchell and bought a cattle ranch up here. That's how we got to Mitchell.

"We've been living on the Jackson Ranch for almost 50 years. We've

---

20 Joe Fitzgerald, life-long resident of the Mitchell area, interview, 1995
21 Audrey Quant interview, 1996

come from the horse and buggy days to the modern days. I drove horse and wagons and teams and nowadays it's tractors with cabs on them."

Ron's wife, Loretta, added: "And some of them even have stereos in them — and air conditioning!"

"This will be my forty-ninth year stacking hay," Ron continued. "It's all machine done now; harrow bed. I used to pitch it on the wagon. Loose alfalfa hay, loose grain hay. At that time, we had a binder to bind grain hay with. Then someone would come along and pitch that on the wagon and pitch it on the stack. We started getting it baled in the late '50s, '60s and we hauled the bales by hand for a long time. We still bale it, but we use a harrow bed now to haul it. Haying has changed quite a bit.

"I used to do a lot of horseback riding. Rode horses and stacked hay. That was mostly my job. I never rodeoed. We didn't have time. Had to work all the time!

"We raise angus and Hereford. They make a good cross. A white faced black calf sells good on the market."[22]

Effie Jackson Carroll, Ron's aunt, was proud of the family ranch, which became a Century Farm in 1992.

"I was born out on the Jackson Ranch 15 miles northeast of Mitchell in a little community called Waldron, which is four and a half miles from Richmond ghost town. It's on the road to Service Creek. Our house has burned down many years ago. We still have our ranch there. It's a Century Farm. My family has had it over a hundred years, and that's why we call it a Century Farm.

"My parents were Martin Joseph and Mary Caroline Stout Jackson. My father came out to this area of Oregon in 1889. And he bought our little Century Farm in 1892. He worked very, very hard to pay for that in ten years. So he paid for it in 1902.

---

22 Ron Quant, long-time resident of the Mitchell area, interview, 1995

"I love horses. You know where Horse Mountain is? Wild horses ran wild up there. And in the wintertime and in the fall, my father would turn our horses out and they would join the wild horses and they would have a free life all winter up there running wild up there on Horse Mountain. There were lots and lots of them — maybe 400 at a time — wild horses on Horse Mountain."[23]

Sandy McKay remembers the wild horses well. He began working on the Muddy ranch when he was eight, in the summer, when he'd herd cattle. "When I worked on the Muddy [ranch], everybody wanted the wild horses off the ranch. You could have them for nothing. They was two guys got a contract together and all the ranchers was supposed to send a man out there. The Muddy asked me if I wanted to go out. I liked that."

Many of the old-timers chased wild horses, or "shitters" as they were often called, for recreation, enjoying the thrill of riding at breakneck speed through the hills, rounding up the animals that, given free range, would eat twice as much feed as a cow. Ridding the country of the feral horses became almost a necessity for the ranchers in the country where overgrazing was fast changing the lush grasslands of the 1860s to bare hills.

"They sold them to the chicken plants. Chicken feed. They was people in Portland. Two or three outfits. I know we wound up with over 500 horses. But the guys over in Shaniko and Antelope, they had over a thousand. All at one time. Homesteaders just turned them loose, is where they come from. On BLM [Bureau of Land Management land]. You could buy a horse, if you wanted, and it cost $5. You could get them cheap. There were some good horses, too.

"When we got the horses, we drove them to Gateway. Took three days. We were at Rileys [ranch] with them. And they had to show them to everybody. There were fifty or sixty men there. And they chicken

---

23 Effie Jackson Carroll, long-time resident of the Mitchell area, interview, 1995.

fed all the horses. Three and a half cents a pound. They weighed them all. Took a couple of days at the stockyards in Gateway to get them all weighed.

"And that wasn't all of the horses. Muddy had a lot of them left. They never got all of them. I was there for about three months, and Muddy paid me for that."[24]

Another old-timer, Carlyle 'Cork' Norton spent his life on his family ranch near the Painted Hills Park. A good friend and peer of Joe Fitzgerald, he was the son of the well-known historian and writer, Ned Norton, who shared many a tale about the folks in the area. Although he hauled logs for 30 years for a living, Cork also raised cows on his ranch and he recalled when many of the ranchers in the area kept dairy cows and sold their cream to a dairy in Prineville.

"On branding and marking calves," Cork explained, "we go by the old Farmers' Almanac. I believe in that. We would mark them when the moon was going down, the zodiac sign, I think, is in the feet, when it is the best. And then, also, I've noticed that sometimes a brand will grow and cover. It'll be twice the size that is a normal size when you brand. Other times, why, it's just the same size as the iron. Branding by the sign makes a difference.

"We wean whenever we can get them in. There is a time when it's supposed to be better, and when to make fence posts, cutting hay, drilling grain or seed. If you go by what is in the old Farmers' Almanac, there's a time for that. And killing weeds. We kinda follow that if we can.

"About milk fever and using a bicycle pump. Putting air in the teats, blowing the bag up, and they'll get right up and go to eating. Baxter Paine did that. He aired up each teat and pumped her bag full of air and it wasn't but just a little bit until that cow was up and eating. He just used

---

24 Sandy McKay interview

that needle that you pump a basketball or football with. He put it up in there and then he had a little hand pump. Now they use medicine from a bottle and you just put a needle into the jugular vein in the neck and then just let that drip in there and it does the same thing.

"Folstons picked up cream cans a long time ago when all the ranchers sold cream to the dairy at Prineville. And then you'd have five-gallon or ten-gallon cans. They'd pick that up at the mail stop.

"Our mail in those days was the same as it is right now, twice a week on Tuesdays and Fridays. And they'd take the cans over and leave them over at the Taylor place. And you'd leave your empty cream cans there. Most of them had their name stamped on it, and they took them into Prineville to Ashbacher's Creamery. A lot of families lived on their cream checks."[25]

Beef ranching is now Wheeler County's largest agricultural crop, though with modern equipment, improved range management, and up-to-date medicines for vaccinations, raising stock is a far cry from what it was a hundred years ago when Gilman and French and Henry Wheeler began their venture. The old-time cowboys are mostly a memory of the past, though there are still those few old-timers who follow many of the practices of their fathers.

The "real thing" is not the typical Marlboro Man of the well-known cigarette advertisements who grandstands for city-folks at rodeos or at brandings. Rather, he is the one who quietly goes about caring for the herd with a sense of pride in a job well done, surviving harsh winters of feeding cows in all kinds of weather and pulling calves reluctant to be born and fighting predators, all the while contending with government regulations and constantly rising costs of production and the often low prices of beef.

---

25 Carlyle Norton, life-long resident of the Mitchell area, interview, 1995

When he loads his calf crop into the big semi-trucks that will haul his young cattle to market, the trailing of cows over a long and hot and dusty road a distant memory, he is hoping the price from the sale will be enough to see him through the year to the next marketing of his calves. He's almost sure, though, that his bank account will be a bit short and he'll soon be visiting with his friendly banker again.

As he unsaddles his work horse and gives him a measure of grain, he surveys the mother cows in his pasture and looks to the sky for signs of a much-needed rain for the parched pasture grass. The silence is broken by the lonesome bellowing of a mother cow searching for her just-shipped calf, and the cattleman counts his riches by the feeling of contentment inside him because he knows he's seeing the dust of a truck full of his prime beef heading down the road. It's not a profitable existence, but it's a fulfilling one, and he wouldn't change his life for all the silver bits in Oregon. It's rewarding to be one of the last of the independent folk.

Chapter 16
Wheeler County's Green Gold

Meyer and Hewot had found good pine for timber in the Ochoco Mountains not far from where they located their fort-house. The men were the first of the early homesteaders who cut down the trees, limbed them, and drug them home with their work horses. The process was as physically hard as it was time consuming, but after hewing the long timbers into shape, they had the logs they needed for completing their fort-house and for constructing the out-buildings on their holdings. With folks frequently passing on the road running through their property, Meyer declared that, for privacy sake, a two-hole privy would be top priority on the list of structures they should build. Soon after their throne was constructed, the two men built a smoke house, a shelter for their animals, and a stable with a blacksmith shop set up on one end.

When they had erected the buildings they felt were essential, the men began using a whipsaw to form planks for flooring in their home. Meyer held onto one end of the long, thin saw and Hewot grabbed hold of the other, and the two men sawed crudely formed boards to make their floor.

"Sure hope some enterprising soul comes along wanting to build a sawmill before long," Hewot exclaimed, wiping away the sweat streaming down his face during the short break he and Meyer were taking away from whipsawing their boards. "This isn't exactly my idea of fun," and he rubbed his aching shoulders. "Guess this makes us the first loggers and sawyers in the area, doesn't it?" he added with a touch of pride in his voice.

"Nah. First loggers were those miners who cut those junipers to make the bridge down there," Meyer reminded him, pointing towards the mouth of Bridge Creek to the north. The two friends sighed in unison and stooped to pick their end of the whipsaw and begin sawing again. Their aching muscles were telling them that being able to claim they were the first of the pioneers in the new country wasn't all it was cracked up to be.

While fortune seekers didn't find the treasures the gold miners were prospecting for in Wheeler County, residents would for a time benefit from what has been termed 'green gold' — the timber industry — and Hewot and Meyer would no longer have to saw their own boards. The Mitchell area could eventually boast of having several mills, and there were mills in the Richmond, Spray, Winlock, and Fossil areas as well.

The hosts at the Meyer fort-house declared the meal was on them when Bud Mealy stopped by for the night, declaring his intention of opening the first operating mill in the county on what would be named Keeton Creek east of Mitchell late in the '70s.

"You're a very welcome man," Meyer grinned, looking ruefully at the roughly sawn floor boards in his home. "Wish you'da come sooner, I do!" When the Keeton brothers, James and John, stopped by the fort-house for a bite and a bed in '77, they put their coins in the saleratus can for Meyer's accommodations.

James T. Keeton's parents were Wesley C. and Elizabeth Keeton, and the family had come to Oregon by train after the Civil War and had settled at Corvallis, their dinner guest shared with Meyer and Hewot.

"Went to Oregon Agricultural College for a while," James said of himself. "Worked as a blacksmith apprentice for a while, but didn't like that. Worked on a farm for a time, clearing land. Didn't like that! So, John and I headed this way. Got to Prineville and saw two men hanging from the Crooked River bridge close to town; they'd been hung for stealing horses. Didn't like that!" and the men chuckled at the comment, nodding wryly in mutual agreement that stealing horses wasn't to be tolerated and that hanging was a just punishment for the offense.

For a time James worked in the Up and Down Sawmill which Bud Mealey had started east of Mitchell, hauling logs with an ox team.[1] James also did ranch work and sheared sheep throughout the area, but he had a hankering for his own land, his own business. A man couldn't get ahead if he just worked for wages.

He and his brother John were drawn to the higher country found about half way between Mitchell and Antone, close to where Mealy operated his mill. Looking for land that would satisfy them, they scouted the area south of the military road in the Ochoco Mountains, often through thick stands of timber and always alongside a fair-sized creek with clear water. They followed the meandering stream for a few miles in search of the perfect space on which to homestead. There was good water in the creek and plentiful timber not only for personal use but also to cut and to sell.

They often scared elk as they rode, hearing more of the large animals crashing through the thickets than they saw. Deer fed in the open meadows, looking curiously at the men riding horse-back through their territory, then nervously moving to the cover of the pine and fir trees.

James and John found home sites on the creek that would become Keeton Creek. In '92, James filed on 160 acres towards the head of the creek[2] while John, in '95, filed on 160 acres located on the east branch.[3] Like many other early settlers, the brothers worked on their holdings for a several years before filing claims for ownership. James built and operated a water-powered sawmill on his land, drawing on his past experiences to help him in his venture. Working mostly alone, he put in long days cutting, trimming, and sawing the rough lumber.

---

1 William Keeton et al., in *History of Wheeler County*, Oregon, p.130
2 BLM Government Land Office records
3 Ibid.

The home James Keeton built his Annie, long after the newlyweds
enjoyed their little house on Keeton Creek.

James built his wife, Annie Younger, a home from the first of the
lumber he milled, making a structure sturdy enough that it would stand
proudly in the Keeton meadow for more than a hundred years before
a leaking roof allowed deterioration to set in. Roughly twenty feet by
twenty feet, the building boasted of a living-dining room combined, the
cook stove which would also provide heat taking up several square feet
in a corner of the room. A combined pantry and kitchen was built just
off the living room.

Unless Annie laid a chair on its side to block the doorway, she knew
she'd often find her curious miniature man in the pantry exploring.
Frank delighted in crawling into the pantry where he had discovered a
large potato bin with an open hopper at the bottom where the potatoes
rolled down to replace those that had been used.

Sometimes, laughing, his mother would allow her son to pull several potatoes out of the bin, amused at his reaction as the mass of potatoes moved down into the open chute with a soft rumbling, startling the
boy. His body would jerk back from the opening, his eyes widen in sur-

prise, no matter how often he repeated the motion. Each time, when the tubers had settled, Frank would give a little giggle, and then pull out another potato or two to start the potatoes rolling downward again. He'd take an occasional bite, his little teeth marks on the potatoes resembling those of a hungry rat who had taken a bite here and a bite there, making a hasty meal before scurrying on to discover another morsel.

A small bedroom was the third room in the house, just large enough for the bed with a woven metal coil spring bottom. James built the small room to the side of the narrow hallway leading from the living room to the back door next to the creek. A cheerful Annie patiently mixed flour and water glue and plastered the walls with well-read newspapers when James was finished with them. Over these she glued pieces of cheesecloth to prepare the walls for the paper she would purchase for adding a bit of color to the room. As she glued the coverings onto the lumber, she knew, too, the layers would help to cut down on the drafts when the mountain winds blew down from the Ochoco Mountains.

"Best part of this sawmill job is that when it gets dark, I have to come home, and I know you're here waiting for me," James told his Annie. His wife, heavy with their second child, sighed and playfully tugged at her husband's bushy mustache as they rose from the plank table in their small home after their evening meal. James had nailed the table to the wall to keep their son from toppling it over when he first began pulling himself upright, using the table legs as a prop.

"This has got to be another boy," Annie said, patting her large rounded stomach. "He's been romping and stomping all day. Must want to hurry and get here and play with little Frank."

"We'll have to get someone to stay with you while I'm gone, closer to time for the little guy to get here," James promised his young wife. "I worry about you being here all alone." He playfully took her in his arms and hummed a few bars of "Annie Laurie", the popular Scottish love song, as he propelled her heavy body around the small room in a clumsy dance, and the two laughed happily in their little homestead home on Keeton Creek.

Annie smiled as she watched her two men go through their nightly ritual, her son laughing and tugging at his father's mustache, his father bouncing him on his knee. "Don't worry about me," she assured him. "The first one's always the hardest, they say. After that, there's nothing to it!"

"Even so, I'd feel better if you have someone here," James replied, handing his sleepy son to his wife. "And, now, it's bedtime for this tired old sawyer. I'm exhausted tonight. I'll have to start coming home a bit earlier, get some more plowing done. Need to get the ground worked up a bit more, get the oats in."

"We'll soon have a regular sawmill crew to help you," she grinned as she wiped the supper dishes in the dim light of the kerosene lamp. "There are a lot of folks that are glad to see you hauling that lumber down the road. You could sell boards as fast as you cut them," she predicted, and James nodded in agreement. The country around them was building up fast and lumber was in great demand. There was a ready market in the area of the fast-growing town of John Day to the east or he could take loads of lumber to the smaller city of Mitchell. He would benefit from help in his mill, but initially, at least, he preferred to work alone. His brother John helped often, though he was busy building up his own homestead.

While James was working further up the creek at his sawmill, Annie took care of their home and garden, knowing her husband would be too tired to help much when he did have a few hours of daylight to help her with her chores. Each day, as soon as she'd finished her breakfast dishes, she would go to the woodshed that was less than thirty feet from the cabin, and she would chop enough wood to last until the next morning.

James had built the structure straddling the creek flowing by so that

The Keeton water-powered mill, 1898. From left, two men unidentified;
Frank Keeton, Jim Keeton, George Vineyard, James Keeton, and Mr. Sasser.
Used with permission by MacLaren Stinchfield

the woodchips could be pushed into the flowing water and carried from the floor of the room, allowing Annie to keep the area free from debris. The flowing water also acted as a coolant to the small space and provided a place to hang a deer carcass so Annie could hack off pieces of meat to cook for their meals.

Bit by little bit, Annie fixed up their home, hanging curtains around the windows James had proudly framed with smooth pine boards. Often, when she had a few minutes to spare, she braided rugs from worn-out garments to place on the floors, and she gathered wild flowers to fill the cup she used as a vase and kept in the center of their kitchen table.

James had plowed a small patch of ground for vegetables, which Annie seeded and hoed in the dark and fertile soil. They had diverted water from the creek to irrigate the small kitchen garden, though the nights were cool and the growing season short. "Afraid we're not going to get much of a crop," she had warned James, and he agreed. Their location was too near the Ochoco Mountains to be very conducive to gardening, but the routine of cultivating a crop had always been an almost mandatory part of their lives. They would enjoy what limited harvest they would have.

During the warmer days, Annie would take Frank outside with her as she hung her family's laundry on the clothesline running from the house to a nearby pine tree, always keeping the little boy near her, protecting him from the brown bears she and James had seen in the nearby woods. Her son loved to play in the large patch of sandy soil close to the cabin and often dug up an arrowhead as he played, proudly showing his mother the shiny black obsidian tools the Indians had formed while camping near the Keeton home site.

Off to one side of Frank's favorite play area, Annie found a round and smooth rock used as a mortar by some Native American woman traveling by. Nearby, she found the accompanying pestle that had been used for grinding grains on the mortar, also left behind. She placed the round rock in the sand and Frank claimed the artifact as his personal seat, proudly sitting on his throne as he leaned over and poked the pestle into the soft soil.

Annie readied infant clothes for her second child, mending Frank's outgrown garments and tearing a bed sheet into small rectangles to be used for diapers for the newborn. Taking minute stitches, she hemmed the tiny gown she'd cut from her shift. "No one will see my petticoat anyway," she had explained playfully to James as she ripped the waist of her undergarment from the bodice, cut out the unborn baby's dress, then gathered the remaining fabric and reattached it to the top of her underskirt.

"Not a soul but me," he'd grinned. "Next time I sell a load of lumber, I'll get you some more fabric for a new shift."

Annie's delivery was not as easy as she had assured James it would be, even though it was her second child. Their son Jim was only a few days old when Annie died, leaving her two boys in their father's care. A grieving

James buried her on his homestead, her grave dug on a nearby hillside over-looking their home in the valley with Keeton Creek running through it.

When he returned home with the white marble headstone he'd had made for his Annie, the marker topped with a snowy ball, he grieved once more, looking at the words etched in the stone: Annie E., Wife of J. T. Keeton, Born July 22nd, 1867, Died Oct. 4, 1890.

As he placed the monument at the head of his young wife's grave, he talked all the while with Frank about his mother, realizing the little boy was too young to understand, yet wanting to explain the cheerful and caring young woman who had died just after the birth of her second son.

After Annie died, he became partners with Ab Campbell and the men sawed the lumber for the Mitchell Baptist Church. James married Janie Hulbert Vineyard in '94[4] and the couple added two girls, Golda Howard and Sylvia Marie, and two boys, Chester and Wiliam (Bill), to their family.

James continued to operate his water-powered mill until 1907, when he converted it to steam. His son Bill was only nine years old when he learned to operate his father's sawmill. James tried to sell the mill several times, but it kept getting turned back to him. When he was not operating the mill, he lived in Mitchell and operated a hotel there, as well as a cabinet shop. In the early 1900s, he owned a hotel and a blacksmith shop at Caleb where he lived for about five years. While there, he was postmaster for a time. He also made coffins on order and Janie was in charge of helping to make the linings and trimming them.[5]

Keeton eventually moved to Mitchell in 1911 to Piety Hill so the family could live close to the school his children would attend while James continued to operate his mill. Once a resident of Mitchell, he became involved in politics and served on the city council for several

---

4 Although the date of marriage is noted as being in 1984 in *Wheeler County History*, Annie's headstone makes the date of '94 more plausible.
5 Keeton et al., *History of Wheeler County*, p. 130

years. He was finally able to get out of the mill business when he sold it to his son Bill and Boyd Erikson, and the mill was moved to the Erikson ranch in the upper John Day basin.[6]

In his later years Keeton was able to share stories of his childhood, as old-timers do. He enjoyed telling the story of how the James boys, Frank and Jesse, who lived near his parents in Missouri, stopped by for breakfast one morning. The notorious James boys' parents had been driven from their home by the Militia and the brothers took revenge and started on their life as outlaws. For a time, the folks in the Mitchell area assumed the Keetons had brought some of the James's acquired treasure with them to hide for the outlaws, and they tried to figure out where the wealth was buried and when the James family would show up to get their loot.[7] The Keeton men had no need of the infamous outlaws' loot; their treasure was the green gold that grew abundantly in the forests on their homesteads and the surrounding hills.

James Keeton's mill was one of the first of many to operate in the area east of Mitchell. Arley Brown & Sons were established in the Mt. Creek area near Keeton's mill in 1929; Boyd L. Erikson in '26; Fred B. Brown & Sons in '25; and the Erickson (Hudspeth Sawmill Co.) in '43. Other mills soon sprung up in the area surrounding Mitchell, with customers clamoring for the lumber produced for the growing population. Among these were small mills owned by Clarence Hudspeth, Charlie Jackson, and Eugene Looney, as well as larger ones operated by Central Oregon Lumber Company, the Leach Sawmill, Misener & Cannon, Misener & Brennan, Mitchell Pine Lumber (Ed Spoo), Rube Rosenbaum, Walter N. Ludwick, and William Farley.[8]

Potter & Shufford Miller built their mill on the Six Shooter in the

---

6 Ibid.
7 Ibid.
8 Martin Gabrio Morisette, *Green Gold*, Martin Gabrio Morisette, Prineville, Oregon. 2005, pp. 389 - 404

1920s and R. T. Brown & Son operated a mill there in addition to the three they had in the Antone area. The E. M. Howell Lumber Company opened their mill in '05 near Richmond and Henry Trent also operated there from '13 to '20. Three operations lasted for only one year in the Richmond area: J. A. Wallock from '13 to '14, John Watson from '07 to '08, and the Powell & Quinlan Sawmill in '41.[9]

The first working mill that was located near Winlock was owned and operated by Nels Nelson. Nelson had arrived in that area in 1906 after traveling from Western Oregon in search of a suitable location for a new sawmill. Many of the nearby landowners in the early 1900s owned 160-acre plots; Nelson bought several tracts of timber from these settlers to incorporate into his holdings. In '13, Nelson moved his sawmill a few miles further up the mountain, and it remained there until '27 when it was moved to Dutch Flat in a location between Service Creek and Rowe Creek; the mill closed in '43.[10]

After Nelson set up his initial sawmill, more mills began to open up to accommodate the need for lumber in that region of the new county. The Black Diamond Lumber Company, the Harry Aken mill, J. A.Veness Lumber Company, the John Wagner mill, O'Connell Lumber Company, and the Table Rock sawmill were all established in the Winlock area.

One of the first sawmills operating in the Fossil region was the Butte Creek Land, Livestock, & Lumber Company in 1901. This was followed by the Charles Prindle sawmill in '15 and the Schmidt & Cooper mill in '17.

Both the E. M. Howell Lumber Company and the G. H. Hayden mills were established in Spray in '01. In '17, S. S. Barry & Company and Q. A. Hayden built mills in Spray. The Spray Lumber Company was built in '41 by Crawford, and was sold to Hudspeth in '48. The Midstate

9 Ibid.
10 Ibid., p.67

The mill town of Kinzua, 1950s. Today, nothing remains;
the area has reverted to its natural state.
Courtesy of the Fossil museum

Lumber Company operated for a year in '51, and Willis Spoo operated a mill there, though the year of his operation is unknown.

In 1927, a pine lumber mill was developed by E. D. Wetmore northeast of Fossil and was named Kinzua, a Seneca Indian name for "a place of many fishes." Wetmore had purchased his 50,000 acres of virgin timber in '09, though he didn't establish his post office until '28.[11] With the opening of the mill on the head of Thirty Mile Creek, Fossil's economy grew rapidly and would continue to thrive until the closure of the mill in '78 when both the mill and the small community of Kinzua were totally dismantled.[12] The mill served to supply lumber during the post-WWII housing boom and the large demand for building supplies, and their motto was "Our goal is permanence." The corporation took their slogan seriously and they were known for being totally self-sustaining.[13]

11 Fussner in *Glimpses of Wheeler County's Past*, p. 38
12 Stinchfield in *A History of Wheeler County*, p. 28
13 Lee Hoover interview, 2010

Enabling the families to also be self-supporting was the large number of deer and elk in the area. "There were kids being raised in Kinzua that never ate beef until they were sixteen or eighteen years old," Lee Hoover declared. Deer and elk were abundant in the area, and Hoover attributes the influx and the increase of the population of elk to the demise of the town of Kinzua.[14]

The sawmill industry was a boon to the growing county; at one time the mill was said to employee as many as 330 workers with many of them helping to increase the population of Fossil. In time, a "box factory" would be added to the operation and there many items made of wood were manufactured. One of the more unique glued-wood items made were women's shoe heel stock.

Thomas Burton, grandson of Mary Jane and T. B. Hoover, was known by friends and family as Burt, was postmaster in Kinzua for twenty-nine years, beginning in the mid '30s. Just as challenging as sorting the mail for the 500 or so residents of the mill town was the task of riding herd on his two children. Youngsters in the community were given their share of responsibilities and, once the family chores were done, they enjoyed the freedom of life in the small town. While Burt focused on sorting mail, his wife, Mary "Gilly," helped to ensure each child had a balance of responsibilities and fun.

"As a child, my best memories were of my freedom," Lee Hoover recalls. "In Grandfather Hoover's back yard, when the Indians would come through picking wool off the fence, I was about six or seven years old. Anyway, there was probably two or three teepees of Indians camped in the back lot of the house. As far as I know, my granddad got along with everybody, including the Indians.

"I can remember as a kid going out there one evening and there was

14 Ibid.

just a bunch of Indians camped around there. I was tagging along with my grandfather and we went in the teepee. We sat down cross-legged around the deal and had a conversation. Half of it was sign language, half of it was English. Once in a while there would be a Warm Springs Indian dialect come out. They'd hash things over for a while.

"I had an old horse. I could get on that damn horse and go anywhere in this world I wanted to," Lee related. From the time he was eight years old, he was responsible for taking care of the nine or ten dairy cows and delivering the milk and cream from the little "jug dairy" every evening. After helping milk the cows, he'd load his carriers with milk and make deliveries on foot, gathering empty jugs as he went.

Lee and two of his buddies, Carl, Jr., and Joe Coleman, had plenty of time after the milk distribution to explore the box factory and sawmill. The young men admired the big, rawboned Swedes who worked as timber fallers. All the work was done by hand, as there were no power saws, and the youngsters were amazed when they saw the loggers wolfing down huge stacks of pancakes and perhaps eight or ten eggs for their breakfast.

The men would build their own lunches, making as many as four sandwiches from the assortment of lunch meats available, paying a set amount for the food and drinks for their noon meal. "I'll bet you they ate at least twelve to fifteen thousand calories a day. Not an ounce of fat on the whole damned bunch," Lee remembered.

A sobering event occurred when Lee was eight years old. He and his buddies had been warned time and again to not play on the logs in the Kinzua millpond. "You'll fall in and drown," Burt and Gilly told him repeatedly. "Stay away from the pond." Like all obedient youngsters, Lee and his friends nodded their heads and stayed away from the millpond — when their parents were around.

Then, curiosity and a sense of adventure lured them to the small body of water where the logs soaked before being sent up the chute and into the mill. The biggest challenge was to walk the logs without falling into the water. Unfortunately, little eight-year-old Ham Boyer fell off a log, apparently hitting his head and knocking himself unconscious as he fell into the pond and drowned. A sobered Lee and his buddies avoided the millpond like the plague for a suitable amount of time.

By the time he was twelve, Lee was large enough to see over the steering wheel and still reach the gas pedal, clutch, and brake while driving the company's half-ton pickup, a '41 Dodge, on the Kinzua Mercantile store's delivery route. On Wednesdays after school he'd head for the store and help load the groceries he'd deliver, and on Saturday mornings he'd again deliver the sacks and boxes full of food before joining his buddies for a day of adventure. Lee knew almost as soon as his father working at the post office did when a new family came to town and where they were living.

When he was about fourteen or fifteen, a family moved to the Kinzua area from Fossil and when he delivered groceries to the family, he didn't realize the thin young girl that helped carry the groceries into the mill-owned house would become his wife. "Of course, I never paid any attention to her. I probably thought that was just another skinny little kid."

Patsy, that scrawny little girl Lee claimed to not have paid attention to, was part of the family that had moved there so her dad, Joe Woods, could help construct Camp 5, or Wetmore, as some called it, an extension of the mill, built to house mill and factory workers and loggers.

Woods had come to Kinzua in '41, a year after his two brothers Roy and Clarence Woods. Joe and the other carpenters would get on the "Speeder" at Kinzua and travel to Camp 5, some ten or twelve miles from Kinzua on the railroad. The little flat railroad car carried people back and forth from the camp to the mill town and earned its nickname from its speed — all of fifteen miles an hour heading down hills if there was a good tail wind blowing.

Lee also delivered groceries to the store in Camp 5, which kept a small inventory of bread and milk and other essentials, and part of the regular delivery went to the cook house, where the loggers ate. The dining hall was made from an old railroad car and it set on the railroad track. There was a kitchen on one end and a dining area on the other. This was where Lee remembered the loggers eating breakfast at 5:00 in the morning; by 6:15, there wasn't a soul left behind as the crummy, or large passenger van, carrying the loggers had left for the job site.

In the summers during haying season, Lee drove his father's old Model B truck to a ranch located on the Fossil to Spray road, and picked up loose hay from a stack the rancher had sold to Bert. Sweating under the hot summer sun, he'd proudly heap a large pile on the bed of the vehicle, carefully packing the load to prevent it from sliding off the truck on the way to Kinzua.

It was a matter of pride to the teenage boy to pile the hay higher and higher without losing it on the way home. Once home, he would carefully and skillfully pack pitchforks full of hay onto the stack, piling it just so to make a compact stack that wouldn't fall apart. Then, observing his handiwork with a proud proprietary eye and leaving behind the ladder he had used to climb to the top of the haystack, he would chug along the dusty, rutted narrow road back to the ranch for another load.

Often, when Lee returned with another load of hay, he would find piles of hay that had slid from the top of the haystack to the ground. Puzzled, but determined to build a tidy, tight stack, Lee would once again fork the hay on top, grumbling all the while.

One day, having pushed his father's old truck to the maximum speed and returning home much sooner than usual, he rounded the last corner before the barnyard and caught the culprits. There on top of the haystack stood a guilty Patsy Woods with four of her friends: Nona Graham, Pep Adams, Steve Harrison, and Don Ostrander. Needless to stay, after discussing the matter with the youngsters, Lee's haystacks no longer slid to the ground once he had stacked them. "Well, the ladder was there. Aren't ladders made to climb?" asked an innocent-sounding Patsy.

The Kinzua Corporation had a big hotel for dining and rooming, and many of the workers stayed in that, though others lived in the bunkhouse provided by the company. Most of the men ate in the hotel, so the delivery of food there was a large one. The logging town had, naturally, the obligatory tavern and meeting rooms, a first aid station, a church and community hall, a restaurant, barber shop, library, and close to 125 homes. In addition to the places of business and worship, there was a grade school; high school students were bussed to the Wheeler County High School in Fossil. For leisure times, there was a six-hole golf course and a trout lake.

During World War II, the folks in Kinzua used ration cards. Meat and other foods were rationed, as were gasoline and tires. "Well, this was in the '40s. '42, '41, and a kid going to high school in an old Model A car was kinda handicapped by being given just three gallons of gasoline a week. Talk about efficiency; I mean, we had it figured out. We didn't drive over 35 miles an hour or you'd get a speeding ticket and you were limited to three gallons of gas a week.

"Of course, Kinzua being critical to the war effort with their wood products, had practically unlimited supplies for operation. So, thanks to Kinzua and the ration board, the kids at Kinzua had access to logging fuel and were home free," Lee remembers. Not mentioning any names, of course, some youngsters would go to where the logging operation was, usually when nobody was around, and help themselves to the jammer or whatever might be about, and fill up their rigs with gas. Lee figured the management knew exactly what was going on and he estimated that sometimes 100 gallons of gas would disappear on a Saturday night.

There was also a movie two or three nights a week, roller skating, and church services on Sunday — all in the Jeff Moore Community Hall.[15] There was a dance in Kinzua practically every Saturday night and the Woods family often provided the music, as did other family bands.

"When we moved to Kinzua, if I wanted to go to the movie, I knew better than to ask Mom for money. She didn't have any," remembered Fred Dunn, whose family lived as did many during the early post-Depression years in the small mill city. "I'd just get my gunny sacks and start down the road towards Fossil. I usually took six gunny sacks and I'd get them about half full of beer bottles and hide them. When I got three of them that way, I'd turn around and go back down the other side and go back to town filling the other sacks. Got two cents apiece for the beer bottles. But, I could get enough so my brother and I could go to the movie."[16]

"I can remember the Slinkards used to play for dances in the late '40s and '50s," Fred recalled. "They left when Kinzua closed down. There was a steel guitar player they had, from Missouri. When he was twelve years old, somebody knocked on the door and his dad opened the door and they shot him three times with a .12 gauge shotgun and then run. And, the kid got to see both of them and he'd been looking for them for years and years. His dad was a moonshiner. This young guy, his guns were always in his hip pocket. When he went to work, he laid them where he could get to them; he wanted to kill those two guys. He thought they'd come west and he kept looking for them.

"In those days, coming to Oregon was a good way to get lost, and I think a lot of people did. Some of them ended up out there at Kinzua and the log camp. But, you'd be working out there in the mill and look up and there were the state police. They wore them high leather boots and the jodhpurs. And they'd be coming through the aisles, just a looking for somebody. They was watching away ahead and if some guy run

15 Lee Hoover interview
16 Fred Dunn interview

out the door and jumped into the bushes, that's where they went because they knew he was guilty of something.

"The winter of '48 — '49, it was twenty-seven below at Kinzua one morning. We went to work at 7:00 and I was loading boxcars. Just about freeze to death out there on that dock a filling them; you worked like mad to stay halfway warm. So, I went home for lunch and Mom had a good dinner cooked for me and I took my plate by the wood stove and I ate, getting thawed out. About a quarter to one, I turned and put my clothes back on, getting ready to go to work.

"And Mom said she didn't want me to go to work, but I told her I had to have money, so I went on back to work. There was only five people standing around when I got there. Bill Wright and Morris Brown and Al Rudd, who was the maintenance man, somebody from Fossil, and me.

"Well, it looked like we was going to get to work and somebody shot; it sounded just like a .30 - .30. And we looked around and we heard some more shots. Someone was shooting. Come to find out, it was so cold the joints in the lines under the mill were breaking. So, I worked all day to fix those. Worked a hundred and five days straight. On the day before Christmas, the foreman gave me $100 to work the next day. Needed to get the pipes repaired so the mill could run again. And, he gave me another $100 to work New Year's Day, just to get things repaired."[17]

About that same time, Lee Hoover was working graveyard shift and he recalled the night being colder than scat — probably twenty below, he said. The tops of the logs in the millpond were frozen and, upon hitting the saws, the blades would wobble into the frozen wood and make rough cuts. His boss thought the water, warmed by the discharge of the mill's steam into the pond, would thaw out the logs to ensure more even sawing.

Not thinking about the fact that the logs had originally settled with

---

17 Fred Dunn interview

their heaviest side down and would always settle back down that way, no matter how many times they were turned, the boss directed Lee to turn over the logs in the millpond. Not one to question authority, Lee began to turn logs. "A man did what he was told first and then asked questions later," he explained. He promptly fell into the water in the sub-zero weather.

The young man, aided by an excited Claude Sizemore, left the pond much faster than he fell in, and then hurried to the break-room to discard his wet clothes and don whatever coveralls he could find so he could warm up, huddling in front of the room's heater. An agitated Claude joined him. Waving his hands rapidly in front of the heater, Sizemore inadvertently got a finger into the heater fan and severed half of the digit. The spurting blood flow was stopped, Lee got dried out and warmed up, and the men went back to work.

During the height of the logging operations in the county, a baseball league was set up and Kinzua would play Wasco, Arlington, Condon, Fossil, and a few other towns. Then, in the fall, the top team would play at a state-wide tournament. Old timers recall proudly that the baseball team Kinzua produced was of the same high quality as the wood products leaving the small community.

"Bush-league players, semi-pros, from around the state would work at Kinzua and play baseball during the summers. "There was some pretty hung-over baseball players around!" Lee Hoover recalled. There were some pretty hard hitters, too; the hours spent in the woods toughened young bodies and sharpened young minds, making the eager loggers formidable opponents.

"Oh, they're good," one old-timer told another. "But, they aren't as tough as they used to be. Remember the time they played Prineville for the championship of Eastern Oregon? That was when men were men!" and the two friends recalled hearing of another local team back in '93.

Nine baseball players had traveled to Prineville, according to an article in the Fossil Journal. Then, "...footsore and weary, they were beaten fairly and squarely by the Prinevilles and to add to their misfortune were compelled, owing to the deplorable state of the roads, to walk upwards to fifty miles through the mud in order to reach home."[18]

When the Kinzua Pine Mills Company was moved to Heppner in '76, all signs of the sawmill town of Kinzua were removed and the area reverted to its original state. The loss of the jobs was a severe economic blow to the county and especially to the Fossil area.

The last of the mills in the Mitchell area, the Hudspeth Sawmill Company, closed in 1960. With the exodus of the mill families, the booming logging town lost half of its population. Kent Powell was one of the last of the loggers to live in Mitchell. He moved to the community after his freshman year in high school and graduated in '44 with two girls, Elsie Fitzgerald and Charcelene Barnes. He attended school until Christmas of his senior year and then, as he had the credits, he graduated and entered the Navy.

"In them days Mitchell was kinda — I don't know how to put it. I guess you can classify it as a pretty wild town! They was lots of sawmills around. I think they was about six sawmills operating here, and we didn't have too much.

"It was considerably different than it is now. They was quite a few more people around in the mill camps and in the town itself. I think the population was close to 400.

"They was quite a bit of logging in this area at the time we moved here because in the old days a lot of it was done with horses. Quite a bit of it. And the trucks were older and stuff and they used to haul what they called 'short log' and they was 16 foot and now all the logs is measured

---

18 Jeanne Burch et al, *Days of Yore and Then Some More, A Celebration of Fossil*, Fossil, Oregon, 1991. p. 15

32 foot. Double the length they was in the old days. They had a trailer, but they just had single axle trucks and single axle trailers. And that was before they come out with the modern trucks, you know, with a dual. The eight-wheelers and all that stuff. But of course they couldn't haul near the amount of logs.

"Then, when they went to long logs, they could haul more logs that way and then they had to devise a way to saw the logs in two because the mills can't cut a 32-foot log.

"They was lots of big trees. When I worked in the woods, I worked mostly with the loading end of it, and in those days, we had lots of days when three logs would make a load. And we would have lots of them kind of loads. In fact, back in the '40s, a lot of the time, they were just taking the select part of the tree. And they'd just go up and when they hit the part where the limbs growed, that's as far up in the tree as they'd go. They'd just leave the rest of it out to rot. They was a lot of waste. We never had to clean up after ourselves. We didn't have to do none of that kind of stuff.

"We'd use the horses to skid the logs down to the landing, before the loaders they have now to load the logs. They had what they call a 'cross haul.' It was just a cable around the logs and then they'd have skids up on the trucks. Of course, this was all the short logs. And, the cable would go around the log and they had a horse on the other side and they would just roll it over on the truck.

"In the '40s, they didn't have power saws. They had crosscuts and it would take two men to a crosscut. And it was just manpower with your arms! And it took quite a few men to fall trees; where one now could fall equal to ten men with crosscuts. That's why it took quite a few more men to cut in them days than it does nowdays.

"All of it's done with power saws now and the saw blades in the bigger timber, they have up to 36-inch blades. But, most of the time it's 30 inch or 32 inch for the bigger timber, because they can cut over the side of the log and back down the other side. But the timber's a lot smaller nowdays and the saws are a lot smaller, too, than they used to be.

"The first power saws come out and me and my brother run one. They had two-man saws. One carried the motor end of it and on the other end, the blade end, they had a handle and they called that the 'stringer handle.' One guy would carry it, and they would fall trees with it. And buck with it, too, that way, you know. And what you'd do, instead of using a saw, you'd just use an ax to cut the limbs off. They was a lot of ax work. Well, there's not any more. I don't even think the new loggers know what a ax is.

"They pretty well quit using horses in the early '40s when they come out with the cats. And, of course, the first one come out and they just improved them as they go along. Get better and more powerful.

"And, then, when they were first loading them with cranes, they used what they called 'bell hooks.' And they'd have two hookers, one on each end and they'd have a rope and each hooker would hold the rope and they'd stick the hooks in the end of the log and then the guy running the crane, he would hoist it up and load it on the truck.

"And they was a man that stood on the ban-board of the truck and he was called the 'gop loader' and selected the logs and was in charge of loading the truck. And it took about two hookers and a top loader and the guy running the crane, and nowdays the man running the crane does it all. See, it eliminated about four people there.

"We had gas-powered trucks at first. Poor brakes! Caused a lot of runaways. There's lots of stories about logging. This mill site down at Bridge Creek down here. Our logs used to go in there. And, the trucks, they had to sit on a little incline to wait. And in them days the trucks didn't really have good brakes on them. They had what you call 'vacuum brakes' and if your motor died, you didn't have no brakes or nothing.

"One of the truck drivers had parked his truck there, waiting to unload, and his brakes leaked off and the old truck run down backwards and run right back down into one of the houses with a load of logs sticking into the house! We had several accidents, but it was just part of the game, I guess.

"Me and Charles Maxwell down here, we worked together. We went to work in the woods at the same time for Hudspeth, in 1948. Carlyle Norton, he started driving truck for us a year later.

"There is a lot more logging going on private ground now since — well, it started with the spotted owl. That made Forest (Federal) timber harder to get and the mills bought timber from these ranchers who have little plots of timber."[19]

Lee Hoover witnessed many changes to the timber industry during his years in Wheeler County. "I was county judge sixteen years," he recalled. "It was a traumatic time in the history of Wheeler County because of the fact that you woke up suddenly one day and you had lost almost 70% of your tax base. Kinzua. People getting laid off. Programs changed, and so on and so forth. Wheeler County found itself with hard choices and they had to be made. Either you like them or you don't.

"And, being a land owner and a property tax payer since 1949 and I worked in the community that received most of its funds from the taxes. Not a single one of the 500 people in the community had seen a property tax statement in their life. But, they would gang up and if there was a tax levy come up for a vote, for ESD (Education Service District) personnel, teachers, and so on, and if you were from Kinzua, they'd make sure everybody voted against it. And there wasn't a person there that got a property tax statement. That's the community I grew up in, and personally, I hate property taxes. Fact of the matter, during my tenure as county judge, no property taxes were raised. I'm proud of it. When I went in, my first two years of county court, property taxes decreased.

---

19 Kent Powell interview

"I read an article just the other day that this country is on its way to annihilation simply because we've got too damn many people for its natural resources. Don't pay attention to what we do. We're well endowed with parks in Wheeler County. We don't have trouble with the parks. We have trouble with the people in them!"

"Look what we do to our national forests. Take a good look at the public lands in the United States. Stupid people running around now, all the BLM and national lands are going to be wild horse grazing lands. What the hell good's a wild horse?" asked the rancher whose family, for several generations, have had cattle grazing on Wheeler County grasses. Lee remembers the days when rounding up wild horses and removing them from the over-grazed hills depleted of the lush grasses of the early 1800s was a necessity for the cow man.

"In the first place, how's a guy that was reared and raised and elected from the state of West Virginia know what's good for Nevada, Arizona, Oregon, Idaho?" asked Lee, easily one of the most independent thinking individuals to set his work-boot clad feet under a supper table in Wheeler County. "He's got a commonwealth in West Virginia. Well, take care of it and leave us alone!"

"I think that Wheeler County pays a whole lot less attention than they should to their natural resources. And, a whole lot more than they need, to their human population. This puts loads on the people who are trying to manage for sustainability. A few old hills of dried bunch grass, a few scraggly-ass pine trees. They'll be merchantable in another fifty, sixty years. There are things like recreation, hunters for a select few; the landowner can maximize their income.

"I guess, basically, my philosophy is, if you try to take care of the natural resources, be a true conservationist, the element will take care of itself." Lee's knowledge of and love for the native forests in Wheeler County led to his being awarded the Oregon Tree Farmer of the Year in the '70s.

"Well, I can remember only one time that I observed something going on that actually made me sick at my stomach," remembered Lee, great-grandson of T. B. and Mary Jane Hoover, as he recalled the destruction of prime forest land that had provided so much for his family through four generations in Wheeler County. "In fact, I stood in the middle of the road and I puked. That was a forest fire going through some timber country that I was really proud of. 600 and some odd acres of it. It was one of my achievements. Going up in smoke. It was a few years ago at the Prairie Ranch. I don't know why, but I stood there and watched it go over the hill and it made me sick."

The three small communities in the county have a common bond in that they have all suffered from the closing of logging operations in the area, making Wheeler County one of the most impoverished in the state. Adding to the lack of logging, technology has caused less need for the large number of farm and ranch workers who were formerly employed, contributing to even smaller numbers of employees in the county.

The future of the county seems unclear at times, but of one certainty the newer residents can be assured: almost one hundred percent of the old-timers know the wisdom of conservation on the land cherished by their ancestors and they are going about doing just that in their uniquely independent way.

Afterword

Christian Meyer was always quick to remind his visitors that he had earned the title of being the first permanent settler in Wheeler County. His good friend Biffle, the first settler to pound stakes around a home section in the area, had died, and Waterman had obligingly, if not reluctantly, moved on and solidified Meyer's claim of being the premier pioneer. The farmer had seen the formation of settlements in the county and the ensuing incorporation of Mitchell and of Fossil and the building of the town of Spray. He had witnessed the results of Indian attacks and floods and fires. He had seen the development of farms and ranches and the beginning of the logging industry. And, he had seen the birth of Wheeler County. The gentle German was content.

"He planted the first garden, raised the first grain, set out the first orchard and through thrift and enterprise he built a splendid home, and accumulated a competency. He remained in this section until Monday, February 3, 1903, when he was called to the realities of the world beyond."[1] "C. W. Meyer; 1820 — 9 Feb 1903 age 83" reads the marker in Mitchell's east cemetery. Christian Meyer would be missed by not only his neighbors but by the travelers who had frequented the military road and had stopped by for a bit of refreshment and for news of Wheeler County.

The only reminders of Meyer's fort house beside the old military road are a scattered pile of limestone rocks and a few ancient locust trees standing guard over the German's home site. The waterway that fed those first crops in Wheeler County has deepened through the years. In 1956, the same destructive thunderstorm that washed away downtown

---

1 Shaver et al., p. 639

Meyer's headstone, found in Mitchell's east cemetery

Mitchell slashed a deep ravine a good fifty feet wide and twenty-five feet deep through Meyer's Gulch and deposited on the valley floor large mounds of dirt carried from further up the creek.

Those who pause to reflect can envision the plans discussed at the crudely made table beside the rock wall of the fort house and wonder at the story they would tell if they could only talk. It would be a story of the county that was born from the long-ago dreams of folks who sat with the German and shared his food and his bottles of whiskey. It would be a unique story, a story of hardships and of small and hard-won victories, a story of heartbreaks and triumphs. It would be a story of newcomers and old-timers, new ideas and old. And, always, it would be a story of an independent folk.

Tom Fitzgerald summed up life in Wheeler County for those independent folks: "I think life is kinda like traveling down the road. If you want to get somewhere fast, you stay on the freeway with most of the traffic and go the most direct way with the rest of them. But, if you want to have a little adventure and see different country than most folks, you've got to get off the freeway and go a different route. It's a lot more interesting!" What you'd find among the resident old-timers in Wheeler County would be "...a singularly independent breed for whom conformity is a virtue only in one's neighbor."[2] They are, indeed, an independent folk.

---

2 Tom Fitzgerald interviews

Bibliography

Abrams, Carle. "The County of Wheeler." *Pacific Homestead, Inland Empire Edition.* 10 Nov. 1904: 35.

Bacon, Dr. Phillip. *The United States, Its History and Neighbors.* Orlando, Florida: Harcourt Brace Jovanovich, Inc., 1991: 435.

Beldon, Mary Christy. Personal Interview. 1996.

Bennett, Addison. "Wheeler County Land of Plenty Without Railroad to Interior." *Morning Oregonian.* 10 July 1913.

Blann, Marbel. *Personal Interview.* 1996.

Bowerman, William J. "James Washington Chambers." *The History of Wheeler County, Oregon.* 1983: 63.

Buhl, Kathleen T. "The Professions; Schools." *Glimpses of Wheeler County's Past.* 1975: 73.

Buhl, Kathleen T. "Sheep Ranching in Wheeler County." *Glimpses of Wheeler County's Past.* 1975: 83 — 96.

Bureau of Land Management Government Land Office Records. 1 June 2011 http://www.glorecords.blm.gov.landpatents.surveys

Campbell, Jane Steiwer. "W. W. and Annie Hoover Steiwer." *The History of Wheeler County, Oregon.* 1983: 215, 216.

Cannon, Bob. Personal Interview. 1996.

Carnes, D. Frederic. "The Pine Creek Valley." *Pacific Homestead, Inland Empire Edition.* 1904: 51.

Carroll, Effie Jackson. Personal Interview. 1996.

Carroll, George Cecil. Written Statement.

Cole, Dale. Personal Interview. 1996.

Cole, Lyle. Personal Interview. 1996.

Collins, Bob. Personal Interview. 2010.

Collins, Jack. Personal Interview. 1996.

Collins, Ruth. Personal Interview. 1996

Cooper, Glenn. Letter to Ruth Wilson. 6 Dec. 1967.

Critchlow, Roy. Personal Interview. 1996.

Donnelly, Linda Gail. "The Donnelly Family." *The History of Wheeler County, Oregon.* 1983: 75.

Donnelly, Linda and Roderick Donnelly. "Fount Watkins." *The History of Wheeler County, Oregon.* 1983: 235.

Dunn, Fred. Personal Interview. 2010.

End of the Oregon Trail Interpretive Center. "Provisions and Places. Prices in Oregon 1852." 13 Jan. 2011. http://www.historicoregoncity.org/HOC/index.

Engelman, Viola Parker. "Henry and Winifred Metcalfe Heidtmann." *The History of Wheeler County, Oregon.* 1983: 107, 108.

Ferenstein, Bobby. Personal Interview. 1996.

Fitzgerald, Elsie. Personal Interview. 2010.

Fitzgerald, Evelyn. Personal Interview. 1996.

Fitzgerald, Joe. Personal Interview. 1996.

Fitzgerald, Tom. Personal Interview. 1996.

Flora, Stephenie. "Emigrants to Oregon in 1844." http://www.oregonpioneers.com/1844.htm.

Fossil Journal. "H. H. Wheeler." *The History of Wheeler County, Oregon.* 1983: 6.

Frank, Pat. "Thomas B. Hoover, 3rd." *The History of Wheeler County, Oregon.* 1983: 114.

Fussner, F. Smith. *Glimpses of Wheeler County's Past.* 1975: 30, 31, 36, 58.

Glover, Irene. "Rock Creek Lake." *The History of Wheeler County, Oregon.* 1983: 16.

Goodman, Betty Jean. "William Warren Johnson." *The History of Wheeler County, Oregon.* 1983: 128.

Helms, Dick and Jessie Butler Sharp. "Anthony Houston Helms, Jr. 'Pike.'" *The History of Wheeler County, Oregon.* 1983: 108, 109.

Helms, Mrs. Glenn. "Samuel Carroll." *The History of Wheeler County, Oregon.* 1983: 61.

Hendricks., H. H. "Fossil, the County Seat." *Pacific Homestead, Inland Empire Edition.* 1904: 38.

Hoover, Lee. Personal Interviews. 2010, 2011.

Hoover, Tom and Pat Frank. "Thomas B. and Bess M. Hoover." *The History of Wheeler County, Oregon.* 1983: 113, 114.

Hoover, Thomas B. and Mary Jane, descendants of. "Thomas Benton and Mary Jane Hoover." *The History of Wheeler County, Oregon.* 1983: 113.

Horn, Ed F. letter. 26 Nov. 1940.

Humphreys, Candy. Personal Interview. 2011.

Humphreys, Virginia. Personal Interviews. 1996 and 2008.

Huntington, Bob. Personal Interviews. 2010.

Jackson, Audrey. Personal Interview. 1996.

Keeton, William et al. "James T. Keeton." *The History of Wheeler County, Oregon.* 1983: 130

Kenny, Judith Keyes. "The Founding of Camp Watson." *Oregon Historical Quarterly.* Volume LVIII, Number 1. Portland, Oregon. Mar. 1957: 5 — 16.

Kenny, Judith Keyes. "Early Sheep Ranching in Eastern Oregon." *Oregon Historical Quarterly.* Volume LXIV, Number 2. June 1963: 101 — 122.

Kenny, Judith Keyes. "Henry Dick Keyes." *The History of Wheeler County, Oregon.* 1983: 136, 137

Keys, Linda. Archives.

Lange, Glenna Potter. Mail Contract Between Boomer and Helms.

McAllister. "Twickenham Stock Farm." *Pacific Homestead, Inland Empire Edition.* 1904: 3.

McCulloch, John. Personal Interview. 1996.

McDaniel, L. E. "The Town of Mitchell." *Pacific Homestead, Inland Empire Edition.* 1904: 46.

McFadden, Ethel. Personal Interview. 1996.

Masiker, William. "Haystack Valley 1860 — 1880." (Previously appeared in the *Spray Courier*). *The History of Wheeler County, Oregon.* 1983: 14, 15.

Misener, John. Personal Interview. 1996.

Misener, Mary. Personal Interview. 1996.

Morisette, Martin Gabrio. *Green Gold.* Martin Gabrio Morisette. Prineville, Oregon. 2005.

Mortimore, Howard. "'Harry' and Elizabeth Mortimore." *The History of Wheeler County, Oregon.* 1983: 167.

Mortimore, Richard. Personal Interviews. 2010.

Naas, Carl. Personal Interview. 1996.

Nelson, Bernadine et al. "Spray." *The History of Wheeler County, Oregon.* 1983: 9.

Norton, Carlyle "Cork." Personal Interview. 1996.

Norton, Ned. "Communities Past and Present." *Glimpses of Wheeler County's Past.* 1975: 39, 40.

Pacific Homestead, Inland Empire Edition. Volume 10, No. 11. Salem, Oregon: 10 Nov. 1904.

Pioneer Resources and Webliography. "Plowing." 2 Oct. 2011. http//www.campsilos.org/mod2/ teachers.

Powell, Kent. Personal Interview. 1996.

Putnam, Mrs. Charles. "Grade." *Glimpses of Wheeler County's Past.* 1975: 37.

Quant, Ron. Personal Interview. 1996.

Schnee, George. Personal Interview. 1996.

Sharp, Jessie Butler. "Jonathan and Sarah Duty Brown." *The History of Wheeler County, Oregon.* 1983: 53, 56.

Shaver, F. A., Arthur P. Rose, R. F. Steel, and A. E. Adams. *Illustrated History of Central Oregon.* Spokane, Washington: Western Historical Publishing Co. 1905: 635, 637, 638, 639, 640, 642, 646, 647, 649, 664, 691

Spray, John F. "The Town of Spray, Or." *Pacific Homestead, Inland Empire Edition.* 1904: 49.

Steiwer, Jack. "Communities Past and Present." *Glimpses of Wheeler County's Past.* Portland, Oregon: Binford & Mort. 1975: 25, 30, 32, 37, 64.

Steiwer, William H., Jr and Jane Steiwer Campbell. "William H. Steiwer, Sr. Dorothy Kerns Steiwer." *The History of Wheeler County, Oregon.* 1983: 215.

Stinchfield, McLaren and Janet, eds. *The History of Wheeler County, Oregon.* Dalles, Texas: Taylor Publishing Company. 1983: 6, 8, 9, 13, 27.

Stirewalt, Effie Snable. "The James McFadden Stirewalt Family." *The History of Wheeler County, Oregon.* 1983: 221

Tipley, Alma Jean and Edgar J. Kelsay. "Bert and Euphrasia (Gillis) Kelsay." *The History of Wheeler County, Oregon.* 1983: 131, 132.

Trill, W. G. "J. H. Parsons." *Pacific Homestead, Inland Empire Edition.* 1904: 55.

Warfield, Rose Spray. "John Charles Fremont." *The History of Wheeler County, Oregon.* 1983: 214.

Waterman, Ralph. "Ezekiel H. and Mary Straud Waterman." *The History of Wheeler County, Oregon.* 1983: 234.

Weaver, O. W., administrator for The Estate of J. C. Biffle, deceased. 12 Feb. 1871.

"William H. Seward." 13 April 2011. http://en.wikipedia.org/wiki/William_H_Seward.

Younce, Grace et al. "Twickenham." *The History of Wheeler County, Oregon.* 1983: 12, 13.

Younce, Patsy. "The Descendants of Charlie and Lizzie Palmer." *The History of Wheeler County, Oregon.* 1983: 178, 179

CPSIA information can be obtained at www.ICGtesting.com
Printed in the USA
BVOW031929201111·

276483BV00005B/1/P